Between Iran and Zion

Between Iran and Zion

Jewish Histories of Twentieth-Century Iran

Lior B. Sternfeld

Stanford University Press

Stanford, California

Stanford University Press
Stanford, California

©2019 by the Board of Trustees of the Leland Stanford Junior University.
All rights reserved.

 This book has been published with financial support from
the Memorial Foundation for Jewish Culture and the
Iran Heritage Foundation.

Printed in the United States of America on acid-free, archival-quality paper

Library of Congress Cataloging-in-Publication Data

Names: Sternfeld, Lior B., 1979– author.
Title: Between Iran and Zion : Jewish histories of twentieth-century Iran /
    Lior B. Sternfeld.
Description: Stanford, California : Stanford University Press, 2019. |
    Includes bibliographical references and index.
Identifiers: LCCN 2018007818 (print) | LCCN 2018011170 (ebook) |
    ISBN 9781503607170 (epub) | ISBN 9781503606142 |
    ISBN 9781503606142 (cloth : alk. paper)
Subjects: LCSH: Jews—Iran—Identity—History—20th century. | Jews—
    Iran—Politics and government—20th century. | Religious minorities—Iran—
    History—20th century. | Social integration—Iran—History—20th century. |
    Nationalism—Iran—History—20th century. | Iran—Politics and
    government—1941–1979.
Classification: LCC DS135.I65 (ebook) | LCC DS135.I65 S74 2019 (print) |
    DDC 305.892/40550904—dc23
LC record available at https://lccn.loc.gov/2018007818

Typeset by Westchester Publishing Services in 11/13.5 and AGaramond Pro

Dedicated with love and admiration to my parents, Zahava and Itzhak Sternfeld,
and to my wife, Sharon, and daughters, Shira, Yaara, and Daniela

Naturally it caused an uproar at the Seder when Father asked Uncle Ardi to read the Ha-Lachma. Everyone burst into laughter, even before he began. He obeyed and read, but not without a touch of subversion, a bit of mischief:

"'This is the bread of affliction'—some affliction!—'that our fore-fathers ate in the land of Egypt. This year we are slaves.' May this slavery never end! 'This year here and next year at home in Israel.' Pardon me for not packing!"

. . . The family dreamed of the land of milk and honey but wanted to wake up in Tehran. . . .

After reciting the Ha-Lachma, Uncle Ardi asked, "So, Hakakian, are your bags packed or is the flight to Jerusalem postponed for another year?"

Father smiled and waved him away, assuming his question had been meant in jest. But Uncle Ardi, without the slightest hint at humor, pressed on: "Really, Hakakian, why say it? Why not leave it at 'Love thy neighbor like thyself!' and call off the rest?"

—Roya Hakakian, *Journey from the Land of No*

Contents

Preface

In summer 2016, I traveled to Paris for two final interviews—one with the first president of Iran's Islamic Republic (following the 1979 revolution), Abolhassan Bani-Sadr, and the other with renowned Iranian intellectual and political lexicographer Daryoush Ashouri. At the outset of our conversation, Dr. Ashouri asked for a brief description of my book. I told him that, generally speaking, the book recounts the story of Iranian Jews in the twentieth century. A shrewd humorist, Ashouri immediately replied, "What about the other 2,600 years?" Ashouri was alluding to the fact that every Iranian Jew begins his or her personal and family history with the Babylonian exile. In a sense, Ashouri's question reflects the current status of scholarship on that sensitive topic, and one of the major reasons I embarked on this journey to write *Between Iran and Zion*.

Writing the story of Iranian Jews in the twentieth century requires juxtaposing 2,700 years of history alongside a mélange of oral traditions, autobiographies, and microhistories. These family accounts and microhistories allow for the refashioning of a contemporary narrative, one that defies the compression of history into a neat, linear record. This new narrative necessarily takes into account social and political developments both in Iran and in the Jewish world and, of course, in the broader Middle East.

Between Iran and Zion examines the development of the Jewish community in Iran, and especially in Tehran, since the early twentieth century. In 1941, following the invasion of the Allied armies as part of World War II, emissaries of the American Joint Jewish Distribution Committee in Tehran reported to their organization's New York headquarters

that about 80 percent of the Jewish communities in Iran were impoverished members of the lower and lower middle classes. These Jews lived in
rural areas or on the outskirts of big cities and, although generally literate,
were unable to break professional and social glass ceilings. Exclusionary
practices, while affecting many individuals in Iran's hierarchical society
(regardless of ethnic or religious affiliation), applied most particularly to
Jews. Only 10 percent, according to this 1941 report, belonged to the
urban middle class, and an additional 10 percent were affluent Iranian
industrialists and bankers.[1]

By the late 1970s, reports from the same organization offered a radically different picture: 80 percent of Jews belonged to the upper middle class,
10 percent belonged to the economic elite and upper class, and only 10 percent
were still classified as belonging to the impoverished lower class. This
change occurred in the course of less than four decades, which is especially astounding in a community of one hundred thousand individuals.
Equally intriguing is that in the 1940s Jews were not thought of as having
any political agency. Conversely, in the 1970s they appeared simultaneously
as avowed Communists or Iranian nationalists, maintained sincere and
close relationships with the Shah and his court, and at the same time also
remained sympathetic to Zionism in its various forms. Such facts allow us
to begin to see the fluidity of identity boundaries within Iran's sociopolitical environment.

This book links the Iranian case to revisionist histories of other
Middle Eastern studies of local Jewish pasts. It demonstrates how minorities should be examined as part of broader Iranian contexts rather than
secluded in space and consciousness. Hence, despite focusing on the Jewish
population of Iran, this research is relevant to Iranian history in general,
particularly to the history of the state and its many minorities. While an
overwhelming number of these minorities are ethnic minorities, some are
both ethnic and religious, and they are insufficiently treated in the narratives of Iranian history. By writing the story of Iran's Jewry more fully into
the Iranian national narrative, this study contributes to a better understanding of Iran's unique social tapestry.

I do not mean for this book to be a definitive history of twentieth-
century Iranian Jews. It is neither a written institutional history of Iranian
Jews nor a comprehensive corpus of modern Jewish history. Rather,
Between Iran and Zion seeks to explore the interrelationship of Jewish
communities—and individuals residing in those communities—with the

broader Iranian society; that is, to illuminate the diverse aspects of Jewish Iranian identity. Should one consider these individuals more Iranian or Jewish, Zionist or Communist? Are they patriots or reluctant participants, or perhaps a combination of all the above, depending on the era and occasion? This book primarily focuses on the historical period following 1941—years of unprecedented urbanization within Iran that translated to new and significant roles for members of the Jewish community. Necessarily, the book's narrative gravitates toward the Jewish population of Tehran primarily and other cities secondarily. Indeed, for the better part of the twentieth century, approximately half of Iran's Jews lived in the capital city.

Between Iran and Zion highlights the social and political transformations Iranian Jews experienced during the twentieth century—and it attempts to shed light on the interconnections between different groups within the Jewish population, as well as their relationships to the greater Iranian society and state. Within each chapter the reader will discover that relevant sociopolitical developments and events almost always had a broader context—one not grounded solely in a Jewish context but also rooted deeply in Iranian contexts.

Acknowledgments

No section of this book brought more joy and stress than writing these acknowledgments. This project became possible thanks to many good friends and colleagues who read, commented, advised, supported, and inspired.

This book project started in the Department of History at the University of Texas at Austin. I am indebted to the brilliant historians who helped me develop this project: Kamran Scot Aghaie, Yoav Di-Capua, Afshin Marashi, Mary Neuburger, and Cyrus Schayegh. They are my role models and incredible mentors and friends. I thank also Houchang Esfandiar Chehabi. Houchang offered me the entry into this project and was always there for brilliant advice.

At Stanford University Press, I wish to thank Kate Wahl for her help, comments, questions, and treatment of this text from the very beginning. I also wish to thank Leah Pennywark and the two anonymous reviewers for their instrumental comments.

Gratitude goes to colleagues and mentors who were part of this project in many capacities: Haggai Ram, who walked me through my baby-historian steps from my days at Ben Gurion University to the end of this project, as well as Ervand Abrahamian, Robert H. Abzug, Shaherzad Ahmadi, Assef Ashraf, Blake Atwood, Benjamin C. Brower, Juan Cole, Hamid Dabashi, Arnon and Bat-hen Degani, Joel Gordon, Rachel Green, Anya Grossman, Atina Grossmann, Mikiya Koyagi, Wm. Roger Louis, Brian Mann, and Ida Meftahi. I am grateful to David Menashri for his assistance along the way, Faryar Nikbakht for sharing his immense knowledge and wisdom on contemporary Jewish Iranian history, and Joshua Schreier, Anousha Shahsavari, and Farzin Vejdani. I wish to thank friends and colleagues who invited me to talk about various parts of this book in lectures, workshops, and panels: Christine D. Baker, Alma Rachel Heckman, Susannah Heschel, Babak Rahimi, Sarah Abrevaya Stein, Rachel Sternfeld, and Fariba Zarinebaf. I likewise thank Orit Bashkin. Her pathbreaking scholarship is second only to her intellectual generosity and kindness. Orit's comments, suggestions, and support were invaluable, and I will always be grateful for all her help.

I thank my Penn State gang, who shared their wisdom: Eliyana Adler, David Atwill, Kate Baldanza, Tobias Brinkmann, Jon Brockopp, Daniel Falk, Lori Ginzberg, Arthur Goldschmidt, Michael Kulikowski, Dan Letwin, Nina Safran, Ben Schreier, and Ran Zwigenberg. I am deeply grateful to all of those who facilitated my research: Carla Darocy and Uri Kolodney from Perry-Castaneda Library at UT Austin, Robin Daugherty from Yale University, Charlotte Brown from University of California, Los Angeles, Misha Mistel and Linda Levy from the American Jewish Joint Distribution Committee (JDC) Archives, and Eric Novotny and Chuck Jones at Penn State Libraries. I also want to thank the foundations and fellowships that funded my research trips: the Churchill Scholarship (British Studies Program at UT Austin), the Fred and Ellen Lewis JDC Archive Fellowship, the Schusterman Center for Jewish Studies, the Center for Middle Eastern Studies at UT Austin, the University of Texas Department of History Research Fellowship, and the Center for Global Studies at Penn State University. I am thankful also to my research assistants, Rabith Mohammad Shaikh at Penn State and, from afar, the amazing Arash Azizi.

I thank my parents, Zahava and Itzhak Sternfeld. They have been my infinite source of energy and encouragement. They taught me all the important things in life, and their selflessness will always be a model that I strive to emulate.

A while ago I read the dedication that Joseph Rotman wrote in his book, and it struck me as the sincerest dedication I have seen. He dedicated his book "to [his] wife and children without whom this book would have been completed two years earlier." On a totally unrelated note, I thank my wife, the love of my life, Sharon. This book would not have been possible without the infinite support, love, wisdom, and care that she gives every day. I also thank my daughters, whom I love more than anything else on this planet: Shira, Yaara, and Daniela.

Note on Transliteration

The transliteration system I use is a modified form of the *International Journal of Middle East Studies* scheme. The exceptions are names and proper nouns that have a conventional spelling in English (for example, Tehran and not Tihran, Ahmadinejad and not Ahmadi-Nijad). I also do not use diacritical marks on those proper nouns and names.

Between Iran and Zion

Introduction

THE INTENSE RELATIONS BETWEEN IRAN AND ISRAEL since 1979 have given prominence to false dichotomies and wrong assumptions that dominate the discourse instead of facts. Relatively few people realize that in the Middle East, Iran's Jewish population is second in size only to that of Israel. The number of Jews in Iran has fluctuated significantly from the early twentieth century to the present time. Due to natural growth on the one hand and migration—mostly out of Iran—on the other, the Jewish population hovered at around one hundred thousand for the better part of the past century; following the 1979 revolution, it dwindled down to twenty thousand to thirty thousand. Today, it is estimated that the number of Jews still living in the country is roughly twenty-five thousand.[1] The reason that this knowledge is scarce stems from our reading of contemporary politics as one-dimensional instead of in the context of the long historical axis of Jewish Iranian history. Iranian animosity toward Israel, necessarily interpreted as anti-Jewish sentiments arising from an acceptance of the Zionist narrative, leads us to think that there is no redemption for (especially Middle Eastern) Jews anywhere but in Israel. Adding the dwindling number of the Jewish population in Iran and the Iranian animosity toward Israel together leaves no choice but to see Iran as inherently anti-Semitic, and Jews, if living in Iran, are locked, oppressed, isolated, and forced to stay put in this long exile.

Iranian historiography, for its part, does not always help us understand Iran better either. Iran is also—to a large extent—a country of minorities. There are dozens of ethnic and religious minorities in the country, and only about half of the population belongs to the Persian-speaking Shi'a majority.[2] Yet the historiography tends to overlook the significance of the ethnic-religious tapestry of Iranian society, and it gives far greater historical agency to the Persian Muslim majority.[3] Every historiographical tradition faces hurdles in regard to Iranian minorities and the state. For example, acknowledging the mere existence of so many minority groups could undermine the century-long project to unify the country under Persian nationalist identity, be it designed along more ethnic-linguistic (pre-1979) or more Islamic lines (post-1979). The same thing goes for other large minorities, such as the Kurds. What kind of minority rights do Iranian Kurds possess compared with their brethren in Iraq or Turkey? How do Kurdish affairs in other Middle Eastern countries impact the Kurdish minority in Iran, if it gets recognized as a national minority?

When studying the history of the Jewish minority, the hurdles are complicated to overcome. Except for a few notable exceptions, Jewish communities in Iran have been studied as *a single* isolated community (rather than taking into account the differences between the many urban and rural communities, such as their different experiences in different times), one that rarely interacted with the broader Iranian society, the majority's society, and other minority communities. Per Iranian Jewish historiography, the community won its redemption, in various forms and ways, with the appearance of Zionism and the "modern secularism" imposed by the Pahlavi monarchy. This book offers an integrative account of Jewish history, one that examines the many Jewish communities as parts of Iranian society and at the same time looks at the intersection of two other historical trajectories: the emergence of Zionism and the subsequent establishment of Israel, and the modern history of Middle Eastern Jewish communities outside Iran. Iran is a country of ethnic diversity, and so are the Jewish communities. This book reveals the inner diversity of Persian, Arab, Kurdish, and Ashkenazi Jews who lived in that mix of Iranian communities. Social movements for the advancement of democracy, socialism, and revolutionary ideals were dominant among Iranian youths and the emerging professional middle class. The same trends took root in the Jewish communities in the cities. With its relations to the Jewish world and Israel, we can see that Zionism did in fact impact Iranian Jews, but it attracted various responses from various groups in the Jewish communities.

Leading to the Twentieth Century

In order to set the stage for a deeper analysis of Jews in twentieth-century Iran, let us briefly explore the pertinent historical events leading up to the beginning of that eventful century. Conceding to older historiographical traditions, I shall begin 2,700 years ago.

The Jewish presence in Iran is usually said to date back to the Assyrian exile in 722 BCE. While being relatively incorporated into society, Jews routinely suffered harassment and forced conversions from the Zoroastrian clergy.[4] It is believed that as a result, in 651 CE Jews welcomed the Arab Muslim conquerors, albeit with mixed feelings, hoping their presence would end institutional discrimination and persecution.[5] The rule of Islam, at least nominally, protected Jews, along with Christians and Zoroastrians, as "People of the Book," in exchange for increased taxation (specifically the poll tax that was levied on all non-Muslim subjects in the Muslim empire, the *Jezyeh*, or *Jizya* in Arabic pronunciation) and relegation of Jews to an inferior sociopolitical status. Being defined as People of the Book allowed these recognized religious minorities to practice their religion relatively freely, as long as they acknowledged the superior legal status of Islam and complied with restrictions on clothing, possession of weapons, and building churches, shrines, and synagogues. They were also spared from forced conversion to Islam, which was obligatory for nonmonotheistic believers who lived under the rule of Islam in the early days. For the following millennium, Jews were not singled out more than any other religious minority, either positively or negatively. Early in the Islamic period, in some parts of Iran (mostly in Khorasan), Iranian Christians and Jews converted to Islam for a host of reasons—among them, to avoid the special taxes, to enjoy the benefit of inheritance laws for Muslims in non-Muslim families, and to get better professional prospects; they even converted for theological reasons, such as the Abrahamic roots of the new religion, which was partly perceived to be an updated message for the religion they were already holding.[6]

A major turning point for Iran and its Jewish population was the establishment of the Safavid dynasty (1501–1736) by Shah Isma'il I, who unified Iran and instituted Twelver Shi'ism as the state religion around 1501. He did so, at least in part, to distinguish his kingdom from the major Sunni forces bordering Iran (namely, the Ottoman Empire).[7] Arguably, the power behind the Safavid project was the formation of religious unity as a source of solidarity, and on these foundations hatred was spread toward any-thing that was not Shi'i.[8] Very little has been written about Jewish his-tory in the Safavid, Zand (1751–1794) and Afshari (1736–1796), and early Qajar eras (1794–1925). A number of documents, mostly written in Judeo-Persian, survive from that period and describe persecution and forced conversions, especially during the reign of Shah Abbas I (r. 1571–1629), Shah Safi I (r. 1629–1642), and Shah Abbas II (r. 1642–1666).[9] However, according to Vera B. Moreen, "the Safavid era cannot be considered a period of total disaster for Iran Jewry. On the contrary, there were numer-ous Jewish communities throughout the kingdom and most of them thrived under fairly vigorous and autonomous communal structure."[10]

The Qajar period brought mixed experiences to the different Jewish communities in Iran. Some communities endured persecution, whereas others enjoyed a period of relative tranquility. Most importantly, Jews did not live primarily in isolation from the broader Iranian society. Therefore, times of hardship for the Jews tended to be times of hardship for other religious minorities as well. One of the most notorious affairs of the Qajar period is the forced conversion of the Jews of Mashhad, who had become *Anusei Mashhad* (the crypto-Jews of Mashhad).[11] However, this was not an emblematic experience for the majority of the Jewish population.

The nineteenth century ushered in significant social changes for Iran's minority communities. The religious minorities accounted for less than 2 percent of the population and lived in cities such as Tehran, Hamedan, Isfahan, Shiraz, Kashan, Yazd, Kermanshah, and Tabriz. These social transformations stemmed primarily from the arrival of European and American Christian missions. Beginning in 1834, missionaries started to work primarily with Nestorian Christians, but later they extended their work to include almost every religious minority in the major cities in the country, such as Tabriz, Tehran, Kermanshah, and Hamedan. The mis-sionaries introduced vast opportunities for social mobility that were con-tingent on religious belief.[12] One interesting phenomenon of that period was the fluidity of religious identity. Vast numbers of Jews voluntarily converted to Islam, Christianity, and Baha'ism to enjoy these opportuni-ties. Conversion became socially acceptable despite some negative conno-tations, and the emergence of Baha'ism in that period attracted many Jews.[13] In the nineteenth century, under Nasir al-Din Shah and his son Mozaffar al-Din Shah, Jews enjoyed more comprehensive legal protection and advancement. With European Jewry's support, they also opened and expanded the network of Alliance Israélite Universelle and other Jewish educational institutions.[14]

In keeping with the development of constitutional trends in the Ottoman Empire, the Constitutional Revolution of 1906–1911 introduced a new civil discourse in which minorities became legally equal to Muslim citizens.[15] A parliament was formed and, after a power struggle with the palace, the governing body wrote and ratified a constitution. After having been requested to withdraw their right to elect representatives in the first Majlis (parliament; 1906–1908), Jews, Christians, and Zoroastrians, not without pains, finally claimed representatives on a national level in the second Majlis (1909–1911), and the political sphere slowly opened for them.[16]

A major turning point arrived after Reza Khan's ascendance to throne in the 1920s. Reza established the last royal dynasty to rule over Iran, the Pahlavi dynasty. Attempting to establish a secular state and society, Reza Shah led a fierce fight against the religious establishment. In the first years of his rule, Jewish institutions enjoyed unprecedented freedoms. However, in the late 1920s and early 1930s, Reza Shah sought to reform and unify Iran's education systems and, in doing so, closed Jewish schools. Overall, the Pahlavi period, with its emphasis on a secular society, brought relief to the Jews of Iran. The Pahlavi return to Persian roots allowed Iranian Jews to claim older and greater belonging to the nation, and they enthusiastically adopted the narrative that portrayed the Iranian Jews as an almost indigenous group that preceded Islam in this land.[17] The tensions that arose between Reza Shah and the Muslim clergy during his struggle to establish a secular state, in which he had the upper hand, emboldened the Jews in their new national path.[18] They now could relate to Iranian culture as a common denominator of Pahlavi society. They felt they could assimilate, as they were able to practice their religion, and they even started leaving the *Mahallah* (Jewish neighborhood) in greater numbers. In this period Jews started to give their children less Jewish and more Persian names to avoid their being automatically categorized as Jews. The ever-broadening interactions with non-Jews ironically encouraged the communities to invest in Jewish institutions so that the younger generation would still develop a solid Jewish identity.[19] The periodic recurrence of anti-Jewish attacks decreased and tended to be local and isolated.

In addition to education reform, Reza Shah's modernization policies included many infrastructure projects, such as railroads and various industrial developments in which foreign consortiums took part. Germany became one of Iran's major industrial partners, a relationship that led Reza Shah to announce Iran's neutral position at the outset of World War II. Nazi propaganda appeared in Iranian public discourse in the late 1930s and early 1940s, but not to the extent that Britain and the Soviet Union claimed in order to justify a military invasion in August 1941.

The Challenges of Writing Iranian Jewish History

Multiple intertwined historiographical problems obscure Iranian Jewish history. First, Jewish history is a field traditionally characterized by a lachrymose historical narrative—one that presents Jewish history as homogenously tragic, regardless of geographical or sociopolitical contexts. We can see the writing about Jewish Iranian history, with a few exceptions, as depicting a 2,700-year stretch of continuous persecution, harassment, pogroms, and various levels of discrimination (I elaborate on this trope later). Second, the much-amplified lachrymose approach to Jewish historiography appeared after the Holocaust and related to the eventual dominance of Zionist historiography in the writing of Jewish history. This historiography denies Jews the possibility of living peacefully and securely anywhere but Israel. Consequently, the literature describing Iranian Jews and other minorities has been highly problematic in that it has not always captured the complexities that accompany their identity politics and their changing circumstances. In his seminal 1928 article "Ghetto and Emancipation," Salo Baron called on scholars of Jewish history to revisit the lachrymose view of Jewish history.[20] Baron wrote this article amid scholarly debates about the period of emancipation for European Jews. He critiqued overestimations of emancipation and the absence of context in other Jewish histories. For example, scholars of Jewish history examined the emancipation period in Europe solely through the prism of Jewish communities. Baron argued that claiming that Jews did not have rights at the time is ahistorical, as no European subject, Jewish or not, enjoyed citizenship rights. He also criticized these historians for not sufficiently covering the (albeit limited) neutral or positive aspects of the Jewish experience of the ghetto and its social structure.

Although I am not claiming in any way that the Jews' position was ideal, or even positive overall, this failure to see the ways in which the communal and social structure simultaneously hurt and benefited the Jews (vis-à-vis the government or regimes) causes scholars to miss the complexity of Jewish life in Europe. The same theoretical and methodological symptoms appear in scholarship concerning Middle Eastern Jewish history as well. These shortcomings emerged, in part, from the tendency to train scholars as Jewish researchers studying specifically Jewish history, rather than as historians studying the Middle East. These scholars then treated Jews as just another specific minority group (hence preserving the "ghetto approach," which prevented them from seeing the larger picture of Jews as part of broader society). Baron's harshest criticism targeted historians "anxious to assist the completion of the process of emancipation with their learning,"[21] which here includes historians who tended to paint Jews as victims who were struggling against a backdrop of anti-Semitism across millennia and safe only in the arms of a strong and Zionist Israel. This bias overlooked the possibilities of a positive Jewish experience—one beyond oppression—within the borders of any Islamic culture at any point in history. Moreover, historians tended to exclude the most recent period (especially after the 1940s), in which Middle Eastern Jews found themselves in a relatively more peaceful and tranquil context than their coreligionists in Europe.[22] Taking into account the structure of relative tolerance that characterized the Ottoman Empire, scholars must carefully revisit the ever-changing nature of the coexistence between Jews and Muslims in the Middle East.

Baron wrote his article before the Holocaust, a trauma that introduced a historiographical mold that portrayed Jews as passive, insecure subjects of whimsical states and populations. This viewpoint forever called into question the Jews' status vis-à-vis the majority of the population and the state. According to this approach, Jews lived in a perpetual existential crisis. This essentially European experience was then overlaid by historians of Jewish history onto the Jews of the Middle East, and of the Muslim world specifically—without sufficient regard for how closely (or not) these cases resembled the European experience. Concomitantly, Zionism became the prescribed remedy for all Jewish communities and the ultimate measure of all things past. Long before the realization of political Zionism, Baron identified the inevitable historiographical challenges it had already imposed in 1928. He maintained, "Zionism wished to reject the Diaspora in toto, on the grounds that a 'normal life' could not be led by Jewry elsewhere than on its own soil."[23]

Iranian Jewish history was also subject to a narrow Zionist perspective that eschewed the possibility of secure and flourishing life in the Iranian "diaspora." Accordingly, significant parts of the Jewish past in Iran seemed to consist mainly of anti-Jewish events. The Zionist perspective dictated that Jewish life in Iran would be viewed as yet another link in a chain of perennial anti-Jewish persecution. According to this approach, when Jews in Iran were politically active, they exclusively supported the Shah's government because of its close relations with Israel. Moreover, it was argued that Iranian Jews largely abstained from participating in national political events such as the 1979 revolution—hence their absence from Iranian national historiography. In fact, Iranian Jewish communities underwent tremendous transformations over the course of the twentieth century, which have been insufficiently addressed by Iranian and non-Iranian scholarship alike.

The Lachrymose Historiographical Tradition

The trend of lachrymose historiography also applies to nineteenth-century Iran. In his important book *Between Foreigners and Shi'is: Nineteenth-Century Iran and Its Jewish Minority*, Daniel Tsadik convincingly asserts that "one can hardly speak of diverse approaches, different schools of historiography, or even major debates among the few scholars who address Iranian Jewry's recent past."[24] This pronouncement in and of itself justifies any new scholarship on Iranian Jewish history. While Tsadik addresses this void in the context of the nineteenth century, a similar gap also needs to be addressed regarding the twentieth century.

The most comprehensive book about Iranian Jewry, written in 1960 by Habib Levy, depicts Jewish life in Iran from the pre-Islamic period (1300 BCE) to 1960.[25] To date, scholars and students refer to it as the most authoritative source of Jewish Iranian history. Writing such an expansive history is a task to be taken seriously. The high status of Levy's book, as well as its embodiment of all the discipline's theoretical and methodological flaws—some of which I mentioned earlier—necessitates a deeper discussion of this book and Levy's personal background. So, who was Habib Levy? Was he right to compress more than two millennia of Judeo-Iranian history into one publication (of three volumes, in the original edition in Persian)? Levy's prominence earned him a biographical entry in the *Encyclopaedia Iranica*. The entry indicates that Levy's family descended from Hakim Eliyahu, who was the court physician of Nasir al-Din Shah (by no means an ordinary Jewish experience in Iran). The entry also mentions Levy's dental

studies in Paris in 1913, his entrepreneurial experience importing pharmaceutical supplies from Paris, his roles as a philanthropist and community
leader, and his service as personal dentist to Reza Pahlavi. In the *Encyclopaedia Iranica* one also finds Levy's Zionist credentials. Levy joined the Zionist
movement following the Balfour Declaration in 1917, was instrumental in
Zionist operations until the late 1970s, built a first-class hotel in Jerusalem,
and eventually, per his request, was buried in Jerusalem. The first sentence
in the entry reads, "Habib Levy, dentist, Zionist activist, Jewish Iranian
historian, was a pioneer in the study of Judaism and Jewish history in Iran."
The final part of this entry explores Levy's many deeds in the field of history
(including hosting the future second president of Israel, Itzhak Ben-Zvi,
who shared Levy's interest in Eastern Jewry).[26]

When covering such a broad historical area, as Levy did in his *Comprehensive History of the Jews of Iran: The Outset of the Diaspora*, some flaws
seem inevitable. Despite his best intentions, this book lacks a strong disci-
plinary methodology and engagement with the dominant historiographical
and theoretical debates of the discipline of history; in addition, it advances
his perception of the entirety of Jewish Iranian history as a series of pogroms
and anti-Semitism. This becomes evident with each and every chapter
and footnote in his three volumes. Interesting as it may be, Levy's book
is valid mostly in the sense that oral traditions are valid in regard to the
nonrecorded past of Iranian Jewry. In his memoir Levy recalls reading
Heinrich Graetz's magnum opus, *The History of the Jews*.[27] As a young man
with significant historical consciousness, Levy was influenced and inspired
by Graetz. Years later, he would set himself what he perceived as a similar
task—recording Iranian Jewish history. Levy relates history through the
lens of anecdotes and unsubstantiated sources, basing his accounts of the
more recent past on his own family or family relatives' stories—mostly
through the prism of anti-Semitic events.[28]

The fact that Levy was a self-proclaimed Zionist potentially creates
a historiographical issue. As Haggai Ram shows, the Zionist paradigm consistently narrates Judeo-Iranian history. With a few notable exceptions,
much of the scholarship on Iranian Jewry has been written by Israelis or
by Jews of Iranian ancestry with connections to Israel. Some wrote from
their personal experiences, and most did not write from within Iran.[29]
While this scholarship provides important information about some aspects
of Jewish life in Iran, it offers an incomplete picture by treating the community as an isolated entity within Iranian society. According to Ram, the

Zionist perceptions embedded in much of this scholarship presume that "the Jewish state is the only place where non-European Jews could escape a bitter fate."[30] Zionist-leaning historiographies, in a sense, deny Jews historical agency by portraying them as passive victims for millennia until their encounter with modern Zionism. For example, Meir Ezri, Israeli ambassador to Iran in the early 1970s, celebrates in his memoir the relations between Iran and Israel and depicts Jewish life in Iran. Yet, for Ezri, the existence of Israel is the only guarantee for the benign treatment of Jews in Iran or for healthy relations between Jews and Muslims in the country.[31] Similarly, Haim Tsadok, the Jewish Agency's 1969–1973 emissary in Iran, hails the Pahlavi dynasty for succeeding in "modernizing" and "secularizing" Iran, though he also mentions the harsh price Iranian citizens had to pay.[32] Tsadok overemphasizes the role that his organization and the Zionist movement as a whole played in revitalizing Iran's Jewish community, and he fails to understand why Iranian Jews would hold any patriotic feelings for a country other than Israel, despite his awareness of the fact that Iran was their homeland for over two thousand years. This approach ignores the common cultural and ethnic traits, real or imagined, that Jews shared with other Iranians, thereby failing to take into account the possibility that Iranian Jews (like religious minorities in other nations) might have felt an affinity with the dominant nationalism of the place they considered their homeland. This approach contradicts general trends in the study of nationalism by ignoring how modern nationalisms compete (more often than not, successfully) with other religious or ethnic communal identities, even in cases in which the dominant group does not treat the minority groups as fully equal members of the nation in question. Moreover, leaving Israel aside, Tsadok believes that "the Jews [of Iran] have, at all times and under all different regimes, been subject to murder, robbery, and plunder."[33]

Levy's Zionist convictions should be taken into account when reading his grand narrative. If one believes, as Levy does, that Jews cannot and should not live in a place other than Israel, then one's entire interpretation of Jewish history (in diaspora) is blurred by assumption. Also relevant is Levy's personal practice of Zionism. While claiming in his memoir to be one of the first true Zionists in Iran and connecting himself to the establishment of every twentieth-century Zionist organization in Iran, he nevertheless consistently chose not to immigrate to Israel, even though nothing prevented his doing so. In fact, when Levy eventually fled Iran, he chose to relocate to Los Angeles, California, and not to Zion, suggesting that even he allowed for different interpretations of Zionism.[34] Iranian Zionism consisted of many streams and interpretations—as this book will demonstrate—and not all of them necessitated en masse migration to Israel. Certainly it did not make individuals any less Zionist if they chose to live somewhere other than Israel, as exemplified by Levy himself.

The Europeanization of the Iranian Jewish narrative also impacted the diasporic Iranian Jewish communities in the United States. Iranian Jews, many of whom emigrated from Iran to the US after the 1979 revolution, including Levy, found themselves to be in a distressing position. Their country of origin, the one they unremittingly claimed as their own, the cradle of their proud culture, was perceived and portrayed in their new homeland as the most heinous of enemies. During the hostage crisis, these expatriates had to distinguish themselves from the frenzied revolutionary Iranians appearing each night on television. One way to do so without forfeiting their Iranian cultural heritage was to emphasize the deep roots of their history; the second way was to forge the strongest link possible to the Jewish American community, which was and still is primarily of Ashkenazi European descent. Although this topic needs to be researched, it appears that the shared memories of rabid anti-Semitism and Eastern European pogroms, as well as age-old connections to Zionism, served as a common historiographical ground for Iranian and European Jews in America.

Yosef Hayim Yerushalmi beautifully explained the role of collective memory in Jewish history: "The collective memories of the Jewish people were a function of the shared faith, cohesiveness and will of the group itself, transmitting and re-creating its past through an entire complex of interlocking social and religious institutions that functioned organically to achieve this."[35] The individual memory—that is, one's personal recollection of events—can and may be overshadowed or modified by the narrative of the community, with no malicious intention to rewrite history. In the case of Iranian Jews arriving in the US, the Jewish narrative of history, characterized by persecution and pogroms, prevailed over narratives that would have challenged this generic Jewish history. Yerushalmi added, and I accept this observation wholeheartedly, "The historian does not simply come in to replenish the gaps of memory. He constantly challenges even those memories that have survived intact. Moreover, in common with historians in all fields of inquiry, he seeks ultimately to recover a total past—in this case the entire Jewish past—even if he is directly concerned with only a segment of it."[36]

A telling example of this may be found by contrasting the Persian edition of Levy's Iranian Jewish history with the subsequent English translation published in 1999. Among many photos of Levy in the Persian edition, there is one simple and beautiful photo of the entrance to the Jewish quarter in Tehran. The caption beneath the photo straightforwardly reads, "One of the entrances to the Jewish neighborhood [Mahallah] in Tehran." The same photo appears in the English edition as well. The caption, however, could not be more different. Under the photo in the English edition, the caption reads, "An Entrance to the Tehran Ghetto." Could the choice of the word *ghetto* after 1945, in a Jewish context, indicate anything other than the Holocaustization of Iranian Jewish history? True, one could argue that *ghetto* could be used in the medieval sense—that is, to refer to a walled and gated neighborhood in which Jews lived according to their own will and in which they were not necessarily placed by force. However, this would require significant qualification, which is clearly not part of this or other texts. Because Levy passed away in 1984, the translation of the term was obviously not his, and perhaps the word choice would have been different had he been alive to review the manuscript. Nonetheless, this example suggests either a subconscious or conscious, fully aware conception of Iranian Jewish history that places it on a historical axis borrowed from a different time and place.[37]

In recent years Jewish histories of the Middle East have received increasing revisionist scholarly attention. A new generation of historians, trained predominantly in the field of Middle Eastern history rather than Jewish studies or Jewish history, have revisited modern and early modern histories of Middle Eastern Jewish communities, making extensive use of their expertise in Middle East languages and scholarship on Middle Eastern societies as a whole, rather than just focusing on their Jewish populations.[38] This trend, to a large extent, departs from the way Jewish (and other minority) histories have been previously written. Historians such as Tsadik, Yeroushalmi, and Mehrdad Amanat have spearheaded a revisionist wave of research on Jewish communities in Iran in the nineteenth century.[39] They have all challenged accepted narratives regarding Jewish existence in Shi'i-dominated Iran (going beyond the practices of impurity and religious tensions) and have revealed the rich and nuanced histories of these communities. Their books notably acknowledge the Jewish community of Iran as part of the broader society, rather than depicting it as a single, "unified" community. Within this context, Tsadik eschews the laboratory-like, somewhat isolated conditions under which Iranian Jewry have been studied. As he rightly observes, "The Jews did not exist in their own universe, separated from Iranian soil and society."[40]

Jews did not live in a different universe, and there was a great deal of mutual cultural influence.[41] The usage of Islamic titles, names, and terms by Jews contradicts claims regarding the social or cultural isolation of Iranian Jews. In fact, Muslim culture in Iran influenced Jews in a variety of ways. Jews gave their children first names that were traditionally considered exclusively Muslim, such as Habib, Abdullah, and Ruhullah. Moreover, Jews who went on pilgrimage to Jerusalem added the prefix *Hajji-* to their names, borrowing from the honorific title assumed by Muslims making pilgrimage to Mecca.

Inarguably, Zionist-centered historiographies have created scholarship focusing on very particular, and somewhat narrow, aspects of Jewish history in Iran—such as incessant persecution, issues of impurity, and Zionist activism—while ignoring other major twentieth-century trends characterizing this population. These overlooked trends include participation by Jews in the political process, Judeo-Iranian patriotism, and nontraditional interpretations of Zionism. Another factor obscuring an integrative account of Iranian Jews lies in those narratives describing national organizations and other agencies in which Jews were active or dominant. These narratives have tended to focus more on the political legacy of those organizations and less on the social, ethnic, or religious characteristics of the people involved.[42]

The study of Iranian Jewish history as part of the analytical category of the "Jews of Islam" is highly problematic, as it lumps together myriad—sometimes conflicted—subcategories, such as Jews in Sunni and Shi'i communities, different regions, different circumstances, and different periods. As a result, the methodology wrongly conflates the histories of the Jews in Arab lands and fails to differentiate or delve more deeply into the radically different histories of Iranian Jewry. Misperceptions of communal stagnation also distort the nuanced social tapestry of Jews in Iran. While other countries in the region saw their Jewish populations diminish, especially after the 1940s, Iran witnessed a period in which Jews thrived more than ever before. Not only did the majority of Jews remain in Iran in the 1940s, but the Jewish community also began to grow and become more diverse than any other Jewish community of the Middle East outside Palestine (or Israel after 1948). Iran and its Jewish population were part of the global and transregional trajectories of displaced persons who found short- and long-term sanctuaries in countries not their own. The transregional nature of the Iranian community, and the fact that the meaning of being Iranian and Jewish changed in twentieth-century Iran, was the result of a commingling of Jewish communities—including European, Arab, and Sephardi communities—during World War II and following the creation of the State of Israel.

This transregional point of view, which takes into consideration the social and political developments in and outside Iran, including the status of Jews in neighboring Iraq or Egypt and the Jewish migration to Israel from all over the Middle East and beyond, seeks to highlight Iran's role and historical agency in global events. As I have stated, World War II sent many Europeans—among them Jews—fleeing to Iran to find shelter from the upheavals in Europe. Another significant group of Jews emigrated from Iraq to Iran in 1941 due to anti-Jewish events. This migration followed that of the 1914–1918 period, during which Iraqi Jews fled to avoid conscription in the Ottoman Army. Thousands of Jews also fled from Iraq to Iran during World War II on their way to Israel/Palestine, where Jewish relief organizations operated transition camps. Jewish immigrants often remained in these camps for long periods of time, depending on the efficiency of the agencies' collaboration with the British Mandate government in Palestine. Many Iraqi Jews chose to stay in Iran with relatives who had already settled, mainly in the borderland between Basra and Abadan. Yet another group of Jewish Iraqi immigrants included those who, after arriving in Israel, decided to return to Iran.

As Jewish demographics in Iran shifted to accommodate immigrants and refugees from diverse ethnic backgrounds, it was not only a Jewish context that came into play but also national, regional, and interregional contexts. Furthermore, politicization of the Jewish population occurred in correlation with that of the non-Jewish Iranian society. When Iranian voices protested the interference of Britain and the Soviet Union, and later the United States, Iranian Jews became part of that movement. When Iranians protested the Shah's dictatorship, Jewish voices also rang out in solidarity, supporting a more inclusive Iranian society. Evidence of this dynamic before the 1979 revolution, during the revolution's immediate aftermath, and even today is irrefutable.

1

Shifting Demographics
The Arrival of Ashkenazi and Iraqi Jews

WHEN IRANIAN MONARCHS sought to modernize Iran in the nineteenth century, they turned their eyes westward and northward. In fact, the premise of the modern Iranian nation-building project was to underscore genealogical relations to Europe—and especially to Indo-European tribes that granted Iran its racial identity as the land of the Aryans. Reza Pahlavi's ascendance to power in 1925 signaled the forceful introduction of the Aryan hypothesis as supreme evidence for Iran's European lineage.[1] This Aryan hypothesis argued that Iranians were genetically, if not culturally, closer to Europeans than to other Middle Easterners.

Reza Shah's vision for modernizing Iran involved industrialization and massive infrastructure projects. These grandiose projects included the trans-Iranian railroad, the development of ports, the expansion of the energy and agricultural sectors, and, of course, the manufacture of machines to serve in developing these venues. He also envisioned expanding research and development at Iranian academic institutions. The presence of European consortia in Iran on such a grand scale had drawn myriads of Europeans to relocate there. Engineers, laborers, scientists, urban planners, architects, aspiring scholars, and romantic students in the respectable field of "Oriental studies" all hoped to live in the place and era they were studying.[2] Political circumstances in the 1930s contributed to an even more interesting demographic mix as young Jews fled the newly established Nazi government. Indeed, many German professionals arriving in Iran were German Jews seeking sanctuary.[3] Ernst Herzfeld, a stellar German archeologist and academic, worked in Iran to excavate and reveal its founding myth, so to speak. Herzfeld, initially condemned as a Jew by Nazi Germany, was subsequently condemned as a German by the Iranians—after being celebrated as a genius by both a number of years earlier.[4] Nevertheless, the arrival of many Jews in Tehran, and the creation of European enclaves with clubs and schools within distinctive communities, contributed to Reza Shah's cosmopolitan vision, as well as to his vision of Iran as a European outpost.

Before World War II, Germany had become Iran's primary trade partner. Relations between the two nations knew ups and downs, but overall, especially after the formation of the Nazi government in Berlin, Iran and Germany formed economic, cultural, and political ties that survived many regional upheavals.[5] It is safe to conclude that any sympathies Reza Shah entertained toward Nazi Germany stemmed from his understanding that a strong alliance with Germany weakened British and Russian influence, globally and in Iran, and that it benefited his overall vision for Iran. As British and Russian empires gained substantial, and some would say catastrophic, influence in Iran, attempts were made to counter this influence by inviting in other Western powers, including Germany and the United States. Reza Shah not only feared usurpation of Iran's oil industry and fishing rights but also resisted recurring attempts to bend the Iranian political system (for example, by swaying Iranian politicians) in favor of Anglo-Soviet interests.[6]

Based on all available records, one can argue that anti-Jewish policies did not inspire Reza Shah, nor did he seek to implement such policies. In fact, Iran was willing to absorb around two hundred Jewish university professors and offered them positions at Iranian universities during the 1930s.[7] By the late 1930s, Iran's population, especially in Tehran and other significant urban centers, had become more diverse and cosmopolitan than ever before. This chapter examines the changing demographics of Iran—and resulting social ramifications—before, during, and after World War II.

In the late summer of 1939, Nazi Germany colluded with the Soviet Union to reorganize Europe, and the two powers signed the Molotov-Ribbentrop Pact of Nonaggression. As the winds of war blew across Europe, the Middle East also became a war theater, albeit a peripheral one. Fascist movements in sympathy with Nazi Germany appeared in the Middle East and gave a localized voice to European fascism. Both fascist and anti-fascist movements gained significant public support. Propaganda machines on both the Allied side and the Axis side engaged in a virtual war through myriad publications, newspapers, and pamphlets. A major turning point came in June 1941 when Germany violated the nonaggression pact and attacked the Soviet Union. This move reshaped the power balance around the world and in the Middle East. The Soviet Union switched sides, joining the Allies against Germany, Italy, and Japan. The Soviet Union recognized the need to open supply lines of oil, produce, and transportation from Iran. Britain, of course, had already established a significant presence in the region. Egypt, for example, was under heavy British influence, especially as far as the Suez Canal was concerned, and the British Mandate still governed Palestine. Great Britain also had military pacts with, and a presence in, Iraq and Jordan while controlling one of the most important wartime assets: the Anglo-Iranian Oil Company, based in Abadan, on the coast of the Persian Gulf.

Reza Shah maintained neutrality from the earliest days of the war. Germany continued trading in increasing volume with Iran, contributing to many industrial infrastructure and railroad projects. From the Shah's point of view, losing a diplomatic relationship with Germany would have threatened Iran's rapid modernization projects.

Nevertheless, Iran's neutrality clashed with Britain's plans, especially following the Soviet-Allied alliance. To end Iran's neutrality policy, Great Britain and the Soviet Union agreed to overthrow Reza Shah and replace him with his son Mohammad Reza. In August 1941 the British and Soviet armies invaded Iran, occupied it with very little resistance, and divided the country into two spheres of influence. The British established their zone mainly in the south, controlling the oil industry, and the Soviets held the north.[8] Interestingly, following the Allied armies' occupation, German citizens in Iran had become enemy aliens and were expected to be rounded up by the British forces for detention in camps, mostly in India. German Jews living in Iran actually begged German diplomats to stamp the notorious *J* in their passports so that they could avoid roundup by the British Army.[9]

After almost two decades of Reza Shah's iron-fisted rule (1925–1941), Iranians experienced new freedoms that, ironically, were contingent on military occupation of their country. This occupation, along with the war, contributed to many other unprecedented developments in Iran. In fact, the abdication of Reza Shah signaled the dawn of the "Liberal Age" in Iran.[10] During this time, great social, cultural, and political transformations were given space to flourish. The presence of up to one million new arrivals—including Allied troops, migrants, and refugees—surely helped the transformation unfold more broadly and quickly.[11] Iran hosted almost a million arrivals, mostly concentrated in major urban centers. According to existing statistics, in 1941 there were almost fourteen million Iranians citizens.[12] Given the wartime influx of individuals, Iran's total population increased by roughly 7 percent; this percentage would have been much higher in the urban centers.

This chapter examines the tremendous changes that occurred following Iran's involuntary entrance into World War II, primarily due to the aforementioned transregional wave of refugees and migrants. The social and political transformations that Iran and its minority communities experienced following the removal of Reza Shah led to greater integration of minorities, as well as increased minority participation in the public sphere. This chapter not only examines the role of immigrants and refugees in the development of Iran's middle class (as well as their contribution to its cosmopolitan nature) but also discusses how their identity was shaped and contested by community groups and the broader society.[13] The geopolitical impact of World War II in the Middle East made Iran an especially interesting ally. Iran played a key role in terms of war infrastructure and supplies and, as will be discussed, became a sanctuary for hundreds of thousands of refugees—and home base for about five hundred thousand British, Soviet, and American soldiers. These shifting demographics forced Iran into a rapid urbanization process that in turn reshaped the political scene for years to come. Due to these massive though largely temporary demographic changes, the Jewish community, while never considered a monolithic, homogenous community, grew more diverse than ever before.[14]

World War II historiography presents a very partial picture regarding Iran. As is the usual case, the focus of such historiography is on Western powers and the European theater. These narratives relegate Iran to a subplot with anecdotes about the Allied occupation and division, or the 1943 Tehran Conference, which hosted Winston Churchill, Joseph Stalin, and Franklin D. Roosevelt. Admittedly, two exceptions may be made: Iranian literature and Polish war historiography. Two Iranian masterpieces bring this historical period to the fore: Iraj Pizishkzad's *My Uncle Napoleon* (1973) and Simin Daneshvar's *Savushun* (1969). *My Uncle Napoleon* humorously discusses Iranian anxieties about the British occupation of Tehran. *Savushun* takes place in Iran under the influence of British, Soviet, and American occupation and reveals the German presence as well. Another major contribution to the conversation about this era is *In the Lion's*

Shadow.[15] In it, Fariborz Mokhtari tells the story of Iranian Abdol Hossein Sardari, who rescued thousands of Jews in Europe. Unlike Oskar Schindler, the German industrialist who rescued a smaller number of Jews and began his operation for less noble and more dubious purposes, Sardari was neither acknowledged nor honored. Mokhtari's point, besides telling a compelling story, was that Sardari could only have executed this operation with the silent consent of the Iranian government. Also, Mokhtari argues that the inherent acceptance or tolerance of Jews in Iran allowed Sardari to openly use his diplomatic connections.

The Arrival of Poles in Iran

Scholarly discussions of the impact of World War II on Middle Eastern populations have recently explored new paths and are increasingly allotting Middle Eastern nations and societies significant historical agency. Broadly speaking, scholarship targeting that specific historical period and region has traditionally vacillated between two themes: its relationship to Nazism (either rejection or acceptance) and its insignificance in terms of geopolitical calculation for either of the belligerent sides of the war.[16] Minorities living in the Middle East for millennia tended to be more vulnerable during that period, and, along with general global instability, a wave of displacement ensued. Jewish and non-Jewish refugees from Eastern Europe and the Balkans made their way to Turkey and other countries in Asia. Poles, Ukrainians, Belarusians, and others were first deported and later dispersed over many regions.[17]

As mentioned earlier, in 1939 Nazi Germany and the Soviet Union partitioned Poland and agreed to occupation zones (Germany in western Poland and the Soviet Union in the east). The Soviet zone of Poland contained approximately thirteen million inhabitants and included important Polish cities such as Vilnius, L'viv, and Białystok. Following the invasion of Poland, the Soviets sought to politically transform the local population; the first step toward "Sovietization" was the expulsion of "anti-Soviet elements" from the Soviet zone.[18] "Anti-Soviet elements" and "class enemies" were fluid and broad expressions for a wide swath of individuals, sects, and political opponents, including—among many others—the bourgeoisie and economic elites. While not all the deportees hailed from elite social classes, a significant number of the 1.5 million Poles exiled to Siberia and other remote locations in Russia belonged to the urban middle class or to the intellectual or aristocratic strata.[19] In short, the Soviets were suspicious of anyone who amassed wealth or held significant property.[20] Beyond the criterion of "class enemy," which served as pretext to expel large numbers of local elites, the Soviets sought to make use of confiscated lands, produce, and animals.[21]

In short, the Soviets sought to cleanse their territory of any potential opponents and ended up deporting 1.5 million Poles from occupied east Poland. Four mass deportations took place between February 1940 and June 1941, sending Poles to forced labor camps—from Siberian Gulags to communal farms in Russia and central Asia. A third of these deportees were children. In mid-1941, after the Nazis invaded the Soviet Union (prompting it to ally with Britain against Germany and the Axis powers), Poles who had been deported from the eastern sector were relocated. Hundreds of thousands were sent to India and Iran.

As previously stated, Nazi Germany invaded the Soviet Union in June 1941, promptly ending their 1939 agreement. Following this invasion, the infamous Operation Barbarossa, Stalin joined Britain against the Axis nations and the new alliance began planning the invasion of Iran, in order to counter Germany's influence. The exiled Polish cabinet, based in London for the duration of the war, asked the Soviet Union to release Polish deportees, now that they were fighting on the same side. Stalin granted the prisoners amnesty, at which point the Soviet Union and Great Britain engineered a plan to support the Allied armies' war effort. The plan allowed the exiled Polish citizens to escape Siberia—or other locations in Russia—and temporarily settle in Iran. The Polish government would appoint an officer to form a Polish army.[22] The healthy and capable men and women among the refugees (deportees and prisoners of war), some as young as fourteen years of age, were conscripted into the Polish force that became known as the Anders Army, under the command of Władysław Anders.[23]

Britain and Russia chose Iran as a refugee destination for several reasons. Both agreed that it was imperative to gain control of Iran since the ruling monarch, Reza Shah, purportedly held overt sympathies for Nazi Germany. Indeed, Iran had become fertile ground for Nazi spies plotting to gain control of the oil fields, transportation routes, and other key strategic resources. British and Russian superpowers needed to secure Iran in order to deliver Reza Shah an ultimatum demanding that he eschew neutrality and join the Allies. When Reza Shah refused to cooperate, the Allies began planning a full-fledged invasion and occupation. Ultimately, Iran (along with British-controlled India, which also welcomed thousands of refugees)[24] became the closest territory outside the Soviet Union to be fully controlled by the Allies and with a relatively reasonable infrastructure to absorb numerous refugees.[25] This was the background of a highly significant wave of migration that Iran received from late 1941 to 1943.

There were other implications of Iran's sudden entrance to the war. Immediately after signing the resolution to free Polish prisoners and to form a Polish military force, the British and Soviet armies, along with the British, Soviet, and Polish governments and relief organizations—such as the International Red Cross and the American Joint Jewish Distribution Committee (JDC)—started arranging the exodus of Poles from Siberia and the Soviet territories. Iran, their destination, was not an easy environment to navigate. There were severe food shortages; famine persisted in some regions of the country.[26] A sudden addition of 5 to 7 percent of the population, in the form of foreigners from Eastern Europe, did not sit well with some of Iran's fourteen million citizens, and it certainly did not simplify things. The British assured the new Iranian government that these refugees would not become a burden on the struggling Iranian nation, and promised to supply all the needs of the refugees and more.[27] Although bread riots erupted in Tehran in 1942, overall the Iranian people generously welcomed the refugees, a phenomenon noted by all the relief organizations.[28] The Christian and Jewish communities established crucial local relief committees to help their coreligionists settle in and adjust. The International Red Cross, the Polish Red Cross, and the JDC were authorized by the British and Soviet authorities to work with the refugees.

Implementation of the resolution held conditions; relief organizations were prohibited from assisting only those refugees who were coreligionists. That is, the Red Cross could not give assistance only to Christians, and the JDC not only to Jews.[29] Refugees arrived in large numbers and exceeded most of the early estimates of the Allies, the Iranian authorities, and the relief organizations.

Polish refugees were transported from Siberia to the Soviet north shore of the Caspian Sea. From there they traveled by Soviet oil tankers and coal boats to Iranian ports, especially Bandar-i Pahlavi, which is known today as Bandar-i Anzali. They were first greeted by aid organizations such as the International Red Cross and the JDC, as well as an array of missionaries. The refugees were allowed to receive assistance from the Red Army and British officials, as long as help was provided indiscriminately (regardless of religion, ethnicity, faith, and so on). Polish army engineers became part of the operation early on and helped to construct the reception barracks.[30] In Bandar-i Pahlavi refugees went through multiple processes, including medical examination, documentation, and the provision of food. It was here the refugees experienced their first taste of freedom. Observers noted that the first thing they did upon landing in Iran was to "kneel down and kiss the soil of a country in which at last they were free."[31] In her memoirs, Irena Beaupré-Stankiewicz, one of these refugees, describes the horrors of the journey from the Soviet territories to Iran, as well as her arrival at Bandar-i Pahlavi:

The port of Pahlavi was an oasis; it was happiness. That same pitiless sun was not so terrible, because there was the sea and palm-leaf mats supported on poles, which gave us shade. We lived under those mats for two weeks, in quarantine. I remember, after leaving the ship, the sympathy on the faces of the British soldiers in charge of the baths. For our first steps on Persian soil led us towards the baths. We washed away the dirt and lice, the last signs of that inhumane land; our rags were taken away and we received clean clothes. The delight of sea bathing, the pleasure of eating our fill, peace, rest, the wonderful feeling that there was nothing to threaten us: here in Pahlavi we were on the road to restored health, a renewal of soul and body, that road, in the end, led me to Isfahan.[32]

Heartbreaking stories unfolded at the port, with scores of refugees arriving critically ill, and many others near death. Some received news of beloved friends and family members who had perished. One of the refugees transported to Iran during this time (and who granted me an interview in 2013) was Roman.[33] He was born in Poland in 1924, not far from the German border. In 1940, at the age of sixteen, he escaped to the Soviet section of Poland and was promptly arrested for not having proof of Soviet citizenship. Soviet citizenship was automatically given to all Poles residing in the occupied Soviet zone, but not to those who left western Poland after the Nazi invasion. In Roman's own words,

I was sent to a Gulag in Siberia because of not having Soviet citizenship, and after a year or so, it was not clear what was going to happen next. When we arrived to the shores of the Caspian Sea we saw stores with food products. We gave military equipment in exchange for foodstuff and flour. I, for example, found a kilo of margarine and ate it all at once. I passed out immediately.[34]

Roman's story is not uncommon. Numerous refugees died at the port after being distributed foodstuffs such as corned beef, fatty soup, and lamb.

Having endured long periods of starvation and accustomed to eating only small pieces of dry bread, the refugees could not tolerate the rich diet, and those who did not succumb to typhus often perished from overeating. Huge cemeteries near Bandar-i Anzali bear witness to the thousands who died upon arrival.

When Roman finally awoke, he was in the Jewish hospital in Tehran: "I later learned that they first sent me to a military hospital, but after being bathed by the nurses they noticed I was a Jew [due to circumcision] and they transferred me to the Jewish hospital. There were many Poles and Jews there." After recovering, Roman joined the Polish Anders Army.[35] Dr. Ruhollah Sapir, a Jewish physician, had established the Jewish hospital after witnessing the mistreatment of a Jewish female patient in another Tehran hospital. The philosophy of Dr. Sapir's institution was to treat each patient with the utmost dedication, never discriminating against anyone for any reason, and especially not for his or her religious affiliation. Tragically, while treating many of the Polish refugees, Dr. Sapir contracted typhus, and he died shortly thereafter.[36] His hospital remains the only Jewish charity hospital in Tehran to this day.

During 1942–1943 about two hundred thousand to three hundred thousand refugees, mostly Polish, arrived. The majority were Catholics; others were Jews. Around thirteen thousand of the refugees were orphans. In a circular arrangement, the Jewish Agency transported 780 of the Jewish orphans to Mandatory Palestine. They came to be known as "Yaldei Tehran" (the children of Tehran).[37] Overall, the Iranians were happy to help refugees and, as previously mentioned, their hospitality was genuine and generous.[38] Stanisława Jutrzenka-Trzebiatowska, one of the Polish refugees who came to Iran from the Soviet Union right before Easter 1942, recounted,

Our arrival in Tehran was full of surprises because it was Good Friday prior to Easter. All kinds of cakes, as well as hard-boiled eggs in great baskets had been brought in large quantities to both the enormous barracks and the air-force buildings. These had been vacated to us—homeless and hungry people. As we made our way through the streets of the town, the Persians threw bunches of flowers from balconies into the trucks, accentuating the friendly welcome. It was not surprising, therefore, that there were tears of emotions and joy, discreetly wiped away, in that pleasant, friendly atmosphere.[39]

The Iranian authorities, however, were not always informed regarding the unfolding developments. As early as March 1942, estimates of the number of refugees needing to be resettled seemed inaccurate. In one week (March 27–April 3) more than forty thousand refugees arrived at Bandar-i Pahlavi.[40] To provide perspective, this number was initially the estimated total of *all* the refugees expected to enter Iran. The Jewish community in Tehran quickly established a Jewish relief committee that genuinely reflected the changing tapestry of the local Jewish community. The members were local Iranians like Loqman Nahurai; prominent Iraqi Jews (from the Jewish Iraqi community that had arrived a short time before) like Sasson A. Kashi, Chaseri Bachash, and Salem Moshy; and even Ashkenazi Jews, represented by Mr. and Mrs. Hirsch Sand.[41] As a result of this tremendous community effort, many Jewish families from Tehran temporarily took orphans into their homes, as well as other Jewish refugees, and cared for them until further arrangements could be made (usually transportation to Mandatory Palestine).[42] Jewish refugees were given accommodations in synagogues and clubs, but also with Iranian Jewish families who could afford to host the refugees. The Jewish Abrahamian family from Rasht had an estate of over seventeen acres and fifteen bedrooms, in which they hosted Jewish soldiers from the Anders Army. Elish'a Pinhasi, the owner of Fadi hotel in Tehran, is said to have hosted Jewish refugees in the vacant rooms at his hotel and collected clothing and toys for them. There are many more stories of generosity within the Iranian communities.[43]

By mid-1942, more than one hundred thousand Polish refugees were already living in Iran, mostly in Tehran and Isfahan. As stated previously, thirteen thousand of these were children, primarily orphans.[44] Polish and British administrators decided to send numerous children to Isfahan, where the climate might help them regain their health. The Christian religious establishment provided essential care for the children, and it is possible that Isfahan was chosen because of the well-developed network of Presbyterian and Roman Catholic missionaries that existed there alongside the thriving Christian Armenian community. In a short time, "Polish Isfahan" came into being, with more than twenty Polish establishments and groups, such as schools, Polish scouts, choirs, and churches.[45] The children, it seems, thought of Isfahan as their home. In her diaries, Beaupré-Stankiewicz recollects, "We left there [for a school field trip] at six A.M. and already at about 11 o'clock we welcomed, with a loud and happy shout, the sight of the majestic silhouette of Kuh-Sofe [*sic*]. 'Oh Isfahan . . . Oh Isfahan!' We were so happy to come back home. For so long Isfahan had been a home to us, that in the end it truly is our home."[46] Efforts to create an environment that would cater to the Polish community—and provide all the necessary amenities for this community to thrive and not just survive—facilitated the creation of a hybrid culture. The newly founded institutions remained Polish to the core in terms of language, culture, and content, but they were careful not to diminish the prominence of Iran, especially given the circumstances under which these institutions had been established. When possible, Poles belonging to or attending these institutions—rather than isolated in Polish enclaves—enriched their cultural experience by traveling around Iran, making efforts to learn Farsi, and engaging with the larger Iranian society.

Polish war literature highlights the importance of Iran in the Polish story. Memoirs, documents, and scholarly works illuminate different aspects of this history. It is noteworthy that historians of Poland and Polish history can relate much more about this period in Iran than historians of the Middle East.[47] Unfortunately, many of these publications, which were originally written in Polish, have never been translated. The ensuing disconnect between the two fields has harmed one more than the other.

From Refugee Camps to Downtown Tehran: Creating Polish Culture in Iran

British Army trucks transported the majority of refugees from Bandar-i Pahlavi to Tehran, where they were initially placed in former military barracks that had been transformed into refugee camps. Stanisław Milewski recalled, "I remember that we were warmly greeted by the Persian people with gifts of food, dates, and clothes. We were simply amazed by the sight of smiling people and a bustling city full of open shops and traffic."[48] The plan was to house them near the outskirts of Tehran, thus allowing relief organizations and military commanders more direct control over the refugees; after all, they might morally corrupt the local population with their habits and leisure activities, which involved, among other things, the consumption of alcohol and dancing.[49] These remote refugee camps did not deter the new arrivals from accessing city life, however. Despite the ineffable hardships they had endured since being forcibly exiled from their homes, the majority of refugees had been members of Poland's elite only two years earlier. They included industrialists, intellectuals, artists, and members of the upper middle class and urban bourgeoisie. Now, after surviving the Gulags and the long journey to Iran, they were going to rebuild their lives the way they wanted and the way they knew. Being placed in a remote location was not going to discourage them. Refugees found ways around rules: "To get outside the camp we needed a pass; often however we managed to get out through the holes in the fence," recalled Milewski.[50] It is important to note that the Polish government supported *only* those refugees who actually lived in the refugee camp, providing them with housing, food, clothing, and cash allowances.[51]

In a fairly short period of time, refugees started leaving the camps and moving to the cities. After all, following two years in Soviet Gulags and a terrible journey to Iran, they were finally free to exercise autonomy and control their own lives.[52] One can only imagine the effect of such an influx of migrants (in addition to many other foreigners) on cities such as Tehran, which at that time was still, to a large extent, underdeveloped. Given their high—almost aristocratic—social status before their forced exile, many of the Polish refugees expected certain amenities from these new places of residence.

An occasional visitor to Tehran would immediately notice an incredible presence of Polish culture around every corner. "Tehran itself is almost a modern city, in many respects, although on very oriental lines," wrote Brigadier General John N. Greely for *National Geographic Magazine* in 1943.[53] Walking around the city, one could easily find a hotel or garden in which one could feast on traditional Iranian cuisine, sip excellent wine "and very high priced European cocktails," and listen to the music of a Polish orchestra.[54] Greely described cosmopolitan Tehran to his readers: "The hotel at Darband and the Firdausi in Tehran proper are gathering places for the growing number of foreigners this war has brought—soldiers, aviators, refugees, newspaper men, diplomats, and others."[55] Iranian newspapers reported on concerts and parties arranged by the Polish community and advertised invitations to the public. On April 30, 1942, the important Iranian newspaper *Ittila'at* announced the opening of a show with Polish artists in Tehran's theater: "A Polish minister and the commander of the Polish forces in Iran will be in attendance, and the public is invited."[56] Similar announcements were published periodically in different Iranian newspapers. A Polish jazz orchestra opened another night of entertainment in Café-Restaurant Shamshad: "A dance party will follow the concert until 2 A.M. All for the price of 15 Rial per ticket."[57]

The new business and cultural endeavors served not only the Polish refugee community but also a myriad of soldiers and military personnel.

In his memoirs, 'Abd al-Rahim Ja'fari, a prominent Iranian publisher and intellectual, recalled scenes of Polish widows and younger women "go[ing] around with" American and British soldiers to cafés and cabarets. He also pointed out the Iranian nationalists' critical view of the moral depravity of these activities.[58] Another type of public criticism appeared in *Ittila'at*, which reported the immoral behavior of a Polish woman who frequented the city with a Polish musician, then went to his apartment. He apparently locked her in, at which point she climbed to the roof, where she threw herself to the street and was injured.[59] The report suggested that this was the inevitable outcome of such immoral behavior. In downtown wartime Tehran, in a basement that has long since housed a chocolate factory and a print shop, one could find the Polonia—a bar where Allied servicemen mingled with Polish girls. Not far from the Polonia, behind the British embassy, Polish prostitutes attracted clients in the alley.[60]

Iran's war economy created diverse business opportunities; the Red Army, for example, brought Russian girls to dance in shows in Tehran.[61] Cafés, ballets, and theaters had surfaced in Tehran beginning in the 1920s, and non-Muslim Iranians, mostly Armenians, overwhelmingly had dominated their development. This urban transformation of Tehran as a city reflected the Pahlavi cosmopolitan vision of the capital. However, the emergence of cabarets as a phenomenon resulted from the social and cultural transformations following Iran's involvement in World War II.[62] Not only did Polish orchestras contribute to the European leisure culture in Iran, but "dancers, singers, and actors put on a vaudeville in French, which was most artistic from a European viewpoint."[63]

Contemporary writers' accounts confirm the Poles' development of a distinct culture—from creating community centers, study groups, newspapers, radio stations, and libraries to building factories and opening places of leisure such as restaurants, bars, cabarets, and beauty salons. A *New York Times* report suggests that Warsaw's leading artists performed in Polish theaters in Iranian towns with Polish populations, as well as for the Anders Army soldiers in Iraq.[64] Some of the younger generation adamantly looked for a way out of the refugee camps. In a report written following a visit to the refugee camp in Dawshan-Tappah, an Iranian Jewish community leader vehemently complained about the immorality of some "young women" who became waitresses and barmaids, despite coming from respectable families.[65] The same sense of immorality existed for some time among other Iranian observers; however, shortly afterward, native Iranian urban elites began to adopt some of the leisure activities the Polish refugees had brought with them.

Joel Sayre, a novelist, playwright, and World War II war correspondent covering the Persian Gulf Command for the *New Yorker*, wrote about the Polish community in Tehran. According to his description, while many Polish men joined the British Army and deployed to other theaters of war, the women stayed in Tehran and ran businesses and pursued other professional opportunities, some of which helped to develop the cosmopolitan environment that characterized the city by the late 1940s. Polish women famously opened a doll factory; others opened successful and popular beauty salons that catered mostly to Iranian women.[66] The turn of events at one of these parlors presents a telling example of the unique Polish-Iranian urban culture:

Another Polish enterprise in Teheran was a beauty parlor opened by three bright girls. Business was good from the start; not only did their countrywomen patronize the establishment but emancipated Moslem ladies of the capital were soon vying with one another for a chance to sit under the drier and read the Persian version of *Screen Secrets*. One day a hard-eyed, swarthy Iranian who vaguely identified himself as an inspector called and asked to see the proprietors' papers. He scowled over them and spouted a long stream of Persian. The girls couldn't understand what the beef was and they became panicky. They asked one of the Moslem clients to interpret. What the man had told them, it developed, was that since Poland was now part of the *Grossdeutchland*, their citizenship was in question. Perhaps it was illegal anyway for a foreigner to conduct business in Iran. Their shop would be confiscated. Recalling that Islamic law permits a man to have four wives, the girls dug up an obliging native bachelor and married him. They continued in business and grew more prosperous than ever.[67]

This incident, along with others, demonstrates the ways these refugees coped with the circumstances created by their imposed reality and exemplifies the cultural fusion or commingling of the period.

In his 1983 film *The Lost Requiem*, Khosrow Sinai, an Iranian documentary film director, traces the legacy of Polish life in Iran during this period. He contributes to our understanding of how the Polish women were viewed at the time: "Polish maids were sought by well-to-do Iranian ladies who wanted to learn makeup and Western fashions from their servants, who often had better backgrounds and education than the employers themselves."[68] Another interesting cultural exchange may be noted in the fact that on Naderi Street in Tehran, Polish teachers taught ordinary Iranians the Polish language.[69] By March 1943, Polish refugees in Iran numbered approximately 150,000, and the influx continued.[70] The JDC envoy reported some 1,800 Jews among the Poles and an unknown number of Jews who were not registered as such on March 8.[71] The JDC contingency in Iran still expected to transfer some 5,000 Jews recently rescued from Nazi-occupied Bulgaria and the Balkan States.[72] In truth, the Jewish authorities had very little idea what to expect. In an internal report they wrote,

The presence of 1,800 Jewish refugees in Teheran, 75% of whom are certificated for Palestine, is in itself not a serious problem. The hundreds of thousands of Jewish refugees still in Russia—whether they remain there or eventually are evacuated—this is the problem. While there are fairly reliable estimates of the number of Polish Jewish refugees still in Russia—200,000–300,000 of whom the preponderant majority [are] in Southern Asiatic Russia (Turkestan)—there [is] no information obtainable about the number or whereabouts in Russia of the Jewish refugees from the Baltic states, Roumania, and other countries.[73]

Reports suggested that the Polish government was negotiating the release of no fewer than an additional 800,000 Poles still dispersed in Russia.[74]

Most of the Jews were in transition to Palestine as part of a three-way collaboration among the JDC, the Polish Red Cross, and the British government, the last of which issued visas to the Palestine-bound migrants.[75] The rest of the refugees, however, prepared for a long stay in Iran. The terms of their stay were not entirely clear, and their status in their newly imposed homeland was constantly negotiated. Given the available solutions for the refugees, a growing number of them decided to work toward making Iran their permanent country of residence.

While accurate numbers are hard to obtain, partial reports from all of the organizations involved are available. For example, in March 1943 word reached JDC headquarters that, out of five hundred Polish Jews surveyed in Tehran, "about 50 of the refugees have established themselves and were seeking permission to remain in Persia."[76] This data suggests that approximately 10 percent of the Polish Jewish refugees may have wished to stay in Iran instead of taking advantage of the opportunity to move to Palestine. A similar ratio among non-Jews would have meant that ten thousand to forty thousand refugees might have sought settlement in Iran. Moreover, in August 1944 the International Red Cross representative in Tehran sent a telegram to the International Committee of the Red Cross in Geneva, informing the committee on recent requests from Hungarian

Jews in Tehran who arrived among the European refugees. These Hungarian Jews asked the Red Cross to urgently help their relatives in Hungary obtain visas to Iran, as Hungary had recently been occupied by Nazi Germany.[77] The response arrived six days later, stating that the British authorities "are not favorable to this immigration."[78]

U.S. brigadier general Greely, like many other observers, believed that the Poles left an undeniable mark on Iran's society and culture. Indeed, many of the wartime Polish institutions, such as art galleries, nightclubs, churches, and synagogues, remained active and prospered at least until the 1979 revolution. Even in Tehran today, at 30 Tir Street, stands Iran's only Ashkenazi synagogue.

Postwar Legacy of Polish Refugees in Iran

The vast majority of Polish refugees living in Isfahan during the war left that city in 1945. Because Isfahan had offered refugees—and especially Polish children—a welcoming, secure home, one can understand how difficult it might have been for them to leave the city only a few years later. Again, Beaupré-Stankiewicz recounts the departure:

I finally left Isfahan on Monday 23rd July 1945. The last day was not pleasant or happy, merely very sad. My nerves let me down completely, and everything else as well—I had a fever, headache, and [was] physically and mentally worn out. . . . In front of the branch office they loaded us onto a lorry in record time, there was not a moment to say goodbye properly in the confusion; we had our last look at Kuh-Sofe, at the blue domes, the green trees of Chahar Bagh, and it was over. Isfahan was behind us, a long (when one is young, everything seems long) three year period of life rich in experiences and attainments.[79]

During the war and immediately afterward, a significant number of Iranians and Poles intermarried. Obtaining the exact number of Polish individuals who sought permanent residency in Iran after marrying is problematic, especially since many of these unions were kept secret, mostly for religious reasons.[80] In the 2008 documentary *My Iranian Paradise*, director Katia Forbert Petersen, the daughter of a Danish engineer and a Polish refugee, recalls her childhood in Tehran.[81] Although born in Denmark after World War II, she grew up in Tehran in a community very much shaped by Polish refugees. In the film she interviews her parents' friends who married Iranian partners, settled in Tehran, and never left. These immigrants discuss the cultural life they created and state that Iran remained their home, their safe place. Petersen herself left Iran in her twenties after the 1979 revolution.

In 2000 Associated Press reporter Anwar Faruqi wrote an article for the *Washington Post* describing a few survivors of the World War II Polish refugee community in Iran, including Anna Borkowska. Especially interesting is the depiction of the contents of her living room: a cheap piano on which she played Polish songs, a pile of Polish magazines, and a variety of photos on display, including ones of Ayatollah Khomeini and Pope John Paul II (who was Polish), as well as portraits of Jesus and Mary. The pictures and images present the range of identities she (and her personal history) contained.[82]

One further example of the temporary integration of Polish and other Eastern European refugees and immigrants may be viewed in *Portrait Photographs from Isfahan: Faces in Transition, 1920–1950*. This book documents the development of studio photography in Isfahan in the twentieth century. Among the hundreds of portraits from the city, several dozen individual and family portraits stand out. In those images, one sees Polish and Russian immigrants in school, attending scout meetings, at home, and frequenting clubs. Isfahan's pioneer photographers documented a wide swath of subjects, including the wartime presence of exiles in that city.[83] One could make a compelling argument that the inclusion of Poles, Russians, and other Eastern European nationals as subjects of Iranian photography during World War II suggests the refugees' successful integration into Iran's social fabric.

Nevertheless, after the war ended in 1945, the majority of refugees left Iran. Regional political instability (even before the war ended), as well as rising tensions between Britain and the Soviet Union, prompted an overwhelming majority of the refugees to leave as soon as Western nations began opening their gates. Those tensions, along with rising political instability in Iran, created a sense of imminent danger for some of the refugees.[84] As suggested earlier, those refugees who wished to stay and marry Iranian citizens did so. It is not entirely clear how the Iranian government considered other refugee applications to remain in Iran. We know that a number of refugees were able to stay even without marrying Iranians; it is likely that their respective religious communities petitioned on their behalf.

On August 30, 1945, a letter was sent to the British ambassador to Iran, Sir Reader William Bullard, on behalf of the Polish refugees of Isfahan. In the letter they express their gratitude for being taken care of by His Majesty's government and ask for this protection to be extended for "as long as it should be necessary." The letter refers to the British plan to evacuate the Polish refugees from Iran and have many of them returned to Poland. In the letter they plead,

Almost all Poles who are in Iran went through Russian prisons, concentration camps and deportations. Subsequently to the extremely hard conditions of life in Russia every Polish family has lost at least one, often more, of its members. . . . We are ready to give our lives for the good of our Fatherland, but nobody can convince us that it should be our duty to increase the number of unnecessary victims by passive submission to a regime introduced against the will of our Nation, and which we learned well from our own experience. Taking in account what we told above, we desire to inform Your Excellency that the Polish refugees do not want to return to Poland as long as the political situation there would not change.[85]

This letter, containing signatures from 351 households, mentions that this was the stance of the majority of refugees in Isfahan. While a small number of refugees returned to Poland, the majority began lives elsewhere. Because of the postwar wave of migration westward, as well as new immigration policies in the United States, New Zealand, Australia, and Great Britain, a significant number of Polish expatriates chose these nations as their final destinations.[86]

Sinai's documentary film *The Lost Requiem* follows in the footsteps of Iran's wartime refugees; for example, Sinai visits the Campolu district in Ahvaz. The name is short for Camp Polonia, one of the primary postwar exit points for Polish refugees leaving Iran. The film, which first premiered in Poland on September 26, 2007, depicts "the destiny of Polish people in Iran; how they arrived, how they lived, how they died, how they married, and where they left to."[87]

Minority Within a Minority: Jewish Emigration from Iraq

Jewish migration to Iran started long before World War II, propelled by a variety of circumstances. During World War I many Iraqi Jews seeking to avoid forced conscription into the Ottoman Army fled the empire, and many of them migrated to Iran.[88] Relations between Jewish communities in Iraq and Iran had enjoyed a long history, revolving around Talmudic centers of religious training (for example, Iranian rabbis were trained in the seminaries in Baghdad), as well as commercial ties. Between 1914 and 1918 the first major wave of migrants arriving in Iran settled mainly in Abadan because of its proximity to the Iraqi city of Basra, which had a large population of Jews. There they established community institutions such as a synagogue and a youth club. These institutions facilitated the second wave of immigration, between 1941 and 1951.[89] The Jewish community of Iraq was generally affluent, overwhelmingly urban, educated, and very much integrated. Its members excelled in commerce and in the financial sectors, and at its peak, it constituted a third of Baghdad's population.[90] Hence, upon arrival in Iran, the community's members practiced their skills and exerted a profound impact. Jewish influence in Abadan, for example, was so strong that it is still visible today. One of Abadan's central city squares is named Maydan-i Alfi, after the Alfi family's department store. The Alfi family, well known today in Israel's performing arts community, immigrated to Abadan from Basra in the early 1940s and subsequently to Israel in 1949.

Many Jews in this second wave of immigrants fled Iraq due to outright persecution and pogroms, most famously, the Farhud of June 1941 (translated from Arabic as "violent dispossession" or "pogrom").[91] Hayyim, one of my interviewees, emigrated from Iraq to Iran with his family. He recounts that

the Jewish Agency and other Zionist organizations wanted to create a mass movement from Iraq to Israel, and they operated openly. This created tensions between the Iraqis and the Jewish community.[92] When the time was right for them, especially after 1948 and the establishment of Israel, Iraqi authorities started to persecute anyone they suspected was related to the Zionist movement, and many Jews had to flee. Where would they go? For many of them there was one option, and that was Iran.

Hayyim's life story sheds light on the connection between Iraqi and Iranian communities. "We were Iraqis for many generations, maybe four or more, but before that, my family came from Iran. My dad had a Persian passport, which later got us into trouble in Iraq."[93] Interestingly, Hayyim's father carried a Persian (Iranian) passport as a memento of the long Iranian-Iraqi Jewish connection. Hayyim's narrative reveals a circular movement between Iran and Iraq that occurred over many generations. In the nineteenth century, for example, Iranian Jews migrated to Iraq for many reasons, including seminary studies and the pursuit of business opportunities.

Their goal was to settle in the most flourishing and dominant Jewish community in the Middle East. Passports had just been instituted at that time; the possession of a passport was far less significant initially than it would become in later decades. However, Jews of Iranian descent kept their Iranian passports and maintained ties with communities across the border. After 1948 about twelve thousand Iraqi Jews bearing Iranian passports returned to Iran, some en route to Israel and some relocating temporarily or permanently in Iran.[94]

This second wave of emigrants from Iraq was far from homogeneous. Thousands of Jews traveled from Iraq to Iran on their way to Israel/Palestine because of the transition camps in Iran operated by the Jewish Agency, the JDC, and other Jewish relief organizations. Jewish immigrants stayed in the transition camps for long periods of time, sometimes up to two years, depending on the efficiency of the agencies' collaboration with the British Mandate government in Palestine. For some Jews, this was the second migration in their lifetimes. Between 1924 and 1928 Russian Jewish refugees arrived in Iraq, seeking relief from persecution in Europe.[95] On June 1–2, 1941, during the holiday of Shavu'ot, a series of violent and often brutal anti-Semitic events (later referred to as the Farhud) erupted in many cities across Iraq, although primarily in Baghdad. These riots occurred during a political power vacuum, shortly after the fall of Baghdad's pro-Nazi government. What followed was a chaotic purge of Jews, who were charged by anti-British forces as being agents of British colonialism. Jewish property was vandalized, synagogues and Jewish establishments were torched, and hundreds of casualties ensued.

Following the Farhud, many Iraqi Jews decided to leave. Some fled to Iran, especially following the Baghdad massacres. Mania Fanahi, for example, was a Russian Jew who migrated to Iraq in the 1920s and then, after the Farhud, to Iran, where she settled and married an Iranian man. She always carried a bottle of poison at the ready in the event that she was forced to return to Iraq.[96] In any case, many Iraqi Jews chose to stay in Iran with their relatives, mainly in the borderland between Basra and Abadan. Another group of Jewish Iraqi immigrants was composed of Jews who had immigrated to Israel, failed to adjust, and returned to Iran.

According to Hayyim, "Many Jews left [Iraq] in 1941, but most of them left later, around 1948 as part of an agreement between Israel, Britain, and Iraq. They were free to leave but had to leave all their belongings behind."[97] The Iraqi and Iranian Jewish communities were intertwined for so long that many Jews of Iranian descent had lived in Iraq for generations:

We stayed in Baghdad until 1952, when we first moved to Israel. My father did not succeed in business and he said: "I have a Persian passport, and I just want to get out." He renewed his passport in the Iranian embassy in Istanbul; he then left for Tehran and felt like it was Baghdad. There was already a large Jewish Iraqi community. The first night he went to a hotel, and the next morning he went to the bazaar where he met a Jewish Iraqi. He immediately invited my father to stay with him in his apartment and after a few months we joined him.[98]

Another interviewee, Daud, also arrived with his family in Iran, but he came earlier, following the Farhud:

My family moved to Iran in 1942. Most of them were from Baghdad and some were from Basra. We first arrived in Khurramshahr [in the Persian Gulf]. My great grandfather (on my mother's side) arrived in the region in the 1920s when it was ruled by Shaykh Khaz'al, and he became friends with him. In Basra we had an import/export business so we knew the area well, and then we settled in Abadan.[99]

The threatening circumstances under which Jews escaped Iraq for Iran left a profound mark on them as individuals and as a community. The representation of Iran as a temporary shelter recurred during my interviews with them. Although they appreciated the relative safety of Iran, the gravity of events, and subsequent anxiety, that had forced these individuals to leave their Iraqi homeland never entirely dissipated—especially among first-generation migrants and their parents' generation. As Hayyim recounts,

We never felt this is our country. Because we got hurt in our homeland, Iraq, we always lived for the moment. We didn't invest in property, because we saw that in a case of emergency it gets stuck, and may leave us behind or [be] left behind. Many of us lived lavishly [spent money on parties, travels abroad, and tuition to the best schools], and wired every extra penny to London. The Persians were the exact opposite. They didn't care for London or America. They cared only for Iran and kept all their money there.[100]

Hayyim's observation is essential to understanding the dominant mindset among Iranian Jews. They viewed Iran as the facilitator of their accumulation of wealth. Iranian Jews felt deeply for Iran and did not want to leave it or to invest elsewhere.[101]

By 1951 the Iraqi Jewish population in Iran numbered fifteen thousand and was indeed a "minority within a minority."[102] Iraqi Jews in Iran developed a hybrid identity in an attempt to preserve their Arab culture and language while making use of the skills, education, and vocations they brought from Iraq, especially in the commercial realm. Cultural tensions arose between native Jewish Iranians and Iraqi immigrants. Iranian Jews addressed newly arrived Iraqis pejoratively as "Arabs,"[103] and in return, the Iraqis labeled their Iranian coreligionists as "'Ajams,"[104] a long-held tradition. Despite this détente between Arabs and 'Ajams, the distinction was not entirely clear for individual families. During my interview with Daud, for example, something interesting happened to illustrate this point. Daud called his elderly father in order to verify a few facts. Overhearing the conversation, I realized that they were using Arabic and Persian interchangeably, pronouncing Arabic words with a deep and beautiful Iraqi accent, and Persian words in a flawless Persian accent. This conversation exemplified the cultural hybridism that they had created and in which they lived. "We had much more in common with the Arabs in Abadan than with the Persian Jews," says Daud. "We spoke Arabic at home, we shared the same background, the same language, and we bonded on that basis. They [the Arabs] too suffered from the chauvinistic nationalist Persian approach and were ill-treated."[105] This problematic relationship with the Iranian Jewish community prompted the Iraqis to develop separate community institutions in the postwar years.

Ettefaq: Iraqi-British Education in Tehran

One of the most fascinating Iraqi educational endeavors in Iran was the Ettefaq School. Established in 1948 by Mayer Abdallah Basson, a wealthy Baghdadi Jew who had come to Iran only a few years earlier,[106] the Ettefaq School embodied educational principles and standards that the Iraqi community had left behind in Iraq. Because the Ettefaq School was fully coordinated with the British Ministry of Education curriculum and exams, its graduates were allowed to pursue academic studies in England. When Iraqi Jews arrived in Iran, they felt that existing Jewish institutions did not meet their expectations, a collective sentiment that propelled Basson to endow the school and attached complex. The complex included a synagogue that adhered to the Iraqi Jewish tradition, as well as an event hall.[107] It housed the Iraqi Youth Club and addressed all the needs of the Iraqi Jewish community in Tehran.

The school's board erected a dedication wall reflecting Ettefaq's mission near the synagogue's eastern entrance. Interestingly, the top of the wall features Basson's curved portrait, accompanied by a short biography in Arabic and Persian at the bottom. In the middle is the school's endowment charter, engraved in Hebrew.

The title of the charter reads, "Mazkeret Netsah" (for eternal memory), and the charter itself explains, "This land with all its buildings and equipment was bought with the blessing of the great philanthropist Mayer Abda[allah] Basson and handed to the Iraqi Israeli community in Iran with the following conditions." It then spells out some of the entailed conditions. For example, the third paragraph emphasizes the importance of the school's financial independence: "The school's expenses will be taken from tuition or revenues from different usage [ventures] of these buildings." This article secures the future of the school for as long as there is a community to use it. The fifth article highlights the school's unique academic program: "The school's curriculum will include Jewish religious studies and Hebrew, along with Persian and Arabic languages and other living languages and the addition of necessary sciences." In fact, Ettefaq's students studied with British textbooks and many of the teachers came from England. While English remained the principal language of instruction, literature and philosophy were taught in Arabic. Other subjects, such as economy and science, were taught in Persian. The next article reads, "It is permissible to build new buildings on school property. All revenues will belong to the school, as do revenues from other events and weddings that will be conducted in school." When the school was built in 1947–1948, it had only ten classrooms, which, at the time, sufficed the needs of the Iraqi community. Basson did not want to limit expansion potential and therefore made it possible to add more space as the need arose—as indeed happened in the 1960s. The final article underscores the administration's belief in the superior status of Arabic over any other language: "The Arabic version of the charter will be superior in the event that any of these conditions need clarification." Even though Ettefaq was a place of many languages, it was first and foremost the institution of a proud Iraqi community. At the bottom of the plaque, all members of the Iraqi Jewish committee in Iran signed as witnesses.

Ettefaq offered a unique educational experience. Although it was built near Jewish neighborhoods, rather than complying with requests from the community (for example, that the curriculum include certain aspects of Jewish education or additional Hebrew instruction), Ettefaq aspired to transform the community. Similar to some private missionary schools across Iran, Ettefaq School made a conscious choice to become an elite Iranian institution. As mentioned earlier, while Ettefaq addressed the needs of the Iraqi Jewish community, its high-end facilities and academic program attracted many Iranian Jews as well. As modeled by other Jewish schools, Ettefaq instituted a tuition waiver program for individuals facing financial hardship. Indeed, approximately 30 percent of students came from poor families and therefore received full scholarships to attend the school.[108]

In 1967 the Ettefaq board turned to Barukh Berukhim, a professor at Tehran University, and offered him the position of school principal.[109] Berukhim agreed, bringing with him a vision of transforming Ettefaq from a community school to a prestigious educational institution. Some of his terms for accepting the position were to double the student population and to accept more non-Jewish students. Ettefaq was already undergoing expansion construction, and, indeed, by the end of the decade it had almost two thousand students, with many more on waiting lists. Berukhim brought as many university colleagues as he could to teach at Ettefaq, with the goal of preparing students for university entrance exams. In very little time, Ettefaq ranked first among schools in Iran.[110]

For the Iranian Jewish community particularly, dramatic changes ensued following the twentieth-century migrations, resulting in a new level of diversity. As we will see in Chapter 3, the Jewish population in Iran evolved from a fairly rural society to an overwhelmingly urban one, from impoverishment and illiteracy to a comfortable, educated position in the middle class.

One might ask, Was the phenomenon of Iraqi and Polish immigrants merely a momentary encounter between Iranian Jews and their non-Iranian brethren? Can one measure the significance of such an encounter in terms of its cultural and religious impact? There may never be a conclusive assessment or answer to these questions. What *is* tangible, and therefore quantitative, however, is the arrival in Iran of international Jewish institutions such as Otsar Ha-Torah (the Jewish Orthodox education network, with anti-Zionism as its core ideology) and the JDC (which continued to have significant involvement in Iran's intercommunal affairs until much later in the twentieth century).

After the war, Iraqi Jews continued to flourish in Iran. In 1949 Jacob Blaustein of the JDC requested an audience with Mohammad Reza Shah Pahlavi; at this meeting, the Shah indicated a willingness to naturalize many of the Iraqi Jews. Although some of these Jews immigrated to Israel, England, and other destinations, their mark remained on the community in Tehran for decades. In 1965 Herbert Katzki (an official of the JDC) reported that there were around four thousand Iraqi Jews still living in Iran. About half had become naturalized citizens. The other half carried Iraqi passports that had been renewed periodically by the Iraqi consulate in Iran. However, in 1964 the Iraqi government began refusing renewal of those passports, leaving many Iraqi Jews nominally stateless. In response, the Iranian government, which favorably viewed the contributions of this community to Iran, applied the same bureaucratic mechanism originally created for White Russians. That is, the Iranian government supplied Iraqi Jews with documents of identification, allowing them to live and work freely. Moreover, they were given Iranian-issued laissez-passers for traveling abroad, when needed.[111]

This chapter has focused on the integral role Iran played during the war, a role traditionally characterized as inconsequential. While major powers did not always consult the Iranian government or its citizens on significant issues—such as allowing the influx of hundreds of thousands of refugees or directing resources for war efforts—both Iranian officials and the Iranian people proved admirably accommodating and welcoming. It should be noted that not all Middle Eastern nations and peoples responded as generously. Corry Guttstadt eloquently points out, for example, that Turkey's government and its citizens were reticent about receiving Jewish refugees fleeing the Holocaust.[112] Given that Turkey was not under occupation, perhaps it could be argued that a "nonoccupied" Iran would have responded similarly. However, historical evidence suggests the opposite. When faced with the unexpected and, inarguably, overwhelming arrival of hundreds of thousands of Polish refugees—Jews and non-Jews alike—the nation of Iran, its people and urban communities, rose to the occasion, not only receiving these refugees with generosity but also strongly supporting their efforts to reclaim normal lives.

2

The Iranian Political Sphere
Shaping a National Identity

THE INVASION OF THE ALLIED armies in 1941, the deposition of Reza Shah, and the more or less coercive opening of the political and journalistic spheres in Iran invited Jews, among others, to take an active part in shaping their nation's new identity. The Constitutional Revolution of 1906–1911 is an apt place to begin because, in many ways, it popularized the notion of a public political sphere in Iran. The revolution created a new notion of citizenship, granted minorities elected representation, and released them from nominal dependency on the Shah (the Qajars, at the time) to protect their rights and communities. Subsequently, minority communities became increasingly politicized. Electing nominees, conducting selections and election procedures, submitting petitions, and contributing to the definition of Iranian national identity—all came out of the revolution and the accompanying political process. As in many other locales in the Middle East and elsewhere (especially Europe),[1] minorities supported parties, usually with community or radical leftist affiliations, that tried to eliminate the role of ethnic or religious identities in articulating the national one. Interestingly, in the first Majlis, the recognized religious minorities (Jews, Armenians, and Zoroastrians) were asked to withdraw their elected representatives and let Muslims represent them. The Jews and Armenians conceded and were represented in the first Majlis by two Muslim clerics, both of whom deeply cared for the well-being of their adoptive communities. Sayyid 'Abdullah Bihbahani represented the Jews and Sayyid Muhammad Tabataba'i represented the Armenians.[2]

The Constitutional Revolution, which was the last nail in the Qajar coffin, symbolized lost dynastic power and the infiltration of modern political ideas regarding state, citizenship, and nationalism. These notions, with varying degrees of European origin, also took root in nearby nations such as Turkey, Iraq, and Egypt. Although the revolution empowered Iranian citizens, and for the first time granted representation in a parliamentary system, it was still primarily an undelivered political promise. Following this period of innovation and experimentation, which was in turn followed by a decade of political strife and instability, a new dynasty was established (1921–1925) by Reza Khan—a dynasty with clear ideas about progress and modernization. With fierce determination, Reza Khan removed any obstacle that stood in his way, including political opposition, instigating an iron-fisted rule that lasted nearly twenty years. In 1941, after his abdication, the political sphere opened once again; new freedoms emerged, including the right of parties, such as the Communist Party, to organize. The political sphere in Iran diversified significantly; a wide array of ideas emerged, ranging from Fascist ideologies to Communism. Nazi propaganda, which served as a pretext for the Allied occupation, continued to thrive in the margins of the discourse.

The next section sheds light on these transformative events, especially the Communist Tudeh Party (which translates as "the party of the masses"), in part through the use of oral histories. Several individuals whom I interviewed are referred to by the first names Pinhas and Habib, again to respect anonymity.

The Tudeh: A Party of Minorities

Communist endeavors appeared in Iran at the turn of the twentieth century; however, these early attempts proved to be minor and scattered. Momentum particularly dwindled during the reign of Reza Shah, when governmental suppression left little room for political discourse or activity. Official government mechanisms dictated new codes that nurtured state ideals and banned large parts of the political spectrum. Of all political groups, the Communist factions probably suffered most under this system.[3]

Reza Shah viewed Communism as a major threat to the monarchy and to the social order he intended to instill. Therefore, he forcefully fought any attempt to establish a party or organization sympathetic to Communism.

Furthermore, Reza Shah revoked school licenses for Armenians, Azeris, and other linguistic minorities under the pretext of the Iranianization of the education system, which in effect meant Persianization. The Shah's vision of a noninclusive, homogeneous Iranian identity was at odds with any potential notion that Iran's many ethnic and religious minorities were integral parts of the nation. Historian David Yaghoubian analyzes the discourse from within the Armenian Iranian community and exposes the contradictions of Zohrab Saginian, the Armenian representative to the Majlis: "It was paradoxical that Zohrab was himself an Iranian nationalist. He considered himself an Armenian-Iranian, and was beholden and loyal to the Iranian nation. He was supportive of most of Reza Shah's secularizing reforms as well as his policies to modernize and strengthen Iran. . . . For Zohrab, the nation would only be cohesive when the state recognized and celebrated the contributions and loyalty of its diverse population."[4] Essentially, Saginian's version of nationalism celebrated the multiethnicity of Iran and viewed it as a strength rather than as a weakness, as the Shah's nationalism implied.

However, Mohammad Reza Pahlavi's ascendance to the throne in 1941 radically shifted Iran's political atmosphere.[5] The political vacuum created by the elder Shah's departure, combined with the chaos of wartime and the lack of effective foreign imposition of a singular political ideology, opened the political spectrum to many, and as a result, a wide array of political parties began to appear. Hundreds of new newspapers, political journals, and pamphlets emerged as well, heralding the beginning of the Liberal Age. This period also witnessed the emergence of one of the most influential parties in Iranian modern history, the Communist Tudeh Party.

With the Soviets in the north and the British in the south, Iran became an occupied nation, divided into two spheres of influence, as Chapter 1 discussed. With Nazi and Fascist threats growing, based on the nominally simple dichotomy of liberal versus Fascist, a new political sphere arose. Increasingly, political parties began to reflect the ethnic and religious diversity of Iran's population. The Tudeh Party appealed particularly to anti-Fascist forces in Iran. Spearheaded by local intelligentsia and workers' unions, the Tudeh Party became a new political home to many minority groups for years to come. In a short time, Jews and Armenians assumed prominent roles in the party. As historian Ervand Abrahamian suggests, minorities' massive engagement and the party's even wider popularity among minorities gained the Tudeh Party a reputation for being the party of Armenians, Jews, and Caucasian émigrés.[6] As was the case in many other countries—for example, Egypt, Iraq, and Morocco in the Middle East and England, France, and Germany in Western Europe—minorities found a way to become involved in the nation's political and social life in Communist parties that, at least nominally, adhered to universalist ideologies.[7]

In 1946 oil workers in the Abadan refineries called the first large-scale strike with active support of the Tudeh Party. British officials quickly represented the strike as a "Jewish-Communist plot to sabotage the AIOC [Anglo-Iranian Oil Company]."[8] This response underscores the extent of Jewish (or rather, minority) involvement in the party's affairs. Shrewdly, in order to discredit the party, British officials (as well as others outside Iran) focused criticism on a visible element also understood to be controversial—namely, the Tudeh's prominent Jewish membership.

Iranian Jews had been involved in leftist parties dating back to the pre–World War II era, forming an anti-Fascist movement as early as the 1930s. The Tudeh Party was certainly one of the oldest political organizations with which Jews sympathized, and they actively supported it. Indeed, the Tudeh Party adamantly opposed Fascism and for years published articles and editorials denouncing the Fascist inclinations of nationalist groups in Iranian society, openly criticizing the prevailing anti-Semitic climate in Iran.[9] The Tudeh Party's enduring defense of the Jewish community and its message of equality for all—regardless of ethnic, religious, or socioeconomic status—attracted many young Jews from Iran's middle and lower middle classes.[10] Iraj Farhoumand, a Jewish Tudeh activist, explained that active Jewish participation in the party was inarguably connected to troubling developments in Europe, Iran's geographic proximity to Russia, and the party's inclusiveness.[11] He references the vast Jewish participation in the 1940s and 1950s and even cites Jews who were members of the party's central committee.[12] In those decades many Jews became loyal Communists for a multitude of reasons, and not merely because of a strong investment in Communist ideology. The specific Iranian context is discussed later, but other global trends also played a significant role.

First is the generational effect directly connected to World War II. Neither exclusively Jewish nor minority related, this generational effect proved to be a global phenomenon. Zygmunt Bauman beautifully frames Jewish acceptance of Communism worldwide as yet another means to break traditional institutions, and Tony Judt explains that images of the victorious Red Army and the brave anti-Fascist and anti-Nazi resistance of Communist parties seduced and convinced this generation to support Communism.[13] Many Jews felt that the Red Army and Communism had saved them from the horrors of the Holocaust. Middle Eastern Jews were well aware of the events of the Holocaust at that point, post-1945. This awareness, combined with the promise of social equality in creating new secular, nationalist societies, heightened the allure of Communist ideology.

The second factor attracting Iranian and Iraqi Jews to Communism was closely tied to regional circumstances. As had occurred in Europe decades earlier among European Jewish youth, Communist activism and ideology offered young Jews not only a path to enter local society as patriots but also the opportunity to rebel against tradition, tight family structure, and religion. Sami Michael, a renowned Israeli Iraqi novelist born in 1926, grew up in Iraq, then fled to Iran en route to Israel. He identifies the youth rebellion against tradition and patriarchal order as a major reason that Jewish Iraqi youths supported Communism or joined the Communist Party. However, he also cites the aspect of adventure in tandem with the realization that Communism was an antidote to the Fascist and ultranationalist tendencies that began to spread in the early 1940s.[14]

An interviewee for this chapter, Pinhas, was born in 1931 to an impoverished lower-class family in Hamadan, one of the oldest cities in Iran. He had eleven siblings and attended a Jewish school until sixth grade. Pinhas's recollection of his first encounter with the Tudeh Party is particularly revelatory:

I left school because we were many children in the house and one income was not enough. I had to get out and earn some money. I had a cart from which I sold anything I could find and a regular spot on the street. Across from where I was standing there was a building with a sign Hizb-i Tudeh, so one day after work I walked in. Inside there were many people—young and adults—and there was a tennis table. They invited me in, and I played for a while. After I finished they invited me to stay for a lecture. I started to go there on a regular basis; to play ping-pong and listen to lectures. They talked about equality and basic economy and taught us all the Marxist and leftist ideals. Until this day, almost seventy years later, I still play ping-pong and I still believe in all these ideals.[15]

The Tudeh "club" welcomed people from all walks of life to socialize and become activists in what became the mission of their generation. Part of the charm was the chance to meet some of the most influential intellectuals of Iran at that time. Not surprisingly, the Tudeh club's appeal also centered on its social and entertainment opportunities.

Doctrinally speaking, the Tudeh was not a typical Communist party. Although secular by nature, it applied religious terminology when needed and lacked some of Communism's most recognizable signifiers. Party by-laws, for example, never mentioned the Marxist slogan "Workers of the world, unite,"[16] an omission that arguably points to the party's local-national goals, which it prioritized over grander global schemes.

Nevertheless, the Tudeh was concerned with the global mission to resist Fascism and to support Soviet victories in multiple World War II theaters. These concerns, however, did not detract from its primary focus on national agendas, such as becoming the party of the Iranian masses. From the 1940s through 1953, the Tudeh enjoyed wide support among Iranian peasants and laborers, and it ultimately became the Iranian intellectuals' party of choice. As mentioned, it appealed to and sought support from people of all social classes. Indeed, many industrialists, as well as individuals who might have been considered bourgeoisie in other nations, joined the party's highest ranks. Iran's Tudeh Party did not emerge out of class struggle, however, and most of the party's supporters in the early years were indifferent to Marxism, to say the least. One historian of the Iranian left, Sepehr Zabih, remarked,

Up to the Iran-Azerbaijan Crisis of 1946, it [Tudeh] was not organizationally or ideologically a true Communist party. While Tudeh generally supported the Soviets, support was strongest when the West (led by the United States and Great Britain) were closely aligned with the Soviet Union against the Nazis, and were actively involved in the enormous war effort enabling the Soviet Union to resist a Nazi invasion, crush the German war machine, and terminate hostilities in Europe. Thus, supporting Soviet policies at that time could not be equated with espousing Marxism-Leninism.[17]

Zabih decouples any kind of support for the Soviet Union during World War II from dogmatic identification with Marxist theories. Iranian leftists demonstrated independent thinking in many other instances as well and, despite self-identifying as a Communist party, paid much more attention to local politics, prioritizing Iran's interests over Soviet interests.[18]

Another interviewee for this chapter, Habib, was born in Tehran in the early 1930s and as of 2017 was residing in North America. At age sixteen he joined the Tudeh and remained an active member for more than three decades. His political activity landed him in Qasr, the Shah's prison, a half dozen times before he left Iran. Habib recalls, "I knew nothing about Marx or Marxism when I joined Tudeh. I joined because this was the only place that they did not call me *Johud* [a derogatory name for Jews]. I learned Marxism in Qasr prison, shortly after I joined the party." Habib's story is by no means unique. Many minorities joined the party to combat the social ostracism they experienced. "We [the Jews] were attracted to Tudeh in order to become more Iranian, and the Armenians also had cultural ties to Russia [the Soviet Union] so they already recognized the political language," concluded Habib.[19]

Yaghoubian provides several explanations for the Tudeh appeal among Christians and especially Armenian communities. Referring to Abrahamian's seminal work, *Iran Between Two Revolutions*, Yaghoubian mentions the Tudeh's commitment to reopening Armenian and Assyrian schools after the 1938 decree.[20] The party also championed other minorities' rights (for example, by adding another Assyrian Majlis deputy), opposed policies that were enacted during Reza Shah's period, and led the movement to offer full citizenship and true equality to ethnic and religious minorities.[21]

Possibly, migrants and refugees from the Soviet Union and Nazi-occupied Europe were more susceptible to radical leftist and Communist politics due to their having experienced the horrors promulgated by Nazis and Fascists. Moreover, since the Soviet Red Army occupied northern Iran, they may have also provided ideological training while attending to refugees. We do know, in fact, that the Soviets were involved in the elections of eight to ten Communist representatives to the Majlis from 1942 to 1948.[22]

Opportunities extended to minorities, first by the Constitutional Revolution (1906–1911) and subsequently by the deposition of Reza Shah (1941), helped to position them as leading figures in their communities. Armenians, thanks to their professional training obtained in community clubs and organizations, schools, and churches, assumed leadership positions in the workers' unions, which became a natural base of support for Tudeh in the 1940s and 1950s. When the opportunity arose to voice protest against the prejudiced tendencies in Iranian society, minorities came together behind the party's leadership. The fact that they served as the leaders of almost all the unions gave the impression of Armenian overrepresentation in the party.

Jews, on the other hand, found their niche in other fields. The curriculum at schools such as the Alliance Israélite Universelle (AIU) and Ettefaq led Jews to master key languages, such as Persian, Arabic, French, and

English, and to write eloquently in these languages. Their linguistic skills were put to effective use in several fields, including international commerce and journalism. Many Jews started writing for the Iranian press, and as a result of their strong presence in the field and their tendency to support the Tudeh Party as part of the anti-Fascist, antiracist front, they were considered, almost exclusively, the in-house journalists of the party.

Jews in Journalism: Tudeh's Newspapers

The importance of minorities in leadership positions was especially apparent in the literary output of the Tudeh's official newspapers: *Rahbar*, *Mardum*, and *Razm*.[23] *Rahbar*, for example, published antiracist editorials and op-eds, and it counted Jewish writers among its regular staff. Shmuel Anvar, a Jewish journalist and Tudeh activist, also established and edited a semiofficial weekly newspaper, *Nissan*. Officially, *Nissan* was an organ of the Cultural and Social Society of Iranian Jews (CSSIJ; Jam'eyat-e Farhangi va ijtima'i-yi yahudiyan-i iran). Prominent Jewish writers including Ibrahim Faiz-Jav and Muhandes Ibrahim Iran-Mehr contributed to both *Nissan* and *Rahbar*.[24] *Nissan* also consistently defended minorities' rights. During periods when *Rahbar* was banned, *Nissan* continued to present the views and opinions of the party's leadership. Indeed, *Nissan* enjoyed wide exposure and far-reaching distribution.[25]

The close association of *Nissan* with Soviet-supporting factions of the Tudeh Party is obvious from articles appearing in the newspaper, as well as from the language used. The ambiguous response of the Tudeh and the Soviet Union to Israel and Zionism was unmistakable—and was presented as a conversation between different streams of thought in the party and in the community. *Nissan* covered local and global political Jewish issues extensively and provided editorial interpretation of ongoing events. It presented Zionism as a "puppet of American imperialism" (*alatidast imperialism amrika*). During the Prague trials of 1953, *Nissan*'s journalists asserted that the "leaders of today's state of Israel have sold themselves to American imperialists and have used Zionist organizations to further American interests in the People's Democracies [the Eastern Bloc]." In this article Zionism is described as the "political and nationalist movement of Jewish bourgeoisies."[26] Moreover, *Nissan* also translated articles from the Israeli press; its editorial board presented what they considered to be fallacies on the part of Israel and the Zionist project. One article examined the rift between two factions of the kibbutzim movement (overwhelmingly perceived in Israel to be leftist-socialist, to varying degrees). The article claimed that the kibbutzim who opposed Prime Minister David Ben-Gurion's anti-Soviet policies were targeted and harassed by the "right-wing" MAPAI (Mifleget Po'ale Eretz Yisra'el; the Workers' Party of the Land of Israel) and its supporters. The article mentioned especially Kibbutz Yad-Hanna, acknowledged to be an ardent Communist kibbutz, and the "left-wing" MAPAM (Mifleget ha-Po'alim ha-Me'uhedet; United Workers' Party) as integral to the Socialist movement.[27]

One could argue that *Nissan*'s interest in Israeli discourse regarding the Soviet Union bordered on obsession. For example, a 1953 article titled "Israeli Press and People Condemn Anti-Soviet Provocations of Ben-Gurion" addresses the deterioration of diplomatic relations between the Soviet Union and Israel (following the Doctors' Plot in Moscow and the Prague trials).[28] The author of this article underscores the Israeli public's resentment toward Ben-Gurion's miscalculated steps—and the widespread agreement among Israelis regarding the necessity for improved relations with the Soviets. The article quotes Dr. Shemuel Elyashiv, Israeli ambassador in Moscow during this time. At a MAPAI meeting in Tel Aviv, Elyashiv is quoted as saying that "the anti-Soviet policy of Ben-Gurion's government will only hurt the existence of Israel, hence showing dissent from within the Israeli political establishment."[29] Understandably, the trials in Moscow and Prague made some Jews wary of developments among Communist movements around the world. In an occasional segment titled "Dialogue with Readers," a reader identified as Mr. Roshan from Kashan praised the role of *Nissan* in "awakening the Jewish community," but he added that he did not understand why the trials would cause "the Soviet government [to] cut its relations with Israel." *Nissan* responded by saying that Zionist organizations were plotting with the US against Soviet interests. Eventually the Soviet government acknowledged its wrongdoing, reversed criminal charges against Jews who had been unjustly accused, and put an end to this trial.[30]

Jewish radicals in Iran had much to process in the early 1950s. First, Israel's ruling government was a self-proclaimed socialist system. An important pillar of Israel's emerging MAPAI (labor-Zionist) coalition was the leftist-Marxist MAPAM, founded in 1930. Second, the Soviet Union had supported the 1947 United Nations Partition Plan. Indeed, one of the declaration signatories had been Meir Vilner of the Israeli Communist Party, and even the Tudeh Party, overall, supported the establishment of Israel. In short, *Nissan* (and Jewish radicals) could not easily dismiss Israel as yet another reactionary force or puppet of Western empires since, to varying degrees, a coalition of socialists and Communists, along with Soviet support, had played a pivotal role in the "state story" of Israel.

In an effort to shed light on the socialist spectrum of Israel's political arena, *Nissan* set the historic record straight in another article published in 1953; the article, titled "A few words on the 'Jewish Question'" argues that anti-Semitism had emerged as a social phenomenon (resulting from the dominance of capitalism) to disunite the workers. The "Jewish Question," therefore, resulted from long years of capitalism, and it had forced Jews to leave Europe. To clarify, the "people's" countries (such as the Soviet satellite states) criminally prosecuted anti-Semitism even as "capitalist" countries (such as Germany and England) helped it come to power.[31]

Although *Nissan* implied that initial immigration to Palestine was justified, the article asserted that "the tyrannical current government of Israel stops economic and cultural integration of immigrants from diverse points."[32] It is interesting to note that in the same *Nissan* issue, two other articles underscore the aforementioned points. One of them celebrates the life of Jews in Socialist Romania, and the other, written by an Iranian Jew, reports on the horrible economic conditions and racial tensions in Israel, the kibbutzim, and Jerusalem.[33] However, another article in the same issue, summarizing the position of the various leftist-socialist parties in Israel regarding the Jewish Question, goes on to acknowledge the role of the Soviet-supported MAPAM, as well as socialist elements, in the establishment of the State of Israel. At the same time it describes the 1948 creation of MAPAM as a "unity of various elements of the Zionist left," a unity that was undesired ideologically and that undermined strong leadership.[34]

Nissan kept its readers informed about ongoing events in the Eastern Bloc and beyond. In a way, the newspaper helped to create the sense that a global Jewish leftist community existed. Its reports from Israel, the Soviet Union, and the Eastern Bloc were enriched at times by reports regarding Jewish matters in the West. *Nissan* turned its readers' attention to political affairs in Hollywood, for example, and specifically to the treatment of Jewish actors and progressive "human-loving" Jews. One article from May 1953 criticized the witch-hunt carried out by the US House Un-American Activities Committee, as well as attempts to intimidate political dissidents in Hollywood. The same article reports that Charlie Chaplin had been denied a reentry permit by the US government in 1952 because Chaplin had allegedly expressed Communist sympathies. The article concludes, "There exists another America too: the America of the lovers of humanity, of people with honor, the America of workers and the oppressed, the America of Charlie Chaplin and the Rosenbergs, human loving Jews who have always been deemed alien by the writers of the Zionist organ, whether in the US or in '*Alim-i Yahud*.'"[35]

Not surprisingly, the US espionage trial of Julius and Ethel Rosenberg piqued the interest of Iran's Jewish community. On June 19, 1953, the Rosenberg, two American Jews, were executed for allegedly spying for the Soviet Union. Their trial raised concerns about persecution based on religious beliefs, and many followed the trial with mixed feelings. On July 29, 1953, the CSSIJ held a memorial ceremony for the Rosenbergs. Over five hundred individuals attended. Homage was paid to the Rosenbergs and their struggle for peace. One attendee by the name of Mr. Amini acknowledged the CSSIJ for providing accurate information about the Rosenbergs amid the deluge of disinformation. Another attendee, Ms. Giahizadeh, spoke on behalf of prominent intellectuals such as Jean-Paul Sartre. The memorial service concluded with prayer and the adoption of a resolution addressed to President Dwight D. Eisenhower that protested the inhumane and unjust decision to execute the Rosenbergs.[36]

Periodicals like *Nissan* changed the political conversation for Iranian Jews. Journalists repeatedly provided reasons for Jews to feel proud, which was especially important in such a highly turbulent political atmosphere. While Zionist organizations laid claim to publications like '*Alim-i Yahud* and *Israiil*, the leftists (Zionist and non-Zionist alike) had another spectrum of opinions to discuss and from which to draw. In fact, the reach of *Nissan* went far beyond Tehran, home to the majority of Iranian Jews. Its readership extended to Hamedan and Abadan as well. *Nissan's* representative in Abadan reported that the paper received a warm welcome in that community. The representative asserted that although other newspapers carried similar messages, they were lacking in journalistic integrity or authenticity and therefore did not resonate with the Jewish community. *Nissan* and *Bani-Adam* (the subject of the next section), so says the author, truly represent the class concerns of the people, enabling these publications to draw a wider audience.[37]

Bani-Adam: Socialist Alliance in Iran, Israel, and Beyond

Bani-Adam, which translates from Hebrew as "children of Adam," enjoyed a primarily though not exclusively Jewish readership.[38] Edited by Loqman Salih, *Bani-Adam* (like *Nissan*) was published by the CSSIJ. However, in regard to a plethora of social and political issues, the two periodicals took different approaches. Although remaining staunchly leftist, the views published by *Bani-Adam* were lenient toward and supportive of Israel—whereas *Nissan's* position continued to be, on the whole, more confrontational. As previously suggested, *Nissan* questioned whether Israel was not merely an agent of European colonialism and American imperialism. In contrast, *Bani-Adam* struggled to present Israel as a complex and multilayered society.[39] *Bani-Adam*, for instance, celebrated Israel's independence day while still hoping to advise Israel on the correct political path globally. In *Bani-Adam's* May 4, 1952, issue, front-page headlines read, "Beginning of the Fourth Israeli Independence Celebrations: Jews Congratulate the State of Israel." The article hails Israel's struggle against British colonialism and depicts the Arab states as English agents. It reads,

England used its Arab agents and servants to provoke the Arab people into a war against the independence-seeking Israelis. It made them believe that the struggle of the Israeli nation aimed to deny the rights of the Israeli Arabs and occupy their country. But the bloody struggle of the Israeli people only sought to drive out the English colonialists. . . . In fact, the Arab nations were happy for the expulsion of English forces from their neighboring country, Israel, and do not see it [Israel] as a threat.[40]

This assessment presents a unique interpretation of the 1948 war, to say the least. While it was not extraordinary to view the Zionist movement as essentially an anticolonial movement, describing belligerent Arab nations as agents of British interests was something new.[41] It should be noted that this assessment distinguishes between Arab leaders (as pawns of the British) and the Arab people, who understood well the challenges of the Middle East and the advantages of collaborating with the new State of Israel. The article concludes by conveying the regards of Iran's Jewish community to the free people of Israel and saluting the Israeli martyrs of the war. The last paragraph presents a plea on behalf of *Bani-Adam*: "Once again we ask the Iranian state to establish political and commercial relationship with the state of Israel, and stop insisting on separation and termination of all relations with the nation of Israel. This path is against the real interest of the

Iranian nation and should not be pursued."[42] Chapter 3 of this book discusses the disruption of diplomatic relations between Israel and Iran, especially during the premiership of Mohammad Mosaddeq. It is worth remarking here, however, that Tudeh—as well as other leftist circles— viewed Israel as a partner in the struggle against Western imperialism. The promulgation of this view was central to their political platform for years to come.

Ha'Olam Ha'Zeh (Hebrew: This world), an Israeli publication founded in 1937, became a paragon of left-leaning activist journalism beginning in the 1950s.[43] Bani-Adam occasionally translated articles from Ha'Olam Ha'Zeh, identifying the progressive leftist forces in Israeli politics and consistently introducing them to the Iranian reader. In 1952, issue 21, Bani-Adam translated the article entitled "Israel and the Movements of Liberation in the Middle East and North Africa." The article raises questions regarding Israeli response to anti-imperialist awakenings across the region and refers to Muhammad Nimr al-Hawari, a Palestinian activist and lawyer who was dedicated to Israeli-Arab reconciliation. Al-Hawari's analysis dichotomizes the Middle East. He views one faction as "working for the interest of imperialism and their personal interests and against the masses of the people" and the second faction as composed of "liberationists who truly represent the genuine feelings of the oppressed masses. They fight against the imperialist domination." The article's initial section concludes with the following assertion:

Israel is a country that is part of the Middle East and cannot remain neutral. Because our fate and their fate depend on one another . . . if Israel will support those [anti-imperialist] freedom movements in their fight for independence and liberty for the peoples of the Middle East, and will solve its minor differences with the Arab world, it will gain the respect of the Arab masses. . . . Israel should not let the enemies of the Middle East abuse the situation and introduce it as an enemy of the Arabs.[44]

Evidently the new State of Israel was viewed as a potential member of the Greater Middle Eastern coalition resisting Western imperialism. Yet where were the voices of these like-minded Israeli comrades? Bani-Adam gave voice to these "comrades" by translating articles, such as the one just quoted, and by printing statements from Israeli politicians as well. For example, excerpted in the same Ha'Olam Ha'Zeh article is an opinion piece by Mosheh Sneh, the renowned leader of MAPAM.[45] Sneh is introduced as the "one of the leaders of the leftist workers' party (MAPAM) and a leader of the Israeli military during the war." Sneh reiterates Israel's need to stand together with the struggling nations of the region: "The Israeli state cannot be neutral toward the historic developments that are today going on in the Middle East," specifically pointing to the oil crisis in Iran and the 1936 English-Egyptian treaty.[46]

On April 25, 1952, the seventeenth Majlis term began in Tehran. *Bani-Adam* underscored the Jewish community's expectations by addressing the Majlis thus: "The issue of recognizing the newly founded Israeli republic is also a question [that Iran's] Jewish community expects the 17th Majlis to address." The editorial goes on to contend that, after years of struggling against the British, Israel's best option would be to establish solidarity with its neighbors, and *Bani-Adam*'s editorial board therefore urges the parliament to form deep diplomatic and commercial relations with Israel.[47] Their demands to the seventeenth Majlis also included directing deputies to "quickly end the poisonous anti-Semitic [*zid-i yahudi*] and anti-racial propaganda." Moreover, they articulated objectives that would remain in radical Jewish circles up until the 1979 revolution; that is, a call to end discrimination by official state bodies against Jews (and other minorities) in education, civil service, and the armed forces.[48]

A close reading of *Bani-Adam* reveals that, along with promoting Communist principles, a primary concern of the Tudeh's leadership was the fight against Fascism. This cannot be overemphasized. One of the Tudeh's founding members and prominent leaders, Iraj Eskandari, wrote in his political memoir that the party was created essentially as an "anti-Fascist" organization. The struggle between these two objectives, promoting Communism and fighting Fascism, surfaced time and again during internal debates at meetings such as the 1952 Tehran provincial conference.[49] Indeed, the Tudeh Party and its related publications worked diligently to demonstrate to Iranian Jews that their struggle—the struggle of the Jewish masses—was not an ethnic or religious one but rather a class struggle. The grievances of the Jewish working class, argued the Iranian Jewish leftist activists, resembled the grievances of non-Jewish Iranian workers. Exploitation of the masses by the ruling class crossed religious borders. On this point, *Bani-Adam* took a firm stand, and it remained steadfast in its opposition to the Jewish political establishment, the Hebra,[50] the Jewish representative to the Majlis, and the many operations of the American Joint Distribution Committee, viewing the JDC as an agent of American imperialism in Iran.[51]

Another newspaper to fly the anti-Fascist flag was *Shahbaz*. Established in 1943 by the prominent intellectual Zabihullah Safa, *Shahbaz* printed the work of Jewish writers and journalists. One such journalist and active member of the Tudeh, Rahim Namvar, succeeded Safa as editor in 1948. Having developed a reputation for voicing leftist-nationalist opinions, *Shahbaz* aligned itself with Jibhah-i Azadi (the Freedom Front), a coalition of socialist and nationalist parties and organizations led by the Tudeh Party. *Shahbaz* rapidly became one of the most popular newspapers of its time.[52]

Questions of nationalism and the resistance to colonialism took front and center in left-wing Jewish Iranian politics. During the struggle for nationalization of the AIOC, the Tudeh Party, along with *Nissan* and *Bani-Adam*, voiced unwavering support for Prime Minister Mosaddeq, who championed this issue. The Tudeh also debated the implications of Great Britain's legal challenge to Iran's nationalization bill. Headlines such as the following took prominence: "Whatever the International Court of Justice in the Hague Decides, the Iranian People Will Not Waver from Their Path." The May 1952 *Bani-Adam* article from which this headline was excerpted reads, "The Iranian nation has time and again declared that it nationalized the oil industry based on the Iranian nation's right to sovereignty over its natural resources and no organ can stop a nation from exercising its right to sovereignty."[53] Bringing attention to the struggles in Abadan, *Bani-Adam* included the perspective of Abadani Jews and revealed the multitude of hardships experienced in Abadan amid the oil crisis. One letter printed in *Bani-Adam* reports the closing of Jewish shops near Shat al-Arab:

Such is the sad and heartbreaking conditions of the miserable Jewish classes who spend their life in wails, sighs, and tears. Yes, this is an example of Jewish life in Abadan; a land that, until a year ago, was immersed in black gold that left on massive ships destined for every corner of the world. Even then, these miserable people did not receive anything but hardship and a burdensome life.[54]

This letter illuminates the status of those Jews shunned from the political and cultural center of Iranian Jewry—exiled, in fact, to Iran's social periphery. However, the political reality brought their plight to public attention.[55] Furthermore, if the goal was to create solidarity between Jews and their non-Jewish compatriots, another letter printed in *Bani-Adam* in June 1952 did just that by reporting the suffering of other Abadanis:

But the majority of our non-Jewish brothers endure even worse conditions. They are all mired in poverty and a sad life.

There are those [non-Communist newspaper publishers and reporters] who speak nonsense. These lackeys of colonialism who fill their moneymaking newspapers with cheap, useless, and half-cooked words, are ordered by their bosses to push people away from the truth, to sow division and enmity among them. They [publishers and editors] should send reporters to see the heartbreaking conditions of these miserable people and not distort the truth.[56]

The letter also discussed the Majlis elections and the campaign of *Nissan* and *Bani-Adam* to get Shmuel Anvar, another Jewish Tudehi journalist, elected. Anvar's platform, which received prominent space in both newspapers, resonated with the clear agenda of the Jewish leftists: to improve relations between Jewish and non-Jewish Iranians in fighting racism, anti-Semitism, and Fascism and to work in solidarity for the betterment of conditions for all Iranians.

Jewish Iranian political activists adopted yet another strategy at this time: using religious holidays to marinate the Jewish population in Iranian nationalism—and perhaps to communicate a message to non-Jewish Iranians as well. At the heart of that message was the idea that Jewish traditions inherently educate the masses appropriately regarding their civic roles, guiding Jewish Iranian citizens to contribute responsibly to their beloved homeland. For example, in June 1952 *Bani-Adam* connected the celebration of Shavu'ot with messages of freedom and liberty. According to Jewish tradition, this holiday commemorates the giving of the holy Torah at Mount Sinai. Jews traditionally view it as the first codification of the Divine Law that the Jewish people (the Israelites) accepted as part of their sacred covenant with the one God. The article reads,

The feast of Shavu'ot, which the Jewish community celebrated two days ago, aims to remember these laws and commemorate them. These laws were like a strong light eradicating the darkness that surrounded us 30 centuries ago, and they surely deserve commemoration. Those who assault Jews everyday with all sorts of insults and accusations—Fascists and followers of the despicable racial theory who take to history to prove their nonsense—these people are afraid of considering historical truths. They are blind and ignore the truth that the Jewish masses, like non-Jewish people, support justice, freedom, and understanding among all peoples and will fight to reclaim these ideals.

They obfuscate truth with a false smokescreen and seek to spread division and enmity among the poor who share the same interests. However, on the one hand, the awakening of people and, on the other, the collective struggle of Jewish progressivists to introduce their community to their fellow compatriots, will neutralize the claims of these division-seekers and will further embolden the friendship and intimacy between Jews and followers of other religions.

We congratulate our brothers on the feast of Shavu'ot and invite our fellow Jews to collectively struggle for the guarantee of justice, fraternity, and freedom.[57]

Bani-Adam and *Nissan* created a genre of Jewish political journalism that sought to bring individuals caught in social and geographical peripheries closer to the center. A primary goal was to engage Iranian Jews politically, not just locally in community institutions but, more importantly, at the national level. Far ahead of the global trend, *Bani-Adam* advocated for women's rights, lent unequivocal support for oil nationalization, and called for action[58] in a variety of key political arenas, such as through wider participation in the Majlis elections.[59]

More than any other venues, *Nissan* and *Bani-Adam* welcomed Iranian Jews into the Tudeh circle while demonstrating the need for radical activism. These publications began by asking the question, How could they transform critical social issues at the local level while integrating Jews more fully into the larger national conversation? Their answer centered on identifying with political forces that sought to include religious and ethnic minorities, forces endeavoring to redefine the boundaries of national Iranian identity. The Tudeh Party, by virtue of being a party of minorities, encouraged its Jewish membership to openly support political and cultural advancement for Jews, to fight Fascism globally, and to eschew distancing themselves from major events taking place in the Jewish world.

At this pivotal time, Iranian Jews were bearing witness to their brethren, the European Jews, slowly emerging from ruins of the Holocaust. They were also witnessing the establishment of the State of Israel and being encouraged by the Tudeh and other Jewish associations affiliated with the Communist Party to recognize Israel as Iran's partner rather than enemy. *Nissan* and *Bani-Adam*, as well as the individuals supporting these papers, wanted to see a transformation of the Jewish community in Iran, a reform movement allowing Jews to fit more seamlessly into Iranian society—one that would guarantee them a place at the table in the Shah's plan for modernization. Following the political and social developments resulting from Mohammad Reza Shah's ascendance in 1941, this movement envisioned rural Jews increasingly moving into Iranian cities and therefore contributing more directly to the urbanization of their nation.

With many books having been written about this period in Iran's history, one questions why there has been so little mention of Jewish participation in Iranian leftist circles. One possible factor accounting for the relatively low visibility of Jews in the Tudeh's rank and file, for example, is their naming practice. Jews were given first and last names that were in many cases indistinguishable from those of their Muslim counterparts. As has been discussed, Jews often had "Iranian" or even "Muslim" names, a practice prevalent in most Middle Eastern Jewish communities. Indeed, the prominent Tudeh journalist mentioned earlier, Rahim Namvar, was Jewish (*Rahim* derives from Arabic, and *Namvar* is a generic Iranian last name). In 1964 Namvar published *Yadnameh Shahidan* (In memory of martyrs) as an official publication of the Tudeh Party. This pamphlet recounted the party's history through a lens of martyrdom. Drawing from Communist and proto-Communist organizations that were active from Reza Shah's constitutional monarchy through the 1960s, the pamphlet included profiles of Tudehis from military and political organizations, labor unions, and supporters of Mosaddeq's struggle in the early 1950s.[60] Interestingly, Namvar is likely the journalist to have coined the term *Shahid* (martyr) in reference to political heroes. Namvar's publication is of great value to anyone wishing to study the Tudeh Party's history. Ironically, his religious affiliation, like that of so many other Jews associated with the Tudeh, is easily misconstrued because of his name. Hence, one finds yet another example of the close ties between Muslimness and Jewishness in the realm of Iranian culture.[61]

Jibhah-i Milli: The Nationalist Option

The genre of journalism emerging from these newspapers reflects how deeply invested Iranian Jews were in both public and political spheres. The newspapers, whose staffs were composed of activist and progressive factions, presented a nationalist ideology focusing on critical issues of the day, including stabilizing the Iranian government and dealing with British control of Iranian oil fields—and most especially Mosaddeq's cancellation of the AIOC's oil concession, arguably the most important political issue between 1951 and 1953.

In the postwar period, yet another Jewish journalist joined the thriving community of Iranian nationalist newspapers and journals. Mushfiq Hamadani, an educated officer in the Iranian army, had been editor in chief of the Iranian daily newspaper *Kayhan International* during the mid-1940s. In 1949 he left that position to start his own venture, the independent journal *Kaviyan*, which quickly became the most ardent supporter of the newly emerging political coalition called the National Front (Jibhah-i Milli). Established in 1949, the National Front represented a broad coalition of left-leaning parties, right-wing parties, and strong religious elements. Mosaddeq, a veteran of the Iranian political elite, led the secular wing while nationalist cleric Ayatollah Abolqasim Kashani headed the religious segment. The party gained prominence following the 1949 parliamentary elections even though it won only a few seats in the Majlis. Nevertheless, the coalition was credited with exerting a pivotal and undeniable impact on political discourse. Hamadani's journal became an avenue through which the National Front developed a wide followership and expanded its support. In 1951 the Iranian Majlis elected Mosaddeq as prime minister and subsequently enacted legislation nationalizing the Iranian oil industry. This included its main component, the AIOC. The cover of *Kaviyan* celebrated the new law, proud to have helped win the hearts and minds of the Iranian people. Mosaddeq apparently celebrated, and was duly pleased with, *Kaviyan* as well. On Mosaddeq's historic 1951 trip to the United Nations, during which he met President Harry Truman, only three journalists were allowed to accompany him—one of the three was Hamadani.[62] While *Kaviyan*, which enjoyed a wide readership beyond the Jewish community, proved to be the most important media outlet for both the National Front and Mosaddeq, other Jewish newspapers also actively supported Mosaddeq. A second newspaper, *Daniyal* (named after the prophet Daniel), was specifically aimed at a Jewish readership. Jewish journalist Yaaqub Orayan published and edited *Daniyal* with the express purpose of deepening Jewish support for the National Front. *Daniyal* also voiced unequivocal support for Mosaddeq, attacking *Bani-Adam*, Jewish Communists, Britain, and the Soviet Union for working against the interests of the Iranian nation.[63]

At this time, the West portrayed Iran's National Front as a fanatical party; as such, the international community dismissed or overlooked many of its valuable social programs. Because of Mosaddeq's political partnership with Ayatollah Kashani, who was arguably anti-Semitic, no one seriously attempted to examine the base of support for Mosaddeq in the Jewish community or even considered the relationship between Mosaddeq's Iran and the fledgling State of Israel. Hamadani's unwavering journalistic support of Mosaddeq deepened the Jewish community's confidence in Mosaddeq and his political enterprise. After the Iranian Majlis nationalized Iranian assets of AIOC in March 1951, Great Britain imposed a series of crippling economic sanctions and also used its warships to blockade Abadan. Iran slid into a financial crisis and was forced to sell government bonds in order to keep the AIOC up and running. In response to this national crisis, Jewish community leaders deployed all the communities' resources in order to facilitate nationalization. On February 4, 1952, students from three different Jewish schools in Tehran and a school in Shiraz participated in a demonstration in Tehran supporting Mosaddeq's government. In his memoir, Chief Rabbi of Iran Hakham Yedidia Shofet provides convincing details regarding Jewish solidarity with Mosaddeq: "Jews of Tehran and other cities, to support the nationalization of the oil industry as well as Dr. Mosaddeq's policy in implementing the national economy plans, purchased government bonds. Even students from Alliance and Koresh schools stepped forward to march. Many photos of Jewish students demonstrating in support of the government—photos taken in Bahman and Esfand 1330 [February and March 1952]—appeared in the country's newspapers."[64] Shofet added that Jewish community institutions decided that every teacher would contribute 200 riyals of their salary toward an organized purchase of government bonds. At the same time, two notably affluent Jews, Morad Aryeh and Hajji Habib Elqaniyan, announced that they would donate 50 million riyals each toward the purchase. "In those days only [Iran's] people could prevent the nation's bankruptcy. For the homeland and in order to maintain independence, we had to act with speed and dedication."[65]

Between August 15 and August 19, 1953, the CIA and MI6 tried multiple times to execute a coup d'état. Millions of Iranians representing different parties and organizations—many in alignment with the National Front and Tudeh Party—took to the streets in protest. The Mahallah (Jewish quarter) was also the site of active resistance. An interviewee for this book, Ardeshir, was born in 1944 in the Mahallah in Tehran. Although only nine years old when the coup and ensuing marches occurred, he vividly recalled the days leading up to August 19: "I remember five or six of our next door neighbors, who were Tudehis, working in the Mahallah to get the youth involved. Their little brothers went to Alliance with me, and it was very exciting."[66]

On August 15, 1953, the CIA and MI6 attempted the first coup, which was unsuccessful. Shofet visited Mosaddeq the day after to convey messages of solidarity and resolute support. A delegation of Jewish leaders joined Shofet and congratulated Mosaddeq on protecting Iran's democratically elected government against usurpation by Western powers. On August 19, 1953, however, American- and British-backed coup forces managed to oust Mosaddeq and reinstall Mohammad Reza Pahlavi's regime.

In the aftermath of the coup (codenamed Operation Ajax), Ardeshir entered his classroom at the AIU school in Tehran and acted in accordance with what he thought was right. "We knew that something big had happened. My dad was Mosaddeq's sympathizer, and so I went to class and wrote on the blackboard: 'U.S. go home!' The teacher was furious with me because the school was supported by American donations. This event left an indelible mark on my political consciousness."[67]

This anecdote is one small example of the Jewish community's participation in, and dedication to, a process to truly democratize Iran's social and political spheres. Jewish writers often portray the early 1950s as the dark years before the "Golden Age"—primarily because of the prominent role Ayatollah Kashani played in the National Front, as well as the fact that Mosaddeq had severed diplomatic relations with Israel.[68] However, the widespread Jewish support of Mosaddeq and of other national movements leading up to the coup tells a different story and points to a meaningful Jewish integration into Iranian society at this crucial postwar juncture.

This chapter has focused on a turbulent mid-twentieth-century Iran—specifically, the Tudeh Party's pivotal role in the early 1950s, its membership, and its philosophy; differing Iranian perspectives on the emerging State of Israel; and the significant number of Jewish newspapers and journalists contributing to Iran's sociopolitical dialogue. The fervor with which Jews participated in the national conversation may be explained, at least in part, by the Jewish community's vision of participatory citizenship, their strengthened Iranian identity, and their hopes for an egalitarian society. These same values convinced many to join left-wing political parties. When the crisis around the negotiation of fair oil revenues with Great Britain reached its peak, Jews gathered en masse to support their legitimately elected leader, Mosaddeq, and to embrace his nationalization project.

Publications such as *Bani-Adam* and *Nissan* engaged in fierce polemical debates with other Jewish newspapers such as *'Alim-i Yahud*, *Israiil*, and *Daniyal*. The mere existence of so many periodicals attests to the intense involvement and engagement of the Jewish community in Iranian politics. All the aforementioned newspapers shared a similar agenda: to politicize Iranian Jews at the local, national, and international levels. I would like to point out that because I hold Israeli citizenship, physical access to archives in the Majlis library in Tehran was relatively restricted. My discussion of *Nissan* especially is based on an incomplete review of the records; nevertheless, this chapter's discourse marks a beginning in terms of historical analysis of these key publications.

Bani-Adam was published between 1951 and 1952. *Nissan* was published in the years from 1948 to 1953. The reader should note that I had no access to issues of *Nissan* published before 1953. During this time gap, in 1952, a political earthquake referred to as the 30 Tir (July 21) uprising shook Iran. This insurrection was in response to the resignation of Prime Minister Mosaddeq, based on the Shah's refusal to allow him power over the Ministry of Defense. Iranian citizens engaged in mass protests, strikes, and demonstrations demanding Mosaddeq's reinstatement. Before 30 Tir, the Tudeh Party supported Mosaddeq but at the same time expressed discontent with many of his measures. After 30 Tir, however, the Tudeh became more conciliatory toward Mosaddeq and increasingly protective of him. The analysis provided in this chapter, at least in part, reveals the full spectrum of Jewish activism, which was outspoken and unfettered, even when resisting the tide of Tudeh politics. In short, before the 30 Tir uprising, *Nissan* took a much more critical approach toward Israel than even the Tudeh's official party line, whereas *Bani-Adam* voiced softer and more conciliatory opinions than the Tudeh.

This arguably reflects the multivocal quality of Jewish leftist politics at that time.

Regarding Zionism, Jewish Iranian publishers, editors, and journalists of this era remained largely indifferent. Although many of Iran's Jewish leaders sympathized with the Zionist cause, their political allegiance belonged first and foremost to Iran. Their priorities included joining leftist Iranian movements, eventually assuming leadership positions therein, and making their journalistic voices heard. Quite naturally, this situation caused major frustration in Israel, a state whose existence was, and still is, premised on the notion that the destinies of world Jewries and the State of Israel are inexorably intertwined.

To say that the predominant Jewish Iranian interpretation of Zionism differed widely from the political Zionism espoused by Israel's establishment is an understatement. The former interpretation did not demand the existence of a Jewish state but instead reflected a religious sentiment, an emotional-cum-spiritual attachment to Zion, the biblical name of Jerusalem. This position was not unique to Iranian Jewry; quite the contrary, it was a commonly held belief among Jews across the Middle East.

This relationship to Zionism remained particularly relevant to Iranians, especially since other Jewish communities (including those in Iraq, Syria, Lebanon, and, after 1956, Morocco and Egypt) significantly disintegrated in the decade following Israeli statehood—primarily due to political fallout resulting from the early Arab-Israeli wars. While many Iranian Jews had relatives in Israel and had visited Israel, the nation itself was not part of their Jewish identity. Although records indicate significant Jewish immigration to Israel from Iran between 1948 and 1953, those Jews who remained in Iran were unequivocally devoted to their beloved homeland. Although they maintained a spiritual relationship to Israel and Jerusalem, as mentioned earlier, Iranian Jews neither shared a political interpretation of Zionism nor invested in the Zionist movement as key to the existence of the modern State of Israel. The history behind, and evolution of, Zionist identity in Iran receives full attention in the next chapter.

3

Iranian Jews and Israel
From Indigenous to State-Sponsored Zionism

Zionist Organizations and the Promulgation of Zionism in Iran

"On the 5th of November [1917], the Jews of Iran were informed of the Balfour Declaration by a telegram sent by Zionists in Petrograd.[1] This telegram was passed on to the religious leader of Tehran by 'Azizallah Tizabgar."[2] Thus begins Habib Levy's description of the first encounter of Iranian Jews with political Zionism. As we have seen in previous chapters, Communism and Iranian nationalism, in particular, aligned well with the Jewish community's experience of political and social life in Iran during this period.

However, the appearance of Zionism in Iran offered—at least until the establishment of Israel in 1948—yet another radical political alternative for Iranian Jews. The movement emerged out of a very specific communal context, in relation, of course, to broader global development of the Zionist movement. Let us first examine the preparedness of Iranian Jews for the general message of "Jewish nationalism," or the embrace of national and religious redemption in a place other than Iran. When introducing the topic of Zionism, Levy discusses religious Zionism, the importance of pilgrimage to Jerusalem, and the nineteenth-century migration of Iranian Jews to Israel, primarily to Safad and Jerusalem.[3] He points to the emergence of Hebrew classes taught in Iranian synagogues and associations specifically established to promote Hebrew education. He also refers to what might have become a massive exodus to the Holy Land. Although this nascent

Zionist movement ostensibly intended to prepare all Iranian Jews to move to Palestine and establish new homes in the ancestral Holy Land, it ultimately focused on Iranian youths, seeking to empower rather than relocate them.[4]

Political activists in Iran's Jewish community established many types of Zionist organizations, such as HeHalutz (the Pioneer), founded in 1905. HeHalutz became the umbrella organization for numerous Zionist youth movements, all of which trained young people to settle successfully in Israel. Generally speaking, Iranian Zionism maintained connections with the World Zionist Organization (for example, whenever budgets allowed, Iranian representatives traveled to participate in meetings). Meir Ezri, who later became the Israeli ambassador to Iran in 1958, wrote extensively of his experiences as a HeHalutz leader, detailing the exuberance of his fellow Iranian Jews toward Zionist activities.[5] Haim Tsadok, an Israeli jurist and politician, echoed some of these same sentiments, although he emphasized difficulties that early Zionism faced because of the Jewish population's dispersal throughout Iran.[6] The historian Amnon Netzer further suggested that "Iranian Jewish youths [were] not only Zionist [*Hovev tsiyon*], but really [were] lover[s] of Zion [*Ohev tsiyon*]."[7]

Arguments regarding the Zionist agenda divided Iran's Jewish community. On the one hand, many individuals supported the outspoken representative to the fifth Majlis, Shmuel Hayyim (known as Monsieur Hayyim). Others backed longtime Jewish representative to the second through the twelfth Majlis, and Zionist leader, Loqman Nahurai.[8] An ardent Zionist, Hayyim supported Zionist ideology only to a point. His concern was that fervent Zionism might result in Jews forfeiting their rights in Iran and, therefore, sabotaging their chances of successful assimilation and integration into Iranian society. Hayyim believed that the Jews' first priority should be involvement in Iranian politics and enlistment in Iran's military. He published the newspaper *Ha-Hayyim* (The life), in which he criticized Reza Shah, the Iranian government, and the Jewish community leadership.[9] At the end of the day, his dispute with Nahurai centered on strategies that allowed Iranian Jews to live with dignity, to develop multilayered identities, and to interpret Zionism in an "Iranian" context. Tragically, in 1926 Hayyim was charged with complicity in a scheme to assassinate Reza Shah, subsequently imprisoned, and finally executed in 1931.[10] After Hayyim's fall, Zionist organizations, along with many other organizations deemed "non-Iranian," shut down operations.

Although the political climate encouraged Iranian Jews not to emigrate en masse *before* 1948, what stopped them from doing so afterward? Indeed, the Iranian regime demonstrated leniency toward the State of Israel and even granted it de facto recognition in 1950. Zionist organizations operated openly in Iran and could have arranged certificates for whomever wished to emigrate. Why, therefore, despite what the predominant Zionist narrative tells us, did the overwhelming majority of Jews choose to stay in Iran—even at the apex of Zionism after 1948? According to this Zionist narrative, between 1947 and 1951, approximately twenty-five thousand to thirty thousand Iranian Jews immigrated to Israel, or about one-third of the Iranian Jewish community. Even though this demographic was ostensibly hyper-Zionist, only a relatively small proportion chose to fulfill Zionist aspirations.[11] Indeed, research reveals wildly differing interpretations of the term *Zionism* among Jews, other Iranians, and various hybrid identities in the social-political atmosphere of mid-twentieth-century Iran. A young Jew in Tehran at this time could be simultaneously considered an Iranian patriot, an avowed Tudehi, and a wholehearted Zionist. The components of one's identity, whether ethnic, multireligious, or political, held multiple possibilities. Furthermore, no inherent contradiction existed within these different components.

One interviewee for this book, Pinhas, regards himself even to this day as both a non-Stalinist socialist and a Zionist. He offers the following explanation: "At the same time [that I went to Tudeh activities] I went to HeHalutz. The three ideals they instilled were Hebrew, hard work, and self-defense. We learned Hebrew from a book titled *Yesodot* [Foundations], we worked in the community gardens—mostly behind synagogues—and practiced self-defense."[12] HeHalutz and Tudeh complemented each other in a way. In the late 1940s, and up until 1967, the Iranian left (like many other Iranian political parties) viewed Zionism as a postcolonial movement and considered Israel a legitimate partner in the nascent "Third World."

Zionist movement officials and emissaries remained in Iran under different pretexts. For example, Solel Boneh, one of the companies under contract with Abadan refineries in the 1940s, was the construction branch of the Hebrew Workers Labor Union in Mandatory Palestine (a syndicate established by MAPAI [the National Council of the Workers' Party of the Land of Israel], the dominant party in the Hebrew *Yishuv*). In this instance,

Solel Boneh laborers and staff worked in Abadan on behalf of the British Army. In Abadan, Zionist workers maintained a good relationship with Iranian Jews (as well as with other recent arrivals from neighboring Iraq), engaged in teaching Hebrew, and related magnificent tales and anecdotes about the Promised Land.[13]

With the overthrow of Reza Shah in September 1941, Iranian Zionist organizations came into their prime, as did the Jewish Agency, which officially opened offices in Iran in 1943. Under the umbrella of the Jewish Agency, Youth Aliyah rescued more than five thousand young Jews from Europe, and, as discussed in Chapter 1, the Jewish Agency took responsibility for rescuing the children of Tehran. One need look no further than Mandatory Palestine—the geopolitical region under British control from 1920 to 1948—to begin to understand how World War II and its devastating results affected the Jewish Agency's operations in the Middle East and in Iran specifically. The relationship between the Jewish Agency in Jerusalem and the Jewish leadership in Iran was especially instrumental in establishing Iran's role as an ally in the early success of the State of Israel.

The Holocaust, the Yishuv, and Iranian Zionism

By 1945 the staggering loss of European Jewry had become clear.[14] The first estimates of six million Jews exterminated turned out to be fairly accurate. Once Zionist movement leaders became aware of the full spectrum of genocide, they had to rethink and restrategize much of the Zionist project. A brief history of the Zionist movement reveals fundamental, all-important facts that shed light on its evolution. The Zionist movement emerged in the nineteenth century in response to two major events: European nationalism and the failure of Jews, especially in Eastern Europe, to assimilate and become part and parcel of modern European societies. Zionism eventually offered redemption to these European Jews by making them "a People." While in Europe they were regarded as outcasts and foreigners and were segregated and persecuted, the Zionist goal was to "Europeanize" them by sending them off to establish a new society where they could finally metamorphose as European.[15] However, the loss of six million annihilated this human reservoir intended for the future state, prompting Zionists to turn eastward to find a proper replacement. In the Middle Eastern regions and in North Africa, the Zionist movement identified approximately one million Jews to relocate. Zionist leaders wholeheartedly believed that they were saving those Jews from an inexorably dark fate of living in backward, ultrareligious, and increasingly hostile Muslim environments. To the Mizrahi Jews of Middle Eastern and North African descent, Zionism offered a quantum leap from a seventh-century reality to twentieth-century modern life.[16]

As mentioned earlier, Zionist activities existed openly in Iran after the Balfour Declaration and after 1941. Youth movements such as HeHalutz and Ha-Shomer Ha-tsair (the Young Guard) were integral to the Zionist campaign not only in Mandatory Palestine but also in Jewish communities abroad, including Iran. Education, as always, was of paramount importance. For example, youth movements were responsible for helping to educate and train Iranian Jewish youths in Zionist and socialist ideals. Emissaries from Mandatory Palestine took it upon themselves to teach Hebrew and coordinate events that would appeal to Jewish youths.[17] Ultimately, a key Zionist goal was to make Jewish youths feel more connected to the dream of living in Israel than to their actual lives in Iran.

The Jewish Agency invested enormous resources in promoting Zionist activities in Iran's urban centers, as well as in remote villages and towns.[18] The sight of European refugees finding shelter in Iran along with Iraqi Jews (who, as part of the "second" wave, had been arriving in Iran since 1941) made many Iranian Jews perceive Zionism as a real solution to a real problem—but not necessarily *their* personal problem or solution. They avidly supported Zionist organizations and operations, donated to the Zionist Congress, and participated in fund-raising efforts for refugees in Iran and for the Jewish National Fund (JNF). Iranian Jews happily opened the doors of their local institutions and synagogues to host refugees and Jews in transition to Palestine, but, regretfully for the Iranian Zionist leadership, this massive support did not translate to en masse emigration. Nevertheless, a number of Zionist organizations and clubs continued operations in Iran and even published the newspaper *Sinai*, which was dedicated to Zionist news and events.[19]

Establishment of the State of Israel

David Ben-Gurion declared the establishment of the State of Israel on May 14, 1948, opening Israel's gates to Jews from every corner of the world. Ben-Gurion referenced the catastrophe of the Holocaust, asserting the need to make Israel equal in status to any other nation in the world. According to his declaration, Israel would be open "for Jewish immigration and ingathering of the Exiles."[20] The 1948 war began the following day, exerting tremendous impact on Jews in the Middle East.[21] In Iran, too, there were voices on the political spectrum, albeit relatively few, rallying Iranians to assist Arab armies and the Palestinians.[22] Simultaneously, Israel began absorbing Jewish refugees, primarily from Europe but also from the Middle East and North Africa. This signaled the end of most Jewish communities in the Middle Eastern region. Iran played a central role in the story of mass migration to Israel, not so much because numerous Iranian Jews emigrated but rather because the Iranian government allowed Israel to use Iranian soil as a way station for migration from other countries, including India, Afghanistan, Pakistan, and Iraq. Tens of thousands of Jews made their way to Iran and to these transition camps, and from these camps to Israel.

In the turbulent decade of 1941–1951, the geography and demography of Iranian Jewry shifted dramatically. Because of industrialization, education, and other internal social developments, countless Jews from provincial towns and villages abandoned their homes and moved to Tehran.[23] In Tehran temporary camps were established in every possible locale. Synagogues, schools, and even Jewish cemeteries turned into lively though overcrowded environments. Between the years of 1948 and 1951, Iran's Jewish population shrunk by 21,832 individuals, all of whom immigrated to Israel. At the same time, some 15,000 Iraqi, Indian, and Afghan Jews were flown to Israel from Iran, though some sources mistakenly categorize them as Iranians.[24] In any case, these numbers undermine the assertion that Iran's Jewish community prioritized a political Zionism, anticipating their redemption in Israel.

Generally speaking, those Iranian Jews who emigrated from Iran to Israel did see their lives improved significantly. The first arrival of Iranians in Israel were those in the direst need—the poorest, most disenfranchised Jews, none of whom had benefited from the social and political developments of the first half of the twentieth century. For them, new beginnings in the Holy Land represented salvation. Aliyah[25] operated primarily under the umbrella of the Jewish Agency and the American Joint Jewish Distribution Committee (JDC). Stanley Abramovitch, one of the JDC directors, wrote to the JDC office in Paris that the Iranian government had been very cooperative in providing passports and proper visas. "There is recognition in government circles," Abramovitch wrote, "that removal of the poor Iranian Jews is no disservice to the country."[26]

A closer look at migration statistics reveals a narrative that may be chiefly Iranian rather than Israeli Zionist. Between 1948 and 1949 there were 1,780 immigrants, or *Olim*, from Iran to Israel.[27] According to 1950's records, 10,526 Olim emigrated from Iran, and in 1951, 9,526 Olim did, according to the records for that year.[28] Therefore, about half of Iranian Jews emigrating in the first three years of Israel's statehood left in 1950. Apparently, 1950 marked a year of immense political instability, as suggested in Chapter 2. This instability, along with rising tensions between Islamist and Jewish/Zionist circles (partly due to the conflict in Israel and Palestine), led to increased discrimination and anti-Semitism in Iran's provinces.[29] When one also considers the almost unfathomable poverty that characterized life in the provinces, it becomes obvious that most people, regardless of faith, ethnicity, or religion, would have sought alternatives. Numerous individuals fleeing these regions account in part for Iran's expansive urbanization at this time, and for the mass migration of Jews from remote villages and towns—first to Tehran and then to Israel.[30] A 1950 JDC document records the debilitating poverty and desolation: "Yet, one must not forget that to some extent this misery, this poverty, and even hopelessness is not confined to Jews only in Iran. It embraces many other sections of the community. The Jew, however, has one advantage over his neighbors, he has hope, almost immediate hope of a solution, i.e. emigration."[31]

This report does not present the departure of Jews from Iran as an idealistic or messianic deed, nor as an ideological or religious commitment to Zionism, but rather as an opportunity to escape irrefutably oppressive political and economic hardships. Further support for this argument may be found in an article published in August 1950 by a *Washington Post* reporter named W. G. Dildine, titled "Persian Moslems Join Jews as Refugees to Palestine." According to Dildine, crypto-Jews and Muslims whose Jewish ancestors had converted to Islam many generations before evidently wanted to leave Iran. They believed that a "Jewish background" would help them procure immigrant visas to Israel.[32]

Letters from Israel

In 1948, as the Olim began to arrive, Israel had to come up with ad hoc housing solutions. The first arrivals received rights to abandoned

Palestinian houses in cities such as Jaffa, Acre, Jerusalem, Tiberia, and Haifa. The vast majority of Olim were initially sent to *Ma'abarot* (Hebrew: transition camps) comprised mostly of tents and makeshift huts.[33]

The Olim from Iran were placed in a number of Ma'abarot; the hardships they experienced in the immigration process proved overwhelming. Within a short time they started writing to Iranian relatives and friends, many of whom were waiting to depart for Israel from camps in Tehran. The letters that Iranian Olim wrote did not have the effect that Zionist officials expected. As mentioned earlier, most émigrés taking advantage of Aliyah opportunities were Jews from Iranian provinces. Persuading these individuals to immigrate to Israel had been relatively easy. However, as letters arrived from Israel one by one, it was clear that expectations of an easier life in the Promised Land had hardly been met. Abramovitch describes warnings from Israel to fellow Jews in Nehavand:

The letters that come from Israel dampen all spirits. The Iranian Jew is not the Halutzic [pioneer] type. The ordeals of present day life in Israel have left him discouraged longing to return to his damp dark ghetto room, for he has been used to that room and even liked it. Food is available in Iran, and though he earned little he lived in an environment that was not strange to him. The language, the people, the life was familiar, Israel is not. As a Persian he is looked down upon. . . . The letters that come back to Iran complain about the shortage of food. Nahavand received a letter and Thora scroll from their brethren in Israel. The Nahavand Jews in Israel signed their names on this piece of scroll and in the accompanying letter they wrote that they took an oath by the Thora from which they sent a piece, that their brethren in Nahavand will not come to Israel now, anyway not until they inform them that the time is more suitable. And Nahavand is a God forsaken place in the mountains of Loristan, cut off from the outside world. . . . Yet their "Landsleit" in Israel advice [*sic*] them adjure them to remain in Nahavand. Another family was advised not to leave for Israel until their son Joseph is married. Joseph is one year old.[34]

This report sheds light on what can only be described as a problematic immigration process. Within a relatively short time, enticing images of the new homeland of Israel, along with tales of assured redemption for migrants, had lost their charm. The report also bears a hint of an insult. Indeed, Jews from a God-forsaken village might do better to remain in that village (forget about moving to Tehran) rather than immigrate to Israel.

Abramovitch cites other situations, as well. For example, the Jewish community from Golpayegan, including many relatively wealthy individuals who owned extensive property, decided to hold off on their plans for emigration. They had sent a community representative to Israel to buy land and "look into the possibility of obtaining a village for [the entire] community." Abramovitch feared that a domino effect based on unsavory reports might occur.[35] And so it did. The Jews of Khomein heard about the Golpayegan decision, as well as the terrible condition in the camps in Tehran, and decided to stay in Khomein.[36] The community of Kashan had a similar experience in 1951 when "one of the members of the committee visited Israel during the summer and, from what I [Abramovitch] could gather, he did not bring back too rosy reports. To us he just said that since they [the Olim] cannot speak Hebrew, it is difficult for them to settle right now."[37] These events led to an unprecedented situation in Iran. That is, although the Jewish Agency prepared passports and exit visas, anticipating unprecedented numbers of Jews to emigrate, most candidates for emigration decided not to leave.[38]

Larger problems loomed ahead. Letters and reports from Israel concerning questionable conditions for Iranian Jews threatened to sabotage the successful collaboration between Israel, the Jewish Agency, and Iranian authorities:

News has reached Tehran that about 1,000 Iranian Jews want to return from Israel. They have approached official Iranian authorities with a request for repatriation. Such news is not helpful and may cause the J.A. [Jewish Agency] a lot of embarrassment. It may not be easy to obtain passports as up till now. The authorities may no longer be as helpful when they see that Jews want to come back. Repercussions are already being felt.[39]

Impoverished Jews from Afghanistan, Kurdistan, and various provinces in Iran continued arriving at Tehran's transition camps. Despite everything they had heard, these individuals could not be dissuaded from wanting to immigrate to Israel. For many, there was no turning back, no place to return to where they would be welcome. In a December 1952 report for the JDC, Abramovitch asserted, "Poorer Jews will immigrate to Israel after Passover if facilities are still available."[40] However, in 1951 Israel and the Jewish Agency revamped criteria for immigration eligibility. Israel now made it clear that it was interested primarily in healthy, young, able, educated, and preferably skilled émigrés. This immediately disqualified many of the potential candidates waiting in Tehran's overcrowded camps. The Jewish Agency now had to deal with "two thousand five hundred people in Tehran and about the same number in the provinces who [had] been told to prepare for emigration, [were] stuck without homes, without food, and with little chance for emigration."[41] By 1952, emigration from Iran to Israel had reached an impasse. Those Iranian Jews considered desirable by Israel were not really interested in relocating to Israel. On the other hand, those who wanted to immigrate were viewed as undesirable.

In 1951, Mohammad Mosaddeq attempted to appease Arab countries in hopes of gaining their support vis-à-vis Iranian oil nationalization. As part of this appeasement, Iran cut diplomatic ties with Israel and closed the Iranian consulate in Jerusalem.[42] As discussed in Chapter 2, Mosaddeq's government directly impacted the Jewish population, especially in Tehran. On the one hand, there was the problematic relationship between the conservative cleric Abolqasim Kashani and Foreign Minister Hossein Fatemi, and on the other hand, there was genuine enthusiasm on the part of many Jews who unequivocally supported Mosaddeq's struggle toward nationalization. There is no evidence that Mossadeq's government had a deleterious effect on Israel's ability to receive émigrés from Iran, or that Iran tried to sabotage Israel's migration efforts in any way.

In the four years following the establishment of the State of Israel, between one-fifth and one-quarter of Iran's Jewish population moved to Israel. This wave of immigration, ironically, improved the situation of Iranian Jews choosing to remain in Iran. The remote villagers, the poor, and the disenfranchised—that is, those Jews who needed the greater community's care—had left. This situation helped to consolidate Iran's Jewish population in major urban centers, primarily in Tehran, Shiraz, and Isfahan. In these cities, Jewish communities reorganized and strengthen their institutions by consolidating resources and accessing the support of Iranian organizations and others, such as the JDC and the Alliance Israélite Universelle (AIU).[43]

Iranian Jewish Zionist: An Identity Mélange

During this period of extensive migration to Israel, even as Iran served as a base for that considerable effort, Zionist and non-Iranian Jewish officials were hardly concerned with the complexity of Jewish Iranian identity. Could Iranian Jews be proud, patriotic Iranians while practicing Jewish traditions? Could they be sympathetic to Zionism and to Israel at differing levels? What about Iranian Jews identifying first and foremost as Tudehi but, in accordance with Tudeh's official party line, strongly supporting the establishment of Israel? For all Iranians, and Iranian Jews in particular, identity categories were not mutually exclusive (in contrast to what had been expected by Israel and modern Zionism). While many viewed the establishment of Israel favorably, and rejoiced over their homeland's good relationship with Israel (at least in the beginning), they had no intention to exchange Iran for Israel. The percentage of Iranian Jews choosing the Zionist option was relatively low, and those who did immigrate envisioned that they would see an elevation in their status by doing so.

The slowdown of immigrants prompted Zionist organizations to investigate and analyze this unexpected turn of events. Ultimately they arrived at the identity issue. In 1953 Habib Levy wrote a comprehensive report on Zionist activism in Iran and submitted it to Israel's president, Itzhak Ben-Zvi, whom he knew from the latter's visits to Iran. President Ben-Zvi forwarded Levy's report to the chairman of the board of the Jewish Agency, Berl Locker. Surprisingly, Levy's tone in this report sharply contrasts with the spirit of his historical writing. In his books (both his memoir and his three-volume history of the Jews of Iran), he praises Iranian Jews' commitment to Judaism and Zionist ideals. Conversely, his report submitted to Israel's president seems rather gloomy:

When news arrived of the establishment of the State of Israel, the Jews rejoiced. . . . 30% of Persia's Jewish communities prepared for their *Aliyah*—in camps without any sanitation, exposed to the death angel on one side and on the other side, greedy officials of the Jewish Agency that in odd ways and on weird pretexts robbed them of their few belongings. Despite life in Iran being comfortable, they [Iranian Jews] went to Israel and were going to forget the bitterness of the *Galuth* [exile]. After two thousand and four hundred years of exile, and after 24 hundred years of suffering and tears, they were drunk from excitement and did not pay attention to obstacles, betrayals, and deeds of pocket-picking. . . . Unfortunately today the excitement has dissipated and their fiery nationalistic and religious feelings that were a source of endless power and energy have faded.[44]

Beyond the serious accusations targeting Jewish Agency officials and Israel (accusations upheld by corroborating evidence), Levy lamented the loss of this rare opportunity to keep Zionist fires kindled in the hearts of Iranian Jews. The rest of the report also bears examination. In analyzing the reasons that Iranian Jews were turning away from or losing interest in Zionist ideology, Levy cites the following: "lack of physical, national, religious, and spiritual guidance or training." In other reports, and as a matter of policy, the Jewish Agency tended to blame insufficient knowledge of Hebrew and the practice of Reform Judaism (as opposed to its Orthodox counterpart) for loosening the bond between Iranian Jews and Zionism/Israel. With that in mind, it is interesting to turn once again to Abramovitch, the JDC observer, whose 1952 report contradicts this assessment. In fact, he describes a heightened emphasis on Hebrew language acquisition and Judaism education among Iranian Jewish youths:

We can point to a whole series of achievements. My recent tour of the provincial towns has been an unexpected pleasure. The younger children, those of the primary schools, not only understood our questions but also answered them correctly. Years of guidance and regular examinations have convinced teachers that our instructions should be carried out, that curriculum we've suggested should be taught, and that idiotic superstitious stories abandoned. Children read correctly; they translate correctly; there is proper order to their biblical stories, as well as sequence in their history and religious knowledge. Mr. Cuenca, A.I.U. director, and Mr. Szyf, who accompanied me on this last trip, were as pleasantly surprised as I was at the answers.[45]

How should we reconcile Levy's and Abramovitch's contradicting reports? One way to square the two is to conclude that there was, in fact, no credible connection between Hebrew fluency and a deep understanding of Judaism's teachings and traditions. Later in his report, Levy offers other fascinating though equally far-fetched criticisms that do not necessarily correlate with his other writings. First, he states that Iranian Jews suffer from the absence of a centralized organization. This unfortunate fragmentation, reflected in the proliferation of small community organizations, meant that Iran's Jewish community lacked a unified front. Without a strong, central organization, Levy opines, requisite political and social influence will never be achieved. Additionally, the majority of wealthy Iranian Jews had distanced themselves from Jewish nationalism. Finally, and perhaps most critically, he laments, "The young Jewish students overwhelmingly [will] tend to support the Tudeh Party, when there is a void of worthy Jewish organizations."[46]

Levy fails to entertain the possibility that Iranian Jews *purposely* avoided creating a strong central organization—which would have distanced their community even further from the larger nationalist sphere. Is it not possible that the Jewish community desired to assimilate, to fit seamlessly into the Iranian social fabric, to count themselves as respected and respectable citizens, and thereby enjoy the same rights and experiences as their non-Jewish Iranian peers? Levy also overlooks key reasons why Jewish students overwhelmingly tended to support Tudeh. As demonstrated in Chapter 2, during the early years from 1941 through 1953, Tudeh offered young Jews a stronger connection to their generation and to Iranian society. Since Tudeh was the largest and single most important political organization in Iran, it is little wonder that young Jews found Tudeh so attractive.[47]

Another section of Levy's report is devoted to the hardships that Jews faced upon arriving in Israel. Interestingly, Levy mentions racism and discrimination toward Mizrahi and Persian Jews, regardless of their social status, education, or training. Levy points out that these émigrés could not speak Yiddish, a strike against them. Also, their places of origin made them especially vulnerable to discriminatory practices. Levy proffers the following example: Iranian Jews wanting to enroll their children in an elite boarding school near Haifa were told that the school was at full capacity. Nevertheless, in the ensuing days and weeks their Ashkenazi neighbors enrolled sons and daughters with no problem.[48] This type of news made its way to Iran, undeniably hurting Israel's already questionable reputation around immigration. During those early years, not only did many Iranians return to Iran but, as discussed in Chapter 1, Iraqi Jews also migrated from Israel to Iran. These Iraqis, after finding life impossible to adjust to in Israel, and legally prevented from returning to their Iraqi homeland, settled on their second-best option. Iran at least provided a somewhat familiar cultural climate, and furthermore, a significant Jewish Iraqi community had already established itself. Therefore, Iran became a preferred destination for many Iraqi immigrants, to the dismay of Israel and Zionist organizations.

Early Israeli Influence on Iranian Jewry

Post-1948 Israel played a significant role in shaping Jewish identities and Jewish life in Iran. This included promoting Jewish and Zionist education, sponsoring youth activities, and sending classroom instructors to strengthen Israeli–Zionist grasp on Jewish education in Iran—all while maintaining close relationships with Iranian Jewish leaders. It is worth the effort, therefore, to analyze the ramifications of this strong Israeli-Iranian liaison, especially through a regional or global lens, in order to assess more accurately Israel's impact on Iran's Jewish community. The complexity of issues, policies, and diplomatic concerns that Israel faced in the 1950s and 1960s reverberated in Iran as well.

The time period from 1949 (the year in which Mosaddeq founded Iran's National Front) through 1951 (when Mosaddeq was elected prime minister) remains one of the least understood aspects of the Iranian-Jewish-Israeli triangle. This extraordinary chapter of Iranian nationalism has been portrayed as a dark age for Iranian Jews—because of the purported anti-Semitism of Mosaddeq's senior partner, Ayatollah Kashani, and because of Mosaddeq's decision to cut ties with Israel. This "rupture" between the Iranian state and its Jewish population, however, cannot be substantiated even by careful research. Once again, those who created the narrative around this alleged rupture were inarguably blind to other phenomena, facts that may have contradicted their own personal beliefs. For example, Meir Ezri, the Israeli ambassador to Iran from 1958 to 1973, wrote in his memoirs that Mosaddeq "successfully instilled the spirit of radical nationalism." Ezri insists that although Mosaddeq was at odds with his (that is, Mosaddeq's) biggest opponent, the Communist Tudeh Party (with whom he disagreed on many matters), clearly "Mosaddeq and Tudeh were united in their hatred of Israel."[49] In reality, as previously demonstrated, Ezri could not have been more mistaken. After 1948, Tudeh enjoyed the support of a significant number of Iranian Jews and forcefully pushed the Iranian government to grant Israel de jure recognition on top of an already existing de facto recognition. Although Ezri had been born in Iran (immigrating to Israel in 1950), his understanding of the Iranian political scene was tainted by total immersion in Israeli politics. In Iran many Jews supported Mosaddeq and many of them supported Tudeh—and many also demonstrated support for Israel, to varying degrees, at the same time.

Another example that speaks to the relationship between public opinion in Israel and Mosaddeq's government is an episode that began in 1951. After Mosaddeq assumed premiership and nationalized the oil industry, he instantaneously attained heroic stature in the postcolonial world (quite naturally, including many Arab countries).[50] His courageous opposition to British exploitation was widely reported globally, as were his diplomatic victories in the UN and at the International Court in The Hague. Indeed, Mosaddeq was celebrated not only throughout the nascent Third World from Delhi to Cairo but also in the West from Frankfurt to Amsterdam to New York. Iran's new prime minister quickly became an icon of New Leftist idealism.

Britain viewed Mosaddeq as a major obstacle to safe and reliable access to Iranian oil and an overall threat to the British Empire's well-being. After negotiations to restore its control of the refineries failed, Britain imposed economic sanctions on Iran, forcing Mosaddeq to seek new markets for Iranian products. Not surprisingly, Western governments collaborated with Britain in upholding economic sanctions while some Arab nations, particularly those supporting the nationalization policy, attempted to expand their volume of trade with Iran. However, Arab support was conditional. The promise to expand trade with Iran would be honored only if Iran severed its diplomatic relations with Israel.[51] As previously noted, Mosaddeq did just that—by cutting diplomatic ties with Israel and closing the Iranian consulate in Jerusalem. This effort to appease his Arab neighbors, however, was largely unsuccessful. Arab nations, fearful of risking beneficial relationships with the West, failed to keep their promises of expanded trade with Iran. When Mosaddeq saw that the Arab pledge had been little more than lip service, and that the governments of Iraq and Egypt, for example, had every intention of remaining loyal to their British patrons, he tried to find ways of rebuilding relations with Israel.[52]

To reestablish trust between the two nations, Mosaddeq offered to supply Israel with its oil needs for 25 percent of market value for twenty-five years. The Israeli cabinet declined the generous offer, based on their determination to adopt an American-oriented foreign policy—which marked a distinct shift as, immediately following 1948, Israel had avoided aligning with either the American or Soviet bloc. This decision ignited a public debate in Israel regarding foreign relations between Israel and its immediate neighbors. Members of the Knesset foreign affairs committee who represented the opposition party Herut harshly criticized the cabinet and prime minister for failing to read the map correctly. Who could deny that Mosaddeq represented emerging progressive forces in the region? An oil deal with Iran, they argued, could cement and secure Israel's position in the Middle East. This mind-set gained prominence only a few years later, when Prime Minister Ben-Gurion enacted the "Periphery Doctrine" (a military and political collaboration between Israel and three non-Arab countries in the Middle Eastern periphery: Iran, Turkey, and Ethiopia).[53]

Arguably, one of the most sanguine voices of the right wing at this time was Yosef Nedava. A journalist and later a chief ideologue for the Israeli right-wing parties, Nedava was quick to realize that Mosaddeq was a new phenomenon, a leader unlike anyone who had preceded him. He also understood that Mosaddeq's actions held the potential to impact not only Iran and Britain but also the Arab Middle East and the rest of the world. In 1951 he wrote in *Ha-Boker* newspaper (identified with the General Zionists Party),

The significance of Mosaddeq is not limited merely to Persia. He has become a pan-Asian personality, and in a matter of weeks he has successfully ignited a revolution that will inspire everywhere on this enormous continent. He has awakened the people! Egypt is already following his footsteps. Regardless of the UN Security Council debates results, the Brits will never return to Abadan's oil fields. Whether Persia can really operate the refineries alone is another question, but as of this moment it is only secondary in importance. The Brits have been expelled from one of their key historic positions in the heart of Asia. Viewed from this aspect, Mosaddeq has already completed his mission. In his various speeches in the Majlis, he has repeatedly said that he no longer fears death. He has achieved what he strived for and now he can die if necessary, for he has paved the road for revolution. Whether or not he is assassinated like Gandhi is of no importance, for the manner in which one dies is of no concern in Persia. In Tehran death walks the streets every hour of the day. But one who has carved his name in the pages of history is no longer to be considered a mortal human being.[54]

This editorial reflects Nedava's deep sympathies toward and respect for Mosaddeq, sentiments uncharacteristic of Israeli political discourse at that time. Only among right-wing supporters and radical leftists (mainly pragmatic fractions of Israel's Communist Party) did one find such language. Mosaddeq had laid the foundation for what later became known as the "Third World"—which largely correlated with the ideas of Menachem Begin's Herut and the more centralist General Zionists regarding foreign and diplomatic relations with the Muslim world. Nedava was among the first to contextualize Mosaddeq in the larger Middle Eastern picture. Again, according to Nedava,

There is a resemblance between Nahas Pasha [the Egyptian prime minister] and Dr. Mosaddeq. They both rely on the masses, they both hate foreigners and foreign governments, they both are highly educated, and believe in the urgency for cultural progressiveness in the East. They both declared war on Britain and, to a large extent, succeeded. Mosaddeq remained standing after the International Court in The Hague handed down its decision, as did Nahas, despite the UN Security Council's opinion on the matter of the Suez, because they both understood the exigency of timing one's actions properly.[55]

The depth of Nedava's insight contrasts with Ezri's misperceptions and negates Ezri's efforts to present a unanimous rejection of Mosaddeq by all Israelis.

To restate, from 1948 until 1977 the ruling party in Israel was the socialist MAPAI. Its dominance in Zionist organizations (namely, the Jewish Agency) gave it carte blanche to dictate the loyalties and political affiliation of its emissaries abroad. MAPAI's senior partner in the coalition was MAPAM (the United Workers' Party). Between the two parties, MAPAM was much more ideologically committed. As a socialist movement, more often than not MAPAM was frequently in alignment with the Israeli Communist Party. MAPAM strongholds included the kibbutzim, Ha-Shomer Ha-tsair youth movement, and the Israeli labor unions.[56] Because of its key partnership with centrist MAPAI, MAPAM dispatched some of its own representatives on missions to foreign countries. While abroad, these individuals tried to establish connections with local populations, as well as with local socialist parties.

MAPAM representatives in Iran found themselves in a swirl of controversy concerning their political activism. They had been sent to Iran to represent Israel, not explicitly the MAPAM movement. In September 1951 a secret cable arrived at the headquarters of the Zionist Organization in Jerusalem. The cable, sent from the Central Committee of the Zionist Organization of Iran, expressed harsh resentment regarding activities of MAPAM emissaries in Iran. To be more precise, committee members resented the contacts MAPAM individuals had established with Tudeh organs in Iran. "As our investigations clearly proved, these people came to Iran to operate in favor of an ideology directly opposed to Zionism and one that works against the Jewish minority," reads the cable.[57] To provide evidence of this accusation, a clip from *Yedioth Ahronoth*, an Israeli popular daily newspaper, had been attached. The title said it all: "MAPAM Is Active . . . in Persia Too." The article reports activities of three Israeli MAPAM representatives, all of whom were on a mission in Iran on behalf of the Jewish Agency but whose dealings went far beyond their designated assignments on Jewish matters; that is, they had attempted to "infiltrate" Tudeh. The three individuals in question had even published a short poem in Hebrew in one of Tudeh's publications. Tudeh's editorial board had welcomed connection with the peace-seeking Hebrews as a goal worth pursuing. "The question is," states the reporter for *Yedioth*, "if such a mission benefits Israel, too, [a mission] that wastes public money while these individuals form ties with those opposing Persia's regime, allowing and facilitating the immigration of [Iranian] Jews to Israel."[58] Once again, one notes the extremely complicated relationship among Iranian Jewish political activists, Israeli political officials, and Iranian non-Jewish (and especially leftist) activists. It is fair to assume that the Zionist committee in Iran clearly recognized the risks inherent in MAPAM activities, as well as activities of other political parties left of MAPAI. Would Iranian Jews find more than one way to reconcile the many ideologies and identities they had already embraced, such as socialism, Iranian nationalism, and Zionism?

Meanwhile, Mosaddeq continued his work to repair relations between Iran and Israel. In May 1953, following months of negotiations, the two countries signed a major trade deal, known as the "clearing agreement." This agreement between the Iranian Bank-i Melli and Israel's Bank Leumi created a payment and credit system to facilitate commerce. In June 1953 Israel and Iran expanded this agreement by establishing the Iranian-Israeli trading company known as IRIS (acronym of Iran-Israel).[59]

Following the overthrow of Mosaddeq, Mohammad Reza Shah embraced a strong alliance with the United States and the West in order to consolidate his power. Iran would become a key outpost for the West in the Middle East, providing strategic access to the Caspian Sea and Persian Gulf and standing as an ally directly on the Soviet Union's southern border. Newly gained access to oil proved another benefit of this relationship. Israel, whose relations with Iran were unstable during Mosaddeq's regime, became an important factor in Iran's regional alliances.[60] Much has been written about the close collaboration between Israel's and Iran's military establishments, but what about their nonmilitary collaboration? What was the role of Iranian Jews in this relationship, and how did it impact them? What effect did it have on their identities?

Iranian immigration to Israel had come to a virtual standstill in 1953. Certainly Jews emigrated from Iran after 1953 but, again, these were generally Jews at the lower end of the socioeconomic spectrum. Because of this slowdown, the Jewish Agency and the JDC separately decided to invest greater resources in Jewish educational systems in Iran, convinced that this investment would influence future generations' identity and loyalties, all of which seemed linked to education.[61] Around this same time, Israeli emissaries in Iran realized that they could no longer address Iranian Jews as they might address other Jewish communities in Muslim territory. After all, the Iranian Jewish community (and again, most especially, the Tehrani community) more closely resembled communities in the Western world and industrialist countries than those in Middle Eastern, African, or Asian communities, where Jews were diminishing in number. This new approach included engaging the Iranian Jewish community with Israel on a variety of levels, not necessarily promoting immigration to Israel. This level of engagement would begin with Jewish educational systems and would necessitate significant investment in Jewish schools to spark the transformation of Jewish Iranian identities.

Up to that point, Zionism had not been an integral part of the curriculum in Iran's Jewish schools. As more non-Jewish students enrolled in these schools (especially toward the 1960s, when non-Jewish Iranians identified Jewish schools as vehicles for upward social mobility), attitudes toward traditional Jewish education and Zionist principles became secondary. Almost all Jewish schools in Iran offered Hebrew and Jewish religious studies as optional courses. As the 1960s unfolded, pressure from the local community or from the Jewish Agency ensured that Hebrew and Judaism studies intensified. The AIU and Obchestvo Remeslenogo Truda (ORT; Russian: Association for the Promotion of Skilled Trades) had no interest in training their teachers to teach these subjects and had hired Otsar Ha-Torah teachers to be responsible for this curriculum.[62] Given Otsar Ha-Torah's position on Zionism, which could only be described as anti-Zionist and ultraorthodox, its presence in the schools provoked controversy and mixed reactions. The Jewish Agency blamed the JDC for undermining the agency's activities, as well as for being anti-Zionist: "JDC does its best to foster dependency and poverty in Iran."[63] In some schools the Zionist organization HeHalutz received permission to operate afterschool programs.[64] No documentation exists that shows whether this program was part of a compromise among the Jewish Agency, the JDC, and Jewish Iranian institutions. What we do know is that tensions existed, resulting in allegations by Jewish Agency emissaries or Israeli officials—allegations directed at Jewish community leaders in Iran to the effect that these leaders failed to actively support Israel and Zionism, or to encourage Zionist activity. According to one JDC report, "Jewish leaders pay lip service" to the

Zionist cause but do nothing to bring the assimilation to a halt, and "thousands of years of living in a Muslim society have taken a toll." Another report asserts, "Immigration to Israel has been desultory for a number of years and is offset by the number of births. There is little impetus to leave, since the Jews enjoy all political and social rights of Iranian citizens."[65]

Elias Eshaqian, teacher and principal at AIU schools in Iran for over twenty-five years, wrote in his memoir, "Iran has been my homeland [*vatan*] and Jerusalem has been the source of my belief in God and the direction of my prayers [*qiblah*]."[66] This quotation suggests yet again that many Iranian Jews held different interpretations of Zionism from the ones advanced by the Jewish Agency and Israel. A role model for many Iranians, Eshaqian clearly kept his religious identity as a Jew from diminishing his national Iranian identity. He proudly projected a combined identity throughout his career, which proved an inspiration and guide to his students.

Iranian Jews and Non-Jews Alike: Connection to Israel

During the mid-1950s Israel's position toward Jews in Iran shifted significantly away from traditional strategies employed with "at-risk communities" in other Muslim countries. Iranian Jews were not waiting to be rescued. However, they were not indifferent to Israel either. While they did not want to immigrate, they still showed interest in Israel's social, political, and economic evolution. The Jewish community of Tehran published pamphlets with news from Israel and the Jewish world. Many Iranian Jews already had friends or relatives living in Israel. For better or worse, Israel became part of their identity tapestry. Their response to events in or involving Israel ran the gamut: they embraced, rejected, adored, and criticized the Jewish state and expressed every feeling in between.

Israel's reputation as an emerging socialist country encouraged left-leaning Iranian Jews and non-Jews to hold Israel in high esteem.[67] Ironically, the same emissaries who enraged Zionist officials in Iran helped to strengthen the relationship between Iran's Jewish community and Israel. Public opinion regarding Israel strengthened even further in 1962. On September 1, 1962, the province of Qazvin experienced a devastating earthquake. More than twelve thousand residents of the region died and thousands more remained without shelter. This earthquake, magnitude 6.9 on the Richter scale, was one of the most devastating natural disasters to ever hit Iran. The Israeli government was quick to respond and, in accordance with Israel's foreign policy doctrine, sent numerous individuals to assist with reconstruction of the region.[68] Israeli planners working on behalf of the Israeli government helped to rebuild the province and modernize its agricultural industry, making Israel somewhat more popular among average Iranians, not just the political and military elites in regular contact with Israel.[69] Israeli companies that had already been established in Iran also took part in the earthquake recovery effort and began reaching out to educated Iranian Jews, hiring them as their people on the ground. This may have had a double effect: it tangibly linked Iranian Jews to Israelis and also enabled Iranian Jews to attain a comfortable upper-middle-class status, given that the type of jobs available paid excellent salaries. Some might argue that this hiring practice made Iranian Jews feel particularly more connected to the renewal of Iranian urban society.

Off the record, the Shah himself once referred to Iran's relations with Israel as an extramarital affair. But even this extramarital affair was a fairly open secret. Friendly athletic competitions were conducted regularly between teams from Iran and Israel.[70] By the 1970s a myriad of Israeli companies worked in Iran in almost every field. The Israeli airline El Al had eighteen weekly nonstop flights between Tel Aviv and Tehran and kept a lavish office on Vila Street.[71]

A primary objective of this chapter is to demonstrate that a positive perception of Israel among the general public in Iran was crucial in helping the Jews welcome greater identification with Zionism and Israel. To qualify that, what mattered most was a positive attitude toward Israel among the Iranian intelligentsia. The opinion of poor or working-class Iranians in remote provinces or urban neighborhoods was of little concern. Since the Iranian intelligentsia and the intellectual circles of Tudeh (and other leftist organizations) largely overlapped, what resulted was, overall, a positive image of the Jew. Since the 1940s translations of Jewish thinkers had appeared and had been widely accepted. Sigmund Freud, Franz Kafka, Karl Marx, and Isaiah Berlin became household names among respected Iranians.

Into the 1960s: The Role of Iranian Intellectuals

Travelogues of prominent Iranian intellectuals like Daryoush Ashouri and Sa'id Naficy reflected positively on Israel, describing the complexity of Israeli society in a new light.[72] As an interviewee for this book, Ashouri recounted, "In my early youth, in 1947 I left the Tudeh Party together with Khalil Maleki, who was our leader, to establish Niru-yi Suvvum [the Third Force]. We felt sympathetic to Israel and to the experiment of socialism there. Especially the collectives in agriculture." He continues, "Our party had openly declared sympathies for Israel, something that was a bit strange in Iran at the time."[73] Based on this newly established rapport, the Israeli diplomatic corps in Iran invited Maleki (along with Jalal Al-e Ahmad, a close associate of Maleki) to learn more about the kibbutzim. In 1961 an Israeli university organized a student congress, inviting students from around the world. "They invited two Iranian students from the Jibhah-yi Milli [the National Front], Mr. Abolhassan Bani-Sadr and Miss Bahreini, and they asked Maleki to send one from the Niru-yi Suvvum and Maleki chose me," says Ashouri. However, Ashouri was unable to attend because, just before the conference, he was arrested by SAVAK [*Sazman-i Ettela'at va Amni-yat-i Keshvar*, Organization of National Intelligence and Security] and imprisoned for demonstrating at Tehran University. His passport was also revoked. He was finally able to go a few months later, in 1962, when someone of "tremendous influence" from within SAVAK intervened on Ashouri's behalf. This intervention came on the heels of a formal invitation from Israel's Foreign Ministry.

Ashouri embarked on his two-week trip to Israel, boarding an El Al flight from Tehran. Once in Israel, accompanied by Israeli students and peers, he visited various kibbutzim, the city of Tel Aviv, and the Israeli section of Jerusalem. During our interview, Ashouri recalled meeting the Persian radio personality Menashe Amir and meticulously taking notes about his experiences. One night, upon his return to Iran, he met with Al-e Ahmad in Maleki's living room. Al-e Ahmad, arguably the most prominent intellectual of his generation, had just received an editing assignment for a journal published by the Kayhan Institute.[74] Al-e Ahmad turned to Ashouri and asked, "Do you have anything for us [for the journal]?" Astounded, Ashouri responded that he had just assembled notes from his trip to Israel, which he promised to organize and send promptly. His notes were published in *Kayhan International* shortly afterward, paving the way for the publication of his travelogue.

Bani-Sadr, the future first president of the Islamic Republic, was a student delegate to this same Israeli conference. Clearly Bani-Sadr came away with an entirely different impression of Israel. Visiting kibbutzim in the north, he concluded that these settlements were established not only to defend Israel's borders but also, and perhaps more importantly, to dominate Arab lands. From a socialist's viewpoint in Iran, this was unacceptable. At the Hebrew University of Jerusalem, Bani-Sadr asked to meet with Arab students. He was told that there were only eight. According to Bani-Sadr, "We fixed an appointment in a restaurant. We maneuvered with care to escape [Israeli] security. And it was there that they gave me a report on the situation of Arabs in Israel."[75]

A onetime member of the Tudeh leadership, Al-e Ahmad gained leftist-internationalist credentials in 1962 with the clandestine publication of *Gharbzadegi* (usually translated as *Occidentosis: A Plague from the West*),[76] in which he criticized the tendency of broad segments of Iranian society to blindly mimic the West. *Gharbzadegi* lamented the inevitable loss of Iranian culture and identity to Western models and paradigms. His publication influenced a later generation of Iranian revolutionaries, including 'Ali Shari'ati and the current supreme leader, Sayyed 'Ali Khamenei. Given his remarkable role in both the evolution of the Iranian Left and the development of contemporary political ideologies, one would not expect Al-e Ahmad to name Israel as a model society. Yet he introduced certain ideas that circulated among Iranian intellectuals before 1967, ideas that brought home the following message: Israel, at its essence, was a cultural and political ally.

Two years after the publication of *Gharbzadegi*, Al-e Ahmad and his wife, Simin Daneshvar, visited Israel. Al-e Ahmad's travelogue, *Vilayet-e Ezrael*, attests to the profound impression Israel left on him. Published in 1964 in the widely read literary journal *Andisheh va-Hunar*—and widely discussed among secular and religious intellectuals—the travelogue exerted an extraordinary effect on Iranian Jews and non-Jews alike. Al-e Ahmad wrote about Israel in nothing less than admiring terms. He described in detail a visit to Yad Va'Shem, the Holocaust memorial museum, and expressed his amazement at the resilience and ability of the Jewish people to recover after the horrors of the Holocaust. Later, in the most positive terms, he broadly discussed the kibbutz in Israel and the state's socialist ideology.

During their visit, Al-e Ahmad and Daneshvar stayed at Kibbutz Ayelet Ha'Shahar in northern Israel. He described this kibbutz for the Iranian reader as follows: "These people in Israel had already laid the foundation for the socialization of agricultural production in a part of the world inspired by the Russian Social-Democratic movement, and not by Stalin."[77] Thus, Al-e Ahmad associated Israel with the "correct" side of Communist ideology, reassuring those individuals in Tudeh and in various coalitions orbiting Tudeh, all of whom were staunchly opposed to Joseph Stalin's legacy.

Another reason for Al-e Ahmad's sincere sympathy for Israel may be found in the following proverb: "The enemy of my enemy is my friend." In his travelogue, Al-e Ahmad depicts Arabs in derogatory terms as ideological and cultural enemies. In fact, cultural tensions between Arabs and Iranians surface clearly in the text. Al-e Ahmad declares, "I am a non-Arab citizen of the East who has suffered much at the hands of the Arabs and still do. In spite of all the services that 'I' [*I* as in "Iran," not the person of Al-e Ahmad] rendered to Islam through the ages and still do, they still refer to me as 'Ajam," which in this context translates to "foreigner," as well as "illiterate one." Similar statements are found throughout the text. Given the strength of Al-e Ahmad's public persona and reputation, his travelogue made an undeniably positive impact as far as Iranian perceptions of Israel were concerned.[78]

Al-e Ahmad left the following remarkable comment in the kibbutz's guest book: "Regardless of the hospitality, I saw people here I never expected to meet. Learned people, understanding and open-minded. In a sense, they are implementing Plato. Honestly speaking, I always identified Israel with the Kibbutz, and now I understand why." Daneshvar added, "As I see it, the Kibbutz is the answer to the problems of all countries, including our own."[79]

Iran's current supreme leader (as of this writing), Khamenei, also read this travelogue, which not only puzzled him but also stirred major controversy among the young clerics in Qom, specifically because of the apparent contradiction between this book and Al-e Ahmad's previous popular writings, most especially *Gharbzadegi*. Al-e Ahmad wrote an additional chapter for his travelogue in 1968, faithfully reflecting the transformation of Iranian attitudes toward Israel. This shift occurred in 1967, of course, a watershed moment in the relationship between Pahlavi Iran and the State of Israel. The Six-Day War, during which Israel invaded neighboring countries and occupied the West Bank, the Gaza Strip, the Sinai Peninsula, and the Golan Heights, transformed Israel into a colonial power in the eyes of Iranian intellectual elites. After the war, many Soviet bloc countries severed relations with Israel, as did their satellite parties, including the Iranian Tudeh.

In his final chapter, Al-e Ahmad portrays Israel as part of a Western capitalist scheme in the region, explaining that reactionary Arab regimes had played into the hands of Israel and the colonial powers. He also criticizes French intellectual elites for their betrayal of the Arabs and support, yet again, of a new colonial venture. His criticism was aimed directly at Jean-Paul Sartre and Claude Lanzmann for condemning French colonialism in Algeria and for being hypercritical of Britain's ventures yet miraculously finding a way to ignore the exact same problems when it came to Israel.[80]

Beyond the sphere of Iranian intellectuals, public opinion toward Israel also changed dramatically in Iran after 1967. One saw this clearly manifest in 1968 when Israeli and Iranian national football teams squared off in Tehran as part of the Asia Cup finals.[81] Habib Elqaniyan, a wealthy Jew and community leader, was said to have purchased a large number of tickets, up to five thousand, so that Iranian Jews might attend and cheer for the Israeli team.[82] When Iran's prime minister and minister of economy called him to inquire whether he had indeed done so, Elqaniyan denied the rumor and insisted that he had had to pull strings in order to get tickets for his own family. The prime minister and minister of economy suggested that their information arrived from the SAVAK itself.[83] This cat-and-mouse game presaged the real game, in which Iranians unabashedly showed discontent with Israel's policy. The Israeli team and their supporters, in order to avoid mob violence, had to be escorted out of the stadium by police. This incident reflected a sea change in the Iranian attitude toward Israel. A onetime favorable partner had become an unwanted foreigner, protected only by the grace of the Shah's iron fist.[84]

Tipping Point: Israeli and Zionist Influence in Iran

Episodes such as the one just mentioned signaled a distinct shift in Israeli-Iranian relations. The only doors remaining open to Israelis in Iran seemed to be those of the military establishment and the Shah's court. Memoirs of Israeli officials such as Ezri and Yaacov Nimrodi depict life in Iran at this time as a James Bond–like narrative; everything was top secret and clandestine, all Israelis were Mossad agents or arms dealers, and there were no further signals from the general public suggesting close ties between the two nations. Both Ezri and Nimrodi underscore the fact that the Israeli flag was never flown over the Israeli embassy in Tehran. Conversations with other Iranians (Jews and non-Jews alike), however, tell a different and less dramatic story. Yes, no flag was flying, but the parties, festivals, receptions, and other public events left no doubt that Iranians from a wide social spectrum continued to mix and enjoy life at the embassy on Kakh Street.[85]

Where should we look for further clues about the status of Israel in the Iranian public sphere? Perhaps public ads might provide more information, ads that shed a positive light on the presence of Israel and Israelis. In 1969, the Moulin Rouge, one of Tehran's most celebrated nightclubs, ran an ad featuring its lineup for the coming month. The headline reads, "Cabaret Dance Hall Moulin Rouge Presents: Israeli Singer Recipient of Rave Reviews in Europe and America." At the top center of this advertisement is a large photo of the Israeli singer Tova Porat. The caption beneath her photo reads, "Tova Porat, international singer."[86] More surprising still is the remainder of the ad. Other prominent singers are listed in the second and third rows. However, in the second row, the ad mentions two singers that at the time were arguably Iran's megastars: Googoosh and Vigan. Porat even recorded an album in Persian on the Monogram label, and the record was released with a B side by another Iranian megastar, 'Aref. In all her public appearances, Porat was marketed as the Israeli star. This was in 1969, when, allegedly, public opinion had turned cold toward Israel and Israelis were invisible in the public sphere.[87]

This is not to suggest that public displays supporting Zionism were welcome or even deemed advisable. Undeniably, the political climate had changed within that delicate Iranian–Iranian Jew–Israeli triangle. The Iranian state had surely begun to distance itself from Israel officially, which magnified tensions between Iranian Jews and Israel.

Other examples of the complex relationship between Jewish communities in Iran and Israel may be found in a series of interactions that took place in the 1970s. With the exception of prominent community leaders, members of these Jewish communities by and large maintained a low-profile relationship with Israel, in a way that Israeli officials could not comprehend. On the one hand, Iranian Jews considered it a high priority to maintain a connection with the Sephardi religious establishment in Israel. The Sephardi chief rabbi of Israel, Rabbi Ovadia Yosef (b. Abdallah Yosef), perhaps the most revered religious figure in Israel during the second half of the twentieth century, was invited to Iran in June 1976 to help resolve Halachic disputes and other matters pertaining to the interpretation of Jewish law.[88] Rabbi Yosef received an exceedingly warm and respectful welcome from Iranian Jewish institutions and individuals. Yousef Kohan,

the Jewish representative to the Majlis, even tried to set a meeting between Rabbi Yosef and the Shah.[89]

However, other visitors dispatched as part of Israel's official Zionist
apparatus stirred disquieting emotions among Iranian Jews. In August 1975
Israel made plans to send a representative to deal with JNF issues and
fund-raising efforts in Iran. The Israeli ambassador in Iran, Uri Lubrani,
responded with an urgent, top-secret telegram to the Foreign Office in
Jerusalem, informing them of the unanimous Jewish community opposition to the arrival of a new JNF person in Iran. According to the telegram,
"Arrival of such a person in Iran would give the impression of total Israeli
disregard for the community's needs and wishes."[90] Also in August 1975
tensions rose, perhaps for the first time, between the Shah's court and the
Jewish community. Inflation at that time had skyrocketed. Ambassador
Lubrani reported that some Jews feared they were under surveillance. Another concern centered on a heavy-handed "request" by Ashraf Pahlavi (the
Shah's sister) that wealthy Jews step forward to raise money to build two
hospitals, one in Tehran and the other in Hamedan. Lubrani estimated
(according to rumors circulating at that time) that the requested sum came
to between $15 million and $70 million. Despite this and other equally
stressful concerns, Lubrani added, there had not been even one applica-
tion for an immigration visa to Israel.[91]

Numerous encounters between Iranian Jews and Zionist emissaries
did not produce the results that Zionist officials expected. An innate dis-
sonance prevailed concerning the place of Iranian Jews and their respective prospects in Israel or Iran. Only in the 1960s did these emissaries realize
that they could not "read" Iranian Jews correctly. In a 1961 report to the
Jewish Agency board, the director of the Aliyah Department in Tehran
wrote, "We have to take into consideration that under normal political
conditions in this country, many years will pass before the majority of
Jews will immigrate to Israel. In that sense Persia is not different from other
Western countries whose Jews would rather stay in the diaspora."[92] The
ongoing struggle and tensions between Israel's officials and non-Israelis in
Iran (that is, the JDC, the AIU, and other Iranian organizations) led to
various misconceptions, fueled by wishful thinking (often on the part of
local Zionist activists and community leaders who were especially sympathetic to Israeli Zionism).

The unique ability of Iranian Jews to develop highly complex
identities—and to be largely successful because of their sensitivity to

nuance—often baffled observers from outside Iran. Jews self-identified first and foremost as Iranian, by virtue of their language and culture. Interestingly, Haim Tsadok wrote that between Iranian Jews and non-Jewish Iranians one found 90 percent commonality, whereas between Iranian Jews and non-Iranian Jews in Israel one noted a 90 percent difference.[93] The phenomenon of commonality led Iranian Jews to fight for assimilation into Iranian society, even while espousing ideologies such as Zionism, albeit in a softer, more spiritual form than practiced at the time in Israel.

Zionism in Iran, therefore, moved along an imaginary axis; one end symbolized "very good idea for other Jews" and the other end, "good plan B in case assimilation in Iran amounts to colossal failure." The 1917 Balfour Declaration, coming fast on the heels of the disappointing outcomes of the Persian Constitutional Revolution (1906–1911), caused many Iranian Jews to tilt toward the "Plan B" option only to pivot back again with the accrued understanding that Zionism better suited twentieth-century Jews living elsewhere, beyond the borders of Iran.

Even organizations that were perceived—often mistakenly—as opposing Zionism, such as various Communist clubs or nationalist circles, did not treat Israel with the level of antagonism that many claimed. As was the trend on the Iranian left, many tried to present Israel as an anti-imperialist partner; hence, these organizations should not be judged solely through the prism of the Israeli-Arab conflict. Israeli observers were stuck in a mind-set that precluded any analysis of the Iranian political sphere in paradigms other than the ones with which they were familiar in Israel (and, to large extent, borrowed from the West). They viewed Communism and radical leftism as inherently anti-Zionist, and even anti-Semitic. Israeli observers tried to repair this left-leaning inclination of Iranian Jews, demanding that Israeli leftists be prevented from traveling to Iran on behalf of the government. It had become painfully clear that sending leftist envoys fed the already existing deep sympathies of Iranian Jewish youths for socialism.[94]

At the same time, Orthodox Jewish organizations such as Otsar Ha-Torah were also perceived as an impediment. Rabbi Isaac Meir Levy, an Ashkenazi Orthodox Jew, controlled Otsar Ha-Torah in ways that did not serve Zionist goals, particularly in the arena of education. He not only forbade his students from attending the semi-Zionist Koresh Kabir club but also imposed certain restrictions on teachers coming from Israel. In Otsar Ha-Torah, Hebrew was taught for prayer purposes only and not as a living language, a practice that ran counter to the hopes and aspirations of Israeli officials. When the Jewish Agency board tried to suggest that Rabbi Levy was not connected to his community, the author of the report rightfully replied, "Not only is he connected to the community, but he also speaks Persian and enjoys a good relationship with them [community members]."[95] The JDC, with its unwavering support of Otsar Ha-Torah, was continually blamed for creating obstacles to successful Zionist outcomes. The Jewish Agency and the Israeli Foreign Ministry suggested, and not for the first time, that the JDC's treatment of Iranian Jews made it more convenient for individuals to stay in Iran rather than endure the unpredictable hardships of immigrating.

Not only did the Zionist dream of mass emigration from Iran to Israel fail to materialize but, equally critical, the steady stream of return migration continued. An article published as late as 1969 in *Kayhan International* highlighted the plight of numerous Iranian Jews who, unable to adjust socially and culturally in Israel, chose to return to Iran.[96] Leaving Israel offered the possibility of joining in the upward mobility of Jewish Iranian communities, benefiting from the fruits of a close collaborative relationship between Israel and Iran, and participating, if they chose to, in the White Revolution.

This chapter calls attention to those external forces that shaped priorities and identities within Iran's Jewish community, especially between 1948 and the 1960s—often inadvertently strengthening the already powerful connection between Iranian Jews and their homeland. The next chapter demonstrates how this multilayered identity played out in the years leading up to the Iranian Revolution of 1979, during the revolution, and immediately afterward.

4

Unintended Consequences
The Lead-Up to the Iranian Revolution

IN THE DECADES LEADING to the 1979 revolution, the Jews of Iran were decisively integrated. This integration manifested itself in the Jews' upward social mobility, their visibility in the public sphere, and their prominent place in the Iranian economy, science, and various political projects (some of which are discussed later). Since 1960 the Tehran skyline had included the iconic landmark of the Plasco high-rise building, built by the Jewish industrialist and philanthropist Hajji Habib Elqaniyan;[1] in her 1959 visit to Iran, Eleanor Roosevelt made a public visit to the Jewish charity hospital in Tehran; the Jewish Nursing School was considered one of Iran's best; the empress Farah Diba Pahlavi visited the fashion students in one of the schools of the Association for the Promotion of Skilled Trades (ORT); synagogues and Jewish religious establishment were lavish, open, full, and spread all over the country; eighteen weekly El Al flights between Tel Aviv and Tehran increased the visibility of Jews and Israelis in the country and turned the Iranian capital into the El Al gateway to the East; Yousef Kohan, the last Jewish representative to the Majlis before the revolution, was also a member of the Tehran city council—a position to which he was elected in general elections with no process of reserved seats of any sort. In short, Jews were part of every walk of life in Iran, visible, prominent, and integrated.

When the anti-Shah upheavals of 1978 erupted, Iranian Jews found themselves, naturally, on both sides of the revolutionary movement: among its supporters and its opponents. As violence intensified, many wounded protesters calling for the establishment of an Islamic Republic found sanctuary from the clashes in a rather surprising place: the Sapir Hospital

(Bimaristan-i Sapir), the Jewish hospital in Tehran.[2] The demonstrations' participants knew that the Jewish hospital would treat them well, unlike the government hospitals. Above all, the facility would not turn them over to the Shah's secret service, SAVAK. This rescue apparatus became widely known thanks to the hospital administration's close collaboration with Ayatollah Sayyid Mahmoud Taliqani. Taliqani, who functioned during that time as Ruhullah Khomeini's representative in Iran, was a popular leader of the revolutionary movement. Together, Taliqani and Sapir Hospital staff operated rescue teams for the protesters and played a meaningful role in Iran's most significant twentieth-century moment.

Let us now examine the political and social activities of Jewish groups and individuals, like the Sapir Hospital staff, during the Iranian Revolution in 1978–1979, during the events of the early 1970s that led to the revolution, and in the early revolutionary period. By this time, Jews were fully integrated into the public sphere, and their identity politics of Judaism and Iranian nationalism played out in interesting ways during this upheaval. Although the Pahlavi period is considered to be the golden age of religious minorities in Iran, Jews overwhelmingly did not appear to support the continuation of the monarchy vis-à-vis the imminent revolution.[3] In some cases, they openly supported the rebellious factions in ways that, when juxtaposed with traditional history, may seem counterintuitive.

Previous chapters of this book have noted several historiographical gaps and attempted to shed light on the inner relatively high diversity among the Jewish minority communities, their running social and communal networks not just to attend to their regular constituency but rather to facilitate better integration and assimilation, and their taking an active role in shaping inclusive Iranian identity. This chapter addresses yet another historiographical challenge. As Chapter 2 argued, minorities overall did not refrain from politics; this chapter narrates their active involvement in the revolution that overthrew the regime that benefited them the most. This paradoxical outcome demonstrates the unintended success of the Shah's most significant project; that is, the full integration of minorities into Iranian society allowed them to operate freely, regardless of the myopic interests of their communities.

The common narrative holds that the Pahlavi era was the golden era for religious minorities in Iran, including Jews. Iranian nationalism at that time revolved around cultural roots, Persian language and ethnicity, and Western-style secularism, which at least in theory allowed non-Muslim Iranians full membership in the national project.[4] The Jewish community did indeed flourish under the Pahlavi regime. Jews became high-ranking bureaucrats, industrialists, and merchants. They amassed wealth and climbed the social ladder, flooding the ranks of universities and professional organizations. The government allowed Jews to practice their faith openly. They also maintained many communal institutions, such as schools, synagogues, newspapers, and hospitals. Nevertheless, it was the earlier Constitutional Revolution, as described in Chapter 2, that had created a civic basis for participation that enabled the minorities a certain degree of assimilation.

David Menashri, a prominent scholar of Iran and Iranian Jewry, notes, "[Jews] were overrepresented among the country's student population and university faculty body, among medical doctors and other professionals. Although there were people of low income among them, the vast majority could be defined as middle class, or upper middle class. Some became very rich, taking full advantage of the freedom granted to them to reform programs, and the growing oil income."[5] In his 1985 research, David Sitton provided similar data, which repeatedly appeared later on: "In 1979 two of the eighteen members of the Royal Academy of Sciences, 80 of the 4,000 university lecturers, and 600 of the 10,000 physicians in Iran were Jews . . . the overwhelming majority of Jews were middle class, 10 percent were wealthy and another 10 percent were impoverished. . . . About half of the Jewish children of elementary school age attended Hebrew schools or received lessons in Hebrew. But the ever-growing Jewish intelligentsia took no interest in Jewish affairs and did not long for Zion. Most of them were radical left."[6] Sitton's data shows the predominance of Jews in the Iranian public sphere, especially among the intellectual elites. As already mentioned, only thirty-seven years earlier the vast majority of the community members had been lower middle class and impoverished, and in less than four decades this reality had changed.

This assimilation led the Jews into political activism that may at first seem counterintuitive. Although much has been written about other sectors' activities during the Iranian Revolution, particularly among students, political dissidents, and clerics, few resources document the activities of the Jewish population and other minorities.[7] As Chapter 2 showed, Iranian Jews have been involved in politics in Iran through different parties and championing different goals. Because of the dictatorship's ban on any oppositional political activity, Jews remained active in student movements, underground Tudeh activities, and the establishment of associations that engaged in politics through alternative approaches, such as community political action societies. As explained before, scholarship about Jewish political activism insufficiently covered the political participation, especially the oppositional side of it, so one can scarcely find information about such participation without going back to the activists themselves, sifting through old publications and memoirs, and reaching out to contemporary observers. At the same time, historiography of the 1979 Iranian Revolution tends to focus on the clerical-religious nature of the movement, pushing aside other partner participants, hence creating a one-dimensional narrative of the revolution. This chapter does not attempt to overturn the metanarrative regarding the Iranian Revolution by attributing the event to Jewish involvement; rather, it seeks to reveal an angle that current research has left undeveloped.

A Generation of Jewish Revolutionaries

"The word 'opposition' had become something students find appealing," a KGB official memorandum explained during the wave of student protests in 1969.[8] Indeed, throughout the 1960s and 1970s students led opposition movements around the globe. These movements, typically leftist with Maoist tendencies, criticized the bipolar Cold War policies, weak proxy governments, and injustice inherent in imperialism and colonialism.

Iranian students, mainly in Europe, became political leftist dissidents and were organized as such since the late 1920s. They had strong ties with socialist and pro-Soviet activists in Iran, and many of them later became leaders of the Tudeh Party.[9] During the reign of Reza Shah, they organized conferences, published newspapers in several languages, and generally publicized to the world the Shah's oppressive policies inside Iran. In this process the German Communist Party supported the Iranian student organizations, a collaboration that encouraged a broad internationalist agenda among the future Tudeh leadership. Following the victory of the Nazi Party in Germany, most of the Iranian students previously based in Germany returned to Iran and tried to reorganize the Communist Party, a goal they achieved in 1941 with the establishment of the Tudeh Party. In 1949 a Tudehi student organization was established at Tehran University, which positioned the party as dominant among the Iranian urban intelligentsia. Leaders and political thinkers such as Mihdi Bazargan and Taliqani were members of this student body.[10] They participated in protests against

Mohammad Mosaddeq's trial and Richard Nixon's visit later that year, among others.

By the late 1950s Iranian students' organizations appeared again in Western Europe and the United States, expressing similar views to those of the Tudeh and the National Front. The Iranian student confederation in Paris, for example, enjoyed the active support of the French Communist Party and the prominent intellectual Jean-Paul Sartre.[11] Mohammad Reza Shah's response to these confederations highlights their significance. After a huge demonstration against the Shah's visit to the American capital that was organized by Iranian students, the Shah avoided visiting countries that had active Iranian confederations and in some instances asked the SAVAK to follow their activities.[12]

These student organizations were part of a global movement and partook in struggles other than their own in the 1960s and 1970s.[13] They participated in the struggles of their host countries' students; however, with the reemergence of the opposition movement in Iran, and especially at Tehran University, they began to sync activities with local Iranian associations in Iran and abroad.[14] In this period, one of the members of the secretariat was a Tehrani Jew, Parviz Ne'eman. Other members, who really illustrate the broad participation, were Abolhassan Bani-Sadr, the first president of the Islamic Republic, and Cosroe Chaquèri, who became a historian of the Iranian Left and the Armenian Iranian community after the revolution.[15]

In the 1970s, along with increased assimilation, Jews were immensely active in student organizations and other opposition movements. Jews sympathized with their compatriots, setting aside their community's alleged inherent support of the monarchy. This mind-set of assimilation (and perhaps the feeling that it had arrived at its ultimate stage) could have stemmed from instilling the liberal nationalist ideals those organizations expressed and promoted. Also, it seems as though these organizations, with their apparent religious and ethnic diversity, allowed Jews to envision a multicultural society in which they, the minorities, would have a central role. The result was growing involvement in existing organizations, such as the student confederations and the Tudeh Party, and the establishment of new organizations. The generation of Jews that came of age during the Shah's White Revolution (after 1963) was already acquainted with socialist theories and politics and expressed its views loudly and clearly as the rest of Iranian society prepared for a revolution.

The connections between the associations in Iran and abroad were very strong. Not only did Iranian students collaborate on operations in Iran and communicate activities to Western outlets, but many of them returned to Iran and became involved in the local chapters once they graduated from institutions in the West. For example, one of the interviewees for this project, Mihrdad, studied in Europe and was part of the European confederation. He returned to Iran from Europe at the time when the opposition inside Iran was becoming more active and more explicit:

When I returned to Iran in 1975, I met an old friend who suggested to set up an organization for the younger generation, rather than the old attachment to synagogues. So we established an organization called Council of Advancement of Jewish Social and Cultural Activism and it became very successful. We held our first events in a hotel, not a community center and it became an attraction for the newer generation. We had very interesting events and lectures, which were not religious or pro-Israel. It was more general on an informative basis. We had intellectuals coming from the politically active community. Our events were full. Soon, the room given to us was not enough. It was the place for the young up and coming Jews to meet each other. . . . It had become a big community. We were both Jews and part of the wider community.[16]

This group's worldview was holistic—that is, they wanted to engage in every aspect of Jewish Iranian social life. The newly established council provided cultural and educational activities to as many Jews as it could find and recruit. Among other operations, it ran a summer camp, which aimed to bring together Jews from all over Iran (and especially Tehran), regardless of socioeconomic status. Mihrdad states,

We organized the camp for 14–16 years old. We mixed Jews from South Tehran, the Mahallah, with Jews from North Tehran, and said there is a dress code: jeans and a T-shirt, and we provide the T-shirt, so there was no room for show off. For three summers successively, in 76–78, there were 1,000 kids going to this camp, and all the parents wanted their kids to come to this camp to get to know the others, because the ties within the community became looser and looser and they thought that this is it. Our success was that about a third [of the campers] came from poor families of Tehran and we did not charge them anything, and charged the others double.[17]

This way the group addressed issues that received wide attention in Iran at that time, such as economic inequality, and in their community found a popular and working solution. Although disparity was a much greater concern in the general public, the fact that the group was able to treat this issue inside the community must have been seen as a message of success regarding their leftist ideals.

The ultimate goal of this council was to connect Jews to broader social movements in Iran and bring them closer to political action. In its deeds the council laid the foundation for a far-reaching organization later that decade, when the revolutionary events started to take place. During the protests of the 1970s, while the Tudeh Party's activity was outlawed, two Jewish activists, Harun Parviz Yesha'ya and 'Aziz Daneshrad, were jailed for antimonarchial activity. After serving their time, they turned to political activity within the Jewish community.[18] Loyal to their leftist tendencies and religious identity, they gathered a dozen like-minded comrades and established the most significant Jewish organization in late 1970s Iran: the Association of Jewish Iranian Intellectuals (AJII; Jami'ah-i Rawshanfikran-i Kalimi-yi Iran). Habib, an interviewee for this project, was a close friend of Yesha'ya and Danseshrad from their days in the Tudeh. He was also one of AJII's founders: "We established our office in an apartment on Firdawsi Street. There were four of us, and we did not know where exactly we were heading."[19] They did not have a well-thought-out plan, but they wanted to politicize the community and connect Jewish values and ideas to the political program of the Tudeh Party. AJII's significance is threefold. First, it organized the Jews under a Jewish ethnic banner to engage in revolutionary activity. Second, in 1978 it challenged the old-guard leadership of the community, which mostly identified with the Shah's regime and had connections with Zionist organizations, and gained control of the Jewish establishment.[20] And third, its weekly publication, *Tamuz*, named after the Hebrew month of July (the month in which its publication started), quickly became a highly circulated magazine that aspired to be a bridge between the Jewish community and the Iranian people. As mentioned before, there were overlaps in some of the individuals' affiliations, and so the association actively welcomed people with different political and organizational affiliations and became the main venue for leftist Jewish activists.

In an article celebrating the third anniversary of AJII, a *Tamuz* editorial outlined the organization's contribution to Jewish involvement in the revolution:

From the beginning of the year 1357 [1978] a group of the Iranian Jews has participated in the great movement against imperialism and dictatorship. From the very beginning we tried to collaborate with the revolutionaries, especially the Muslim clerics in different levels, and we have done this work ever since. And at last in the month of Shahrivar 1357 [August 1978] a Jewish group joined the protest for the first time under an Iranian-Jewish banner, and this group, in the month of Azar 1357 [November 1978], met with the late Ayatollah Taliqani, and announced the[ir] common goals.[21]

This quote shows that AJII was a much more sophisticated incarnation of the previous attempt. In November 1978 these groups believed that the revolution was about to happen and that the Shah would soon be overthrown, but it can still be regarded as a bold policy to approach a revolutionary figure such as Taliqani for collaboration and give publicity to such support.

Indeed, AJII was formed to show Jewish discontent with the monarchial regime. The organization was established in March 1978, as revolutionary events were already unfolding. The group immediately began collaborating with other rebelling factions, including Muslim Iranian activists (most notably Ayatollah Taliqani): "We formed this group in order to show the rest of the people in Iran that we Jews were not woven from a different fabric of society than other Iranians, but that we also supported [the new government's professed] goals for democracy and freedom," says Sa'id Banayan, one of the association's founding fathers.[22] AJII became the most vocal supporter of the revolution among the Jewish community. Hushang, an interviewee for this project and a prominent figure in AJII and the Jewish community during the revolution, stated, "AJII was the most important Jewish organization during the revolution. At the core of it were left-leaning intellectuals and students, and later many other Jews joined in."[23] Initially, the Jewish community did not welcome the new AJII leadership and tried to prevent them from gaining influence in the *Anjuman*, the traditional community organization. However, after the elections for the Anjuman's council in March 1978, the new AJII leadership succeeded in establishing a "revolutionary" committee to run Jewish affairs.[24] Some AJII members had served time in the Shah's prisons during previous turmoil, where they had become acquainted with other political dissidents who were later involved in the revolutionary movement. The most significant relationship was with Khomeini's close ally, the popular thinker and a chief ideologist of the revolution, Taliqani.[25]

AJII saw indifference, separatism, and corruption as the main obstacles to advancement within the Jewish community. In order to win the hearts and minds of Jews, the association invested in many activities that correlated with their ideals. It sponsored activities with Muslim activists during the revolution and established a lecture series hosted in local synagogues that featured presentations from secular Muslim advocates of the revolution and high-ranking clerics who were deeply involved in the revolution.[26] For example, Hidayatullah Matin-Daftari, one of the National Front's leaders, came to talk about how important it was for the Jews to contribute to the revolution and participate in building a new Iranian society.[27]

The official AJII bylaws reflect hybrid identities that were, in many ways, unique to Iran. They contained sentiments of nationalism and radical socialism, all mixed with Muslim and Jewish religiosity. Some of the articles in the AJII bylaws expressed this approach with a call for political action and Iranian social solidarity. Article Three, for example, reads, "[We encourage] active participation in the social life of the Iranian people, and the creation of a Jewish society that will struggle shoulder to shoulder with our Iranian brothers for the ultimate victory of the revolution and the building of a free and progressive Iran." Article 4 presents the utopian vision of creating a new society, describing the organization's commitment to "efforts to preserve the fruits of the revolution of the Iranian people in regards of the social and personal rights and including those of the Iranian Jews in the Islamic Republic of Iran." Article 5 distinguishes between Jews and Zionism, since during the revolution there were factions that intentionally conflated the two. The article declares the organization's commitment to waging "war against imperialism, and any form of colonialism, including Zionism, and revealing the relationship between Zionism and world's imperialism," as well as waging "war against any sort of racial discrimination, racism, and anti-Semitism." Article 6 talks once again about the revolutionary utopia, encouraging the community to adapt "to the new reality in Iran, by enjoying all the opportunities to have better conditions to religious and cultural life and welfare of the Iranian Jews."[28] These bylaws' articles efficiently reflected the mind-set of the leftist movements in Iran during the revolution. They envisioned a sort of model society in which universal values of solidarity would yield a just and open community, and in which the Jews would be equal citizens.

AJII clearly envisaged a utopian republic of endless opportunities, which would be made possible only by disposing of the monarchy and establishing the Iranian republic. The vision of a republic that emphasized fraternity, solidarity—particularly with Palestinians—and freedom for minorities is representative of the cultural identity that AJII members aspire to create. This cultural identity is primarily Iranian but expands to include the Arab Middle East and Third World countries. By positioning the organization as anti-imperialist and anticolonialist, AJII became relevant not only to the Iranian context but even to the broader Middle East.

Sapir Charity Hospital, the Revolution, and Ayatollah Taliqani

AJII pulled members from a variety of political realms; state employees, merchants, industrialists, community activists, and Sapir Hospital staff. Some of the senior officials in the hospital were involved to some extent in AJII, sympathized with its causes, and assisted the revolutionaries for various reasons. These facilitators included Gad Naim, who was part of AJII leadership and a senior administrator in Sapir hospital;[29] Dr. Manuchihr Aliyasi, who was also among the hospital's senior staff and an AJII sympathizer;[30] and Yesha'ya, who was among the founders of AJII and *Tamuz* and became the hospital director after the revolution.[31]

On September 8, 1978, mass demonstrations erupted in Tehran. The Shah sent the army to shoot live ammunition at the crowd of protesters. This event became known as Black Friday and coincided with the active involvement of the hospital in events. "That Friday the head nurse, Ms. Farangis Hasidim, called me and told me that they are bringing many casualties to the hospital," recalls Dr. Jalali, one of the senior officials in Sapir Hospital at that time. "I drove to the hospital but the Zhalah [avenue] was blocked, so I went by foot and there was shooting. . . . Since I was friendly with the ambulance services people, almost ninety percent of the injured people came to Sapir hospital, where we treated all of them in our four surgery rooms." At this point Jalali referred to the growing involvement of Ayatollah Taliqani and his personal relationship with him, which proved to be essential later on: "Five months prior to the revolution [following Black Friday] I had a building next to my office, I dedicated it to 'Taliqani Support Group' [in Persian: Guruh-i Imdad-i Taliqani]. . . . After 'Black Friday' he called me and told me how he appreciated all the humanitarian work we did there. And yes, everybody knew about it."[32]

Guruh-i Imdad-i Taliqani became an important apparatus that helped first responders to treat the wounded protesters in the big cities, especially Tehran. According to the Iranian press, there were two first response groups reporting to Taliqani. They had a relatively large staff of volunteer physicians, nurses, ambulances, and other staff, and their contributions toward ensuring the continuity of the protests cannot be overrated.[33]

The acquaintance of Taliqani with Jewish leaders in Tehran extends beyond his friendship with Jalali. Upon Taliqani's release from prison, a group of prominent Jewish figures went to visit him and stayed in close contact with him until his death in 1979. Taliqani became one of the foremost advocates for minority rights in postrevolutionary Iran.[34] Although Jalali was politically affiliated with AJII, some of the doctors were not. The story of the hospital is mostly a humanitarian one.

On December 11, 1978, one of the largest demonstrations against the Shah took place in Tehran. Newspapers called it a "demonstration of millions," and it set a milestone in the struggle against the Shah's regime. Jewish participation set records as well; according to some sources, five thousand Jews participated in these protests.[35] Other estimates were much higher. Hushang, a longtime leftist activist in the Jewish community and AJII, helped organize the massive Jewish appearance that day: "According to press reports close to twelve thousand Jews participated in these protests that day," he says. "The Jewish religious leaders marched in the front row and the rest of the Jews followed them, showing great solidarity with our Iranian compatriots."[36] The religious leadership sided with the young radical group and in a sense "legitimized" them. "From the first days of the revolution we had considerable support from religious leaders. Hakham Yedidia Shofet, Hakham Uriel Davidi, Rabbi David Shofet, Hakham Yosef Hamadani Cohen, and others attended and supported. . . . Other key figures were Parviz Yesha'ya, 'Aziz Daneshrad, Ya'qub Barkhurdar, Hushang Melamed, Dr. Manuchihr Aliyasi, and Ms. Farangis Hasidim, all played a major role," Hushang says.[37] According to him, the activities of AJII helped to reduce tensions between the Muslim majority and the Jewish minority. However, not all of the religious leaders who joined that day did so wholeheartedly. "It was my assignment to convince Hakham Shofet to join us, to get him in the picture," said Mihrdad. "He was sympathetic to the cause but felt heavy hearted. He was reluctant to come and we told him that it was for the sake and safety of the community. We even found rabbinic writing and Halacha ruling that say that if the community requires you to do such and such you do it not because this is your belief but because the decision would be for the good of the community. So he said he would come out."[38] Shofet, then, participated despite early reservations, which makes him a unique case in this story. Loyalty to both the Shah and the community meant a great deal to him. He came out that day and afterward not because he looked to facilitate integration of the community into the broader society but rather to seek protection for the community in a rapidly changing reality.

Habib's memories of this demonstration help us to understand the profound impact it had on the participants: "We met by Darvazah-i dawlat synagogue in south Tehran and joined the main demonstration from there. . . . Our signs and chants were: Yahudi-musalman hambastigi-i mubarak [Jewish-Muslims blessed solidarity]. It was so exciting, I could not stop crying." Hakham Shofet's recollections of this day express the same sentiment:

In every place we live we must respect the majority's opinion and approve and respect their leadership [not necessarily the elected or ruling leadership]. Because of this rule, in those days, with respect to these people, we joined them in marching for the Tasu'a [the ninth day of the holy month of Muharram; in Shi'a tradition it symbolizes the day before the battle of Karbala and the preparations of Hossein] in 19 Azar Mah 1357 [December 9, 1978]. Muhandis Daneshrad and other members of the Jewish Community [Anjuman] board were on my side. . . . It was constructive and inspiring. Many of the Muslims that led this great march and were responsible for it, welcomed us warmly, among them were many Shi'i clerics.[39]

This memory is interesting, especially because of the fact that he did not openly oppose the Shah. There are multiple accounts of Shofet positively commenting on the Shah's period as unprecedented for the Iranian Jews and expressing his fear of the unclear future. In an interview, one of the people who made Shofet join the march said that Shofet stated he would do it for the sake of the community, but he wanted the march organizer to know that every Saturday when he is offering prayers for the health of the Shah, he means it.[40]

Muslim protesters greeted the Jewish group by chanting, "Jewish brother, welcome, welcome" (Baradar-i yahudi khush amadi, khush amadi).[41] When they passed by Madrasah-i 'Alavi,[42] they chanted, "Khomeini's leadership is the basis of national unity" (Rahbari-yi Khomeini asas-i vahdat-i milli). "That day," Habib says, "we all had tears of happiness. We were all in support of democracy, and freedom, and the revolution."[43]

Despite the presentation of national unity in the demonstration, given past experiences, it was obvious that the protest was not about to end peacefully. Sapir Hospital's personnel were well prepared for the events of Tasuʻa and ʻAshura. "That morning they called me from Madrasah-i ʻAlavi and asked to keep all the staff and doctors for the day. I received seventy or eighty percent of the injured from all over the city. All of them went either to Sapir, Kurush-i Kabir as it was called back then, or the Imperial Medical Center, this situation lasted for seventy-two hours," recalls Jalali.[44]

In its second issue, *Tamuz* published a two-page story titled "Sapir Hospital During the Revolution" (Bimaristan-i Sapir dar jarayan-i inqilab) that described the services provided by Sapir Hospital to the revolutionaries: "In the turbulent months of our revolution, Kurush-i Kabir hospital, which after the revolution was renamed after Sapir, became one of the places that, through taking personal risks for the sake of the revolution, treated and facilitated the revolution."[45] The article cites anecdotes from senior hospital officials, such as the head nurse, Farangis Hasidim, who, speaking about the events of Black Friday and ʻAshura, said, "This day unfolded in unexpected ways. I went to see a rebel that arrived with a bullet injury in his leg, and he was bleeding. I immediately took him to the surgery room. I had not finished treating him, when another patient came in, and every minute more and more injured arrived. For many hours the hospital looked like the frontlines of a war zone."[46] The hospital staff also had to cope with the Shah's security officers who came to search for rebels in hiding: "One day we heard great noise from the hospital's back yard and I saw a myriad of people in uniform and plain clothes [that is, secret police] looking for rebels. . . . For twenty-four hours guards circled the hospital, but we did not hand them anyone. . . . During Tasuʻa and ʻAshura the entire hospital staff stayed in the hospital for more than twenty-four hours. The hospital's ambulances cruised the streets to pick up wounded protesters and bring them to the hospital to get treatment."[47]

Following these events, in late 1978 a delegation of the Jewish community went to Paris to meet the leader of the revolution, Ayatollah Khomeini. The tacit purpose of this trip was to ensure that Jews would not be regarded as enemies of the revolution but rather as its supporters. This meeting was the first of many between the Jewish leadership and Khomeini.[48] Shortly after, the hospital received its first recognition from Khomeini: "For this reason [the humanitarian help] Imam Khomeini, before his return to Iran, had sent a letter of gratitude to the director of the hospital, recognizing his help and support for the wounded revolutionaries," said Dr. Siamak Moreh-Sedeq, one of the hospital's leaders and the current Jewish deputy in the Majlis in an interview. He described the assistance given to the revolutionaries and confirmed, once again, the story of the Shah's army siege in 1978.[49] Receiving Khomeini's recognition is not a small feat. In many ways it secured the future of the Jews under the leadership of the revolution.

"Jews Are Not Zionists," Said the Imam

Throughout the revolutionary events, there was a continuing attempt by both revolutionary factions and the Jews to draw a clear distinction between Jews and Zionists. This would be a theme well into the early revolutionary period, but even from the time of the protest there were multiple occasions on which revolutionaries and nonrevolutionaries provided ways to tell the difference.

On September 1, 1978, a few days before the escalation of Black Friday, Yousef Kohan, then the Jewish representative in the Majlis, and another member of the parliament, Ahmad Bani-Ahmad, met the Grand Ayatollah Muhammad Kazim Shari'atmadari. The purpose of this meeting was to have the respected ayatollah stopping the incitement against Jews, which was becoming a problem in some of the provinces in Iran. In his memoir, Kohan described the efforts.

At 1:30 in the afternoon of that September 1st, Bani-Ahmad called me and said, "Kohan! Put on your clothes and come to me immediately. Bring your documents with you." Those days, Bani-Ahmad was in danger, because he was seriously opposing the Shah's regime. I took the address of his secret location, which was the home of one of his fellow Azeris, and took off immediately. Outside the house, a group of tough Azerbaijanis were standing and I could tell they were armed. I asked Bani-Ahmad what was going on. "We want to go visit His Eminence Ayatollah Shari'atmadari," he answered. In any case, all the issues were humbly reported to him on that day in Qum. The Ayatollah was inclined to proclaim that the lives of Jews were protected unless if they were agents of Israel. Bani-Ahmad recommended that "even though this is correct but mentioning it will cause the malefactors to take the life of any Jew they want and then claim that he had been an Israeli agent. It would be better if His Eminence issued a general, unconditional and unambiguous command." Many reporters and correspondents from major international news agencies were constantly on the alert at Shari'atmadari's house with their cameras, because that location was the epicenter of Iranian politics, which was of interest to the whole world. That evening, the Iranian radio and television broadcasted this proclamation of the great Source of Emulation of Iranian Muslims:

"Reports are reaching us that a series of written threats against religious minorities who are recognized by the Constitution and respected by the Iranian Nation, have begun under the name of the Clergy and the banner of Islam. Iranian minorities, have all the liberties and the rights imaginable for the people of Iran. On the other hand, according to the ruling of Islamic commandments, personal rights of all the people of the world and even the human rights of our enemies have been recognized. Religious Minorities, which have been identified in the Constitution, have been shoulder to shoulder with the struggle of the Iranian nation as far as I remember. They accompanied the people in every step of the momentous events of the Constitutional Revolution. I shall never accept the smallest threat or intimidation against them under the name of Islam. In fact I consider such actions as an anti-Iranian and anti Islamic conspiracy. We must know that irresponsible people with missions of sabotage are on the prowl and are hoping to spread the seeds of hate and disunity."[50]

Such a proclamation from a prominent religious leader like Ayatollah Shari'atmadari was a major achievement for the Jewish leadership and in fact was crucial at a moment when Israel was brought up more often as part of the anti-Shah slogans and some Iranians could not tell the difference between Jews, Zionists, and Israelis.

Later that month, during the events of Black Friday it was rumored that the Shah deployed Israeli soldiers to confront the protesters. This rumor, of course, had no basis, but it promptly became an issue demanding attention on behalf of the Jewish leadership.

In the 2013 documentary *Before the Revolution: The Untold Story of the Israeli Paradise in Iran*, Nissim Levy, one of the Israeli embassy's security officers, recalls that as he drove through the streets of Tehran right before the ultimate victory of the revolution, he saw graffiti that read, "Kill Every Israeli—But Do Not Harm the Jews."[51]

Immediate Aftereffects of the Revolution

Shortly after the 'Ashura events, the revolution took a dramatic turn when on January 15, 1979, Mohammad Reza Pahlavi left Iran for good. "Shah Raft" (The Shah left), announced the newspapers the next day to the overjoyed crowds, and about two weeks later they announced that the Imam had arrived (*Imam amad*). All major minority groups came to the airport to welcome Ayatollah Khomeini back to Iran. The Jewish delegation coordinated their participation with another prominent leader of the revolutionary movement, Ayatollah Mohammad Bihishti. According to Mihrdad, "Bihishti knew Yesha'ya from the time they were in jail together and helped to bring the Jewish community on board of the welcome ceremony." This acquaintance facilitated bringing the Jewish representatives into the reception plans.[52]

After the installation of the new regime, the hospital encountered controversy. Jalali states, "One night after the revolution they called me to tell that a group of people from the regime came and changed the name of the hospital to 'Khusraw Golisurkhi Hospital.' A member of the left, Golisurkhi had been executed by the shah.[53] It took us a long time, together with Parviz Yesha'ya to change it to 'Dr. Sapir Hospital.'"[54] Simin, Sapir's relative, explained how they petitioned the government to have the name changed to Dr. Sapir: "I collected evidence from people that got treatment in the hospital, collected newspaper stories, letters from clerics about the hospital during the revolution, and gave it to them in a big box. After a short discussion they pronounced him a Shahid, a martyr of the revolution, and ordered to have the name changed to Dr. Sapir Hospital."[55] This episode of the name change became significant as the Jewish community retained management of the hospital and the government acknowledged the role the hospital had played during the revolution. Still today, at the entrance to the hospital, there is a sign welcoming patients, staff, and visitors. The sign reads, in Hebrew and Persian, "Love thy neighbor as yourself" (Hebrew: *Ve'ahavta le're'acha kamocha*; Persian: *Hamnow'at ra mesl-i khodet dust bedar*), and this essentially captures the philosophy of this hospital from the days it was established by Sapir and onward. "Love thy neighbor as yourself" is a very charged command in Judaism. This phrase, "V'ahavtah l're'achah kamochah, Ani Adonai" ("You shall love your neighbor as yourself, I am the Lord"; Leviticus 19:18), is regarded as a Mosaic commandment in Jewish tradition. According to the Midrash, the great Tannaitic scholar Rabbi Akiva regarded it as the Torah's "great principle" (Palestinian Talmud, Nedarim 30:2). When asked to summarize the entire Torah, Rabbi Hillel the Elder coined a variation on this phrase and stated that "what is hateful to you, do not do unto others—this is the entire Torah, while the rest is commentary. Now go and learn it!" Due to the centrality of the principle, many Jewish communities adopted the custom of starting the daily morning service by declaring, "I hereby accept my Creator's commandment, to love my neighbor as myself. By this merit I shall open my mouth." While most Halakhic scholars viewed the commandment as applicable only toward fellow Jews, some rabbis—notably Italian scholar Eliyahu Benamozegh (d. 1900)—saw it as a universal commandment, obligatory for all people.[56]

Politics continued to play out in the Jewish community after the revolution. The cooperation between the hospital and the AJII was reaffirmed in early 1982. AJII held weekly meetings that were open to the public and often included a guest lecture, either on revolutionary topics or on Jewish topics during the Jewish high holidays. In January 1982, the executive board of Sapir Hospital came to participate in the weekly meeting. The next day's issue of *Tamuz* reported on the visit, depicting the recent history of the hospital and its plans for the future. Dr. Mansur Sharim, the director of the hospital, told the paper that, as always, Sapir Hospital continued to serve the Iranian people regardless of their faith.[57]

As already seen, Jews were active in all-Iranian organizations—such as the Tudeh—and, of course, in sectarian, explicitly Jewish groups, such as the AJII. However, Jews participated even in almost exclusively Muslim organizations, such as the Mujahidin-i Khalq (the People's Mujahidin of Iran). The Mujahidin-i Khalq was established by members of the intelligentsia—engineers, doctors, university students, and the intellectual elites of the nationalist opposition factions. Ayatollah Taliqani and Bazargan (the future prime minister) were among its prominent sympathizers. This organization employed a fascinating combination of Marxist and Islamist discourse in its articulation of a revolutionary ideology.[58] The Mujahidin-i Khalq was one of the key opposition organizations in the 1970s until the revolution.[59]

One of the Jewish activists in Mujahidin-i Khalq was Edna Sabet. Sabet was born in 1955 to a Jewish Kermanshahi family that lived in Tehran. Her family belonged to the middle class in the city, and many of her family members were American-educated engineers and industrialists. During her college years at Ariyamihr Technical University in Tehran, Sabet became politically active and joined an underground organization, Paykar. She promptly became a member of its central committee in Tehran. In Paykar she met Ghulam Husayn Salim Aruni, whom she married later.[60] Aruni was Muslim and became attracted to the Mujahidin-i Khalq.[61] Soon he joined the organization and Sabet followed suit. They were both prominent activists in the movement, and their story was widely circulated among the Tehran groups.

The institution of the interim revolutionary government prevented the Mujahidin-i Khalq from participating in the April 1979 elections. As a result, the group turned against the newly forming Islamic Republic's government. Iran's new revolutionary guards arrested (and even executed without trial) the Mujahidin-i Khalq members who only a short time before had fought with them against the Shah's oppressive regime. In 1981 Aruni was captured, arrested, prosecuted, and executed in the infamous Ayatollah Sadegh Khalkhali's court. Sabet was arrested a few months later. Evidence later showed that Sabet never faced court on any charges. She was tortured in prison but remained resilient and confident. She was executed on February 12, 1982, when she was only twenty-seven years old. A fellow comrade from her days in the Mujahidin-i Khalq said, "She was everything the new Islamic regime feared: A brave woman, a Jew, a leftist fighting uncompromisingly against the very core of the Islamic Republic."[62] Sabet was one of the Jews who were members in an almost exclusively Muslim organization. Despite her tragic ending, Sabet's story illustrates yet another facet of the complex identities and allegiances that characterized many of her generation. Her affiliation with the Mujahidin-i Khalq and the story of Sapir Hospital during the revolution exemplify the breaking of the traditional frameworks of this community's assimilation. These instances show yet again that in the late 1970s, most of the Jews in Iran favored their countrymen's interests over their own good or narrow communal benefits.[63]

The same events, wars, philosophies, and ideologies that shaped revolutionaries elsewhere in the world inspired the generation that came of age in the 1970s in Iran. It was the time when American students demonstrated against the war in Vietnam and Sartre and Michel Foucault incited European students and supported various goals of Third World identity groups. At the same time that many countries experienced their first moments of independence, the Iranian students' local project was to struggle against the American-backed monarchy in Iran and institute a functioning socialist republic instead. This kind of republic, obviously, would be founded on the ideals of an egalitarian society, where religious or ethnic affiliations play no part. The promise, thus, was to create an Iranian multiethnic, multireligious society.

The involvement of the Jews can be explained by the level of assimilation that they had reached by this crucial moment. Whereas members of their parents' generation in the late 1960s and early 1970s spent their own youths paving the way to leave the ghettos and the Jewish traditional life in order to pursue education and careers in the private and public sectors, their children felt they had to fight not for their status as a marginal minority but rather for a better society for Iran. The Jewish identity at that point served as another component and possible affiliation in the greater social tapestry of minorities in Iran.

Jewish participants in the student movements, both in Iran and abroad, belonged at that point to the nationalist bourgeoisie, whether they recognized it or not. Their assimilation efforts were fruitful, and Jewish culture and identity were just additional labels they carried and that perhaps rooted them deeper in the Iranian soil. It is within this context that we can begin to understand the establishment of AJII, initiatives such as the ones involved Sapir Hospital during the revolution, or the participation of Jews in Muslim revolutionary movements. These all represent the entire spectrum of national belonging, from the decision of AJII's members to profess Iranian nationalism as Jews, to Sapir Hospital's efforts to form a partnership to provide humanitarian assistance (again, even when some of the collaborators evidently supported the Shah), and to Sabet's choice to assimilate through the adoption of all the identifiers of Iranian and Islamic symbolism and rhetoric.

The large level of participation in the demonstrations may suggest that the majority of the Jewish population, although they did not take an active role in the events leading to the revolution, realized its inevitable victory and embraced the opportunities and blessings it might bring to the community and its future in its homeland.

What Is the Place of Non-Muslims in the Islamic Republic? Postrevolution Dilemmas

"Revolutionary crises are not total breakpoints in history that suddenly make anything at all possible if only it is envisaged by willful revolutionaries," wrote Theda Skocpol, referring to popular revolutions and the sobering moment after the revolution itself when utopian visions face reality.[64] The Iranian Revolution definitely experienced such a moment. Even though the nascent regime and elites aspired to replace the old, corrupt order with a new, idealized one, the transformation was difficult at some points and impossible at others.[65] The removal of the Pahlavi dynasty and the establishment of the interim government opened the Iranian political sphere and heralded an attempt to create a new society, established on the same ideas as the revolution: equal society, freedoms, rights, and democracy. However, chaotic struggles between rebelling parties ushered in this transitional period.

It was obvious that the fighting factions, from Communists and Marxists to nationalists (various offshoots of the National Front) and religious Islamists, would soon face a struggle over the character of the revolution and, ultimately, the character of Iranian society. After the revolution, the Iranian nation found itself once again defining its boundaries and identity. Jews had to find yet a new way to deal with changing national ideals, which were now defined by the new revolutionary elite.

Unlike under the Pahlavi regime, the intercommunal relations in the postrevolutionary society were in disarray. Different parties inside the Jewish community encouraged their peers to consider different political allegiances, while a myriad of ideologies continued to thrive among the Jews, such as socialism and religiosity. Many opted to temporarily leave the country until things returned to normal; Zionist agencies helped those who wished to move to Israel, and Jewish organizations assisted with migration to the US. The political activists who steered the community during the upheavals made the first calls. While they remained the spokespersons for their organizations, they had to understand how to navigate in the new political order.

The postrevolutionary journey began for the Jews shortly after the Shah left the country. On February 13, 1979, almost two weeks after Khomeini's return to Iran and two days after the victory of the revolution, the Jewish leadership showed support en masse for the revolution and welcomed the country's new leader.[66] AJII members were involved in the movement so deeply that they attended some historical milestones of the revolution. For example, on February 27, 1979, the keys of the former Israeli embassy on Kakh Street were given to the Palestine Liberation Organization representative, Hani al-Hassan. AJII members were there to welcome al-Hassan, and later that day, in a reception in the prime minister's office, they delivered a written statement in support of the Palestine Liberation Organization and against Israel and Zionism.[67] The Palestinian struggle against Israel occupied a fair amount of space in their rhetoric at that time, which served to draw a clear distinction between the AJII and any representation of Israel. They identified the Palestinian struggle as one of the issues the Iranian regime should support strongly and emphasized their stance on this matter.

Another way for AJII to position itself in opposition to Israel was to show that Zionism had long forgotten and abandoned any kind of Jewish ideals. AJII's official newspaper, *Tamuz*, continued to make correlations between radical socialism and Jewish religiosity. On November 22, 1979, *Tamuz* published an expanded interview with Rabbi Ovadia Yosef.[68] Yosef was the chief rabbi of the Mizrahi or Sephardic Jews. He was born in Baghdad in 1920 and served as a chief rabbi in Egypt and then in Israel. He was known for his relatively progressive rulings, and in many cases he advanced the Mizrahi cause by opposing the line he was expected to follow—namely, Zionism. In this interview, Yosef repeated his most recent ruling at that time, that "in order to prevent bloodshed [Israel] is allowed to retrieve occupied territories."[69] The significance of such a ruling stems from the Zionist and (to some extent) Jewish theological understanding that the territories occupied in 1967 are part of the "forefathers' land" that modern-days Jews inherited through birthright.[70] Menachem Begin, the right-wing leader, headed the Israeli government, and his official stance was that the territories gained in 1967 had the same legal status as those that belonged to Israel after 1948. Yosef's ruling, therefore, illustrates both his pragmatism (by leaving the ultra-Zionist camp) and his religious tolerance (by agreeing to give up parts of the holy land)—two qualities AJII was happy to emphasize.

Initially, AJII was well coordinated with the new regime. Yet any hope for Iranian Jewish-Muslim rapprochement was quickly snuffed out. Just a few months after the revolution, on May 9, 1979, one of the Jewish community's philanthropists and leaders, Elqaniyan, was executed after being accused of spying for Israel and acting against Islam and the revolution.[71] Many Iranian Jews suspected that the revolutionary court and the new government had framed Elqaniyan, and they feared a new era of persecution against Iran's Jewish population. Many Jewish supporters of the revolution felt betrayed by their Muslim compatriots. Three days later, a small delegation, led by Hakham Shofet, traveled to Qom to meet with Ayatollah Khomeini. The Iranian media widely reported the meeting, which successfully established ground rules regarding the relationship between the Muslim majority and the Jewish minority. Khomeini distinguished between Judaism and Zionism, allegedly ending the widespread speculation that all the Jews were undercover Zionist agents. In his proclamation, Khomeini acknowledged the deep roots of the Jewish community in Iran, underscored the elements of monotheism present in both Judaism and Islam, and distinguished between Zionism and Judaism: "We know that the Iranian Jews are not Zionist. We [and the Jews] together are against Zionism. . . . They [the Zionists] are not Jews! They are politicians that claim to work in the name of Judaism, but they hate Jews. . . . The Jews, as the other communities, are part of Iran, and Islam treats them all fairly."[72]

A detailed article in the nationally distributed newspaper *Ittila'at* reported that a Jewish delegation came to meet the Imam in Qom, citing the mutual proclamations of the Jewish leaders and Khomeini. Jalali was also among those leaders. "We Consider the Jewish Community to Be Non-Zionist," proclaimed the title of the article. The following day, Elqaniyan's execution and the meeting of the Jewish leaders with Khomeini were still in the headlines of the newspapers. *Ittila'at*'s editorial on May 14 discussed the harm Zionists were doing to the Iranian Jews. "The Zionists Are Shedding Crocodile Tears over the Iranian Jews," the headline of the article announced. It read, "The truth is that the Muslim community in Iran has never had a dispute with its Jewish brothers, and their collaboration during our protest and revolution against the dictatorial regime, is one example of this." In addition, the author singled out Israel as having double standards because it pretended to care for the Jews while profiting politically when they suffer.[73] Another story related to Elqaniyan's execution might illustrate the complex identity of those juggling Iranian, Jewish, and Communist affiliations. Shortly after Elqaniyan's execution, Amnon Netzer met Hakham Shofet and asked him who was caring for Elqaniyan's corpse and funeral arrangements. Shofet replied that since many members of the community feared the consequences, the only one who came to care for and say Kaddish over the body [a highly religious burial ceremony] was an AJII leader, the Communist Daneshrad.[74]

This confusion between Zionism and Judaism ignited a sort of fascination in the early postrevolutionary public conversation. The need of the broad public to understand the difference between the two was great. Mihrdad, one of the AJII founding members, recalls,

During the first 3–4 months after, on state television whenever they had a [talk show] program they tried to bring one of the members of Jami'ah-yi Rawshanfikran [AJII].

We were in half of the programs, which was way too much. The first event was in Pessah [Passover]. After the revolution they wanted to compare Pessah to the Iranian New Year, that was a few days earlier, and to know how Jews celebrate it at home. . . . While it was not taken over by the Islamists there was a very big reception of the fact that Jews were part of the movement.[75]

This recollection attests to the increased interest of Iranians in Jewish Iranian culture and demonstrates acceptance of Iranian Jews as a piece of the new Iranian puzzle.

Another instance developed rather differently. A few months later, on June 29, 1979, another talk show hosted two prominent Jewish leaders who were known to be in the social circles of AJII members: Rabbi David Shofet and Daneshrad. The show invited the two to speak about Zionism. Shofet, who was the son of Hakham Shofet and the first Iranian rabbi to be ordained in the United States, intended to talk about religious Zionism. Shortly after the show aired, *Tamuz* provided an account of the televised roundtable: "On Friday 8/4/1358 the second television roundtable debate about Zionism took place. Rav David Shofet and Mr. Muhandis ʿAziz Daneshrad provided valuable observations on differences between Judaism and Zionism."[76]

In the program Shofet explained that the name Zion stems from the name of a mountain in southeast Jerusalem that is a holy place for Jews because it was the location of the temple. He provided the biblical context and quoted from the biblical scrolls of Ezra and Nehemiah that contextualize the Babylonian exile and Zion. Furthermore, he explained that the Jewish religion requires no action by humans in regard to the creation of a Jewish center in Zion. Shofet pointed out that the religious Jewish vision of the Messiah's return includes not only Jews but all humanity.[77] Ishaq, a member of the Jewish community in Tehran who is active in the religious establishment, remembers the debate vividly and, in his interview for this project, recalled, "The interviewer asked Rav Shofet if it is true that all the Jews are Zionists, he waited a second and answered: Jerusalem, Zion, for me is like Mecca for you! Jerusalem is the place to which I make pilgrimage, a place I address my prayers to. If this is what you may call Zionist— then I am a Zionist."[78]

Yet again, one can see the fluidity of the term *Zionism*. While the conventional wisdom defines the term as political Zionism as professed by Israel, we see here (as we saw in other chapters, especially in Chapters 2 and 3), that the term yields several interpretations. The one used here invokes religious sentiments regarding Jerusalem and the word *Zionism*, completely detached from the political context.

Later in the discussion, the host asked Daneshrad about political Zionism. Daneshrad explained that Zionism emerged in Europe alongside European classic nationalism and as a solution to tragedies such as the pogroms in tsarist Russia. Daneshrad explained, "The Zionist movement suggested that the liberation for Jews is impossible with their compatriots, but that they all have to go and gather in one land (then Palestine was chosen), and establish a state."[79] This message resonates clearly with AJII's priorities: to have a role in shaping postrevolutionary Iran, to act for equality and unity, and to construct a democratic society with the members' Iranian compatriots.[80]

The Assembly of Experts and the Draft of the First Constitution

AJII's efforts to be part of the rebuilding process came to partial fruition when Daneshrad was appointed to the Assembly of Experts and the constitution-drafting committee, representing the Jewish religious minority. In July 1979 general elections for the committee took place, and the committee subsequently began its work. Four out of seventy-three representatives were elected on behalf of minorities to fill the quota of one representative for every recognized religious minority (with the exception that one representative served both Assyrians and Chaldeans). On the committee with Daneshrad, Sargon Bayt-i Ushanakugtappeh represented the Assyrian and Chaldean communities, Hara'i Khalatian represented the Armenians, and Rustam Shahzadi represented the Zoroastrian community.[81] Daneshrad was a longtime political activist and the head of the Jewish community at that time. He was also well connected with some of the revolution's leaders and had been elected as the Jewish representative to the Majlis. During the meetings of this assembly, Daneshrad tried to change the precedents for minorities' representation in the parliament. The Constitutional Revolution established that every recognized religious minority would receive seats in the parliament according to population size, with one representative for every one hundred thousand people. Jews and Zoroastrians received one representative each, the Armenians had two, and, as mentioned, a single seat represented both

Assyrians and Chaldeans.[82] This measure was intended to assure minorities that the government would never disenfranchise any recognized minority group.

Minorities' representation in the new constitution remained a conversation among Jews in Iran during the work of the committee. *Tamuz*, thus, became the venue for debates among the Jewish leadership regarding the direction of and reactions to the new constitution. The different opinions were brought forth in columns and op-eds by Daneshrad and others who were involved in it. Shortly after the constitutional assembly first convened, on July 4, 1979, Daneshrad published his lengthy proposals for amending the constitution. In particular, he identified articles he thought should do more to emphasize equality for the religious and ethnic minorities. The article "Nazariyat-i Jami'iah Rawshanfikran Yahudi Iran Dar Barayi Qanun-i Asasi" (AJII's observation of the constitution) details the historic situation of minorities in Iran, and religious minorities in particular, before predicting the effects of the coming constitution. Daneshrad tried in this article to articulate the argument for the Jews, and he began with the historical background and the dominant Iranian identity of the Jews and their complete integration: "Iranian Jews trace back to the eighth century B.C. when groups of them were brought by the Assyrian government. . . . Bigger groups were brought by the Babylonian government and they settled in different Iranian cities. These groups effected social transformations that took place during the centuries and have been transformed by the different communities in Iran."[83] He later presented the articles of the constitution that were in dispute and his proposal for revisions. In many instances the corrections merely stressed the equality of all citizens regardless of their faith, race, social, or economic status before the law. However, in his article, Daneshrad also describes his egalitarian vision for the government:

In article 50 of the constitution it is written that Zoroastrians and Jews of the country will have one representative elected, and Christians will elect two representatives. This proposition is drawn from years of tyranny and strangulation and the being of the country dependent upon identification of the religious minorities and the national majority. . . . AJII believes that every Iranian, of any religion or ethnicity or race, must have the right to vote for every competent Iranian of any ethnicity and race. This right must be implemented by mutual understanding between all ethnic groups and followers of all the religions in the country.[84]

The Jewish revolutionaries envisioned a democratic republic for the new Iranian nation, one that needed no protected quotas of representation. Hoping to have a democratic society that eliminated religious or ethnic distinctions, Daneshrad suggested ridding the minorities of special representation and allowing full and equal participation by all citizens in the general parties. Mihrdad, who advised Daneshrad in his capacity as a legal scholar, recalls,

We went to Bazargan and told him we do not want the secured member in parliament. He told us that we [the Jewish community] are too small, and that we will never be represented. So we said that we want to have equal rights; if we are good enough we will be elected and have more than one representative in the parliament, but we do not want to be disenfranchised otherwise, having one member representing us.[85]

This conversation between the Jewish leaders and the sitting prime minister indicates that the latter had more doubts regarding the direction of the revolution, or the possible shortcomings of major amendments to the proposed constitution. Although the Jewish leadership was optimistic about Jews' chances to remain represented in the framework of existing parties, without quotas, Bazargan was more skeptical, as well as more aware of the dominant factions in the postrevolutionary provisional government.

Because of these debates, in the assembly's debates Daneshrad did not broach this topic again. He continued to participate in debates regarding Article 64, which has been revised twice for matters not directly related to minorities. However, Daneshrad did not limit himself to dealing with minorities' issues exclusively, and his political and ideological background served him well in discussions on social and economic issues. He argued and fought to establish the state's social responsibilities toward workers and the poor, as well as the protection of national and cultural assets.[86] During the debates on Article 14, which makes the recognition of religious minorities official, the deputy from Baluchistan, Molavi Abdol-Aziz argued against Iran's decision to recognize the official religions of Israel and America (countries that were nominally enemies of Iran) while not recognizing his Sunni Islam. Daneshrad asserted that "the Israeli government is a government of no religion and its foundation is not based on religion but on the politics of usurpation which is hated by all believing Jews."[87]

Brothers in Arms: Challenges During the Iran-Iraq War

With the outbreak of the war with Iraq in August 1980, the postrevolution took another turn. The war became a galvanizing experience and put to the test the loyalty or the patriotism of the minority groups. Radical yet popular factions of the regime began treating Jews suspiciously and suggested that Iranian Jews were serving as agents for Israel. To prove their loyalty, the Jewish establishment engaged in two activities almost obsessively: supporting the Iranian war effort against Iraq and criticizing Israel while espousing a strong pro-Palestinian stance.

Iranian Jews expressed pro-Palestinian sympathies by attacking Zionism as a whole, providing critical analysis of Israeli society (mostly through *Tamuz*), and aligning with the Islamic Republic's official policy. For example, the Jewish community organized demonstrations against Israeli air raids in Lebanon in the early 1980s and more vehemently against the Israeli invasion of Lebanon in 1982. The critical analysis came in the form of interviews, such as the one mentioned earlier with Rabbi Yosef, or in writing about Israel's most recent population crisis, as the number of Jews leaving Israel was greater than the number of Jews immigrating to the country. The *Tamuz* article on the issue was titled "Reverse Migration from Israel: The Zionists Are in Complete Deadlock."[88] The article analyzes the identity crisis that ended the trend of Jewish migration to Israel. As for the alignment with the Islamic Republic's official policy regarding the Palestinian struggle, on Ruz-i Quds (Jerusalem Day) in 1981 AJII published an announcement condemning Israel and expressing support for the Palestinian people and the Iranian leadership in this campaign. The language used in this article is astonishing: "Zionists employ Nazi-style attacks on defenseless people," reads one sentence. The article also indicates the disconnection between world Jewry and Israel and Zionism. The announcement ends with "Hail to the Heroic Palestinian People" and "Victorious Common Struggle of Muslims, Christians, and Jews Against Imperialism and Zionism."[89]

The second part of this AJII strategy was the unequivocal support within Iran of the war effort against Iraq. During the Iran-Iraq War, AJII committed once again to connecting the Jewish community, especially the younger generation, to the ideals of the revolution. They published articles encouraging the community's youths to engage in political activity or to join the combating forces. Relying on the blood covenant established during the revolution, several authors called on young Jews to help in the new struggle: "Jewish Iranian youth, before and after 22 Bahman 1357 [February 11, 1979], joined their [Muslim] compatriots in the struggle against the shah's regime, and in this way sacrificed [members] for the revolution. After the victory of the Islamic revolution and the stabilizing of the Islamic Republic of Iran, the Jewish youth has to go again to the field and participate with its Muslim brothers and sisters in the holy war against Iraq."[90] Official numbers of Jews who joined the army are difficult to obtain, but judging by the articles in *Tamuz* and other unofficial sources, a growing number of Jews volunteered to join the army. On the home front, Sapir Hospital once again was recognized for the efficient first response it provided to wounded soldiers and civilians during the war.[91] In 2011 the Ministry of Culture and Islamic Guidance published a memorial book for the sacrifices of religious minorities during the Iran-Iraq War. The book, *In the Memory of the Sacrifices of Our Christian, Zoroastrian and Jewish Fellow Compatriots*, recounts the stories of the war heroes among the religious minorities. This publication praises the contributions of Sapir Hospital; Siamak Moreh-Sedeq, a frontline physician; Mansur Sharim; and Jihanbakhsh Qihrmani, a pharmacist who served in the army and was severely wounded in the war.[92]

Naturally, Jewish and other minority soldiers died in the war as well, and the revolutionary government erected a mural in their memory. The enormous mural shows the faces of five of the martyrs and presents a quote of Khomeini: "Religious minorities have special respect in Islam and essentially they are in one line with the Muslims in serving the country." Irony, however, may have played a role in the location of the mural. It sits at the visible intersection of Vali-asr Avenue and Mirdamad Street in North Tehran, across the road from a famous business and complex of residential buildings, the Eskan project. The Shah built the entire complex through the Israeli contractor company Solel Boneh. The site is thus a reminder of the flourishing relations between Israel and prerevolutionary Iran.[93]

Despite becoming bitter enemies, Iran and Israel continued to pursue—to a large extent—the same geopolitical policies that they had pursued before the revolution. The countries negotiated military connections and large-scale arms deals with active involvement of the United States. Israel continued this relationship partly because the country believed that Khomeini's revolution would not last long. Iranian Jews who migrated to Israel and the US successfully convinced policy makers in Tel Aviv and Jerusalem that this revolution contradicted the Iranian national identity and therefore would not take root in Iran's culture.[94]

The nation-building project of postrevolutionary Iran challenged the minority groups. In the immediate postrevolutionary period, some believed that the revolution had ceased to be "Iranian" and become "Islamic" instead. The spaces or positions minorities aspired to claim had to be found in the midst of postrevolutionary chaos, due to domestic tensions between competing factions and external concerns, such as the war taking place. The actions of AJII in regard to the war coincided with the policies it professed before the revolution—that is, to assimilate to any form of society that was shaped after the success of the revolution, be it an Iranian republican society or an Islamic state.

Building the postrevolutionary society entailed certain challenges no one had foreseen; the Islamic movements that got the upper hand, did so despite earlier convictions that postrevolutionary Iran would become an inclusive society based on social justice and indifference to religious or ethnic identities or prerevolutionary social status. The new nation-building project privileged religion over political ideology and pushed religious minorities to the social periphery again, thus reversing the minorities' achievements in the past three decades.[95]

However, the reality was that the place minorities had already obtained in public life and the public sphere was not easily taken by any government. Moreover, the postrevolutionary government encouraged this participation by reserving seats in the committee that was entrusted with creating the founding document of the new Iran, the constitution. As this chapter has shown, when discussing the character of the society, government-social affairs, and the economy, the religious identities played a small role, if any.

When the war with Iraq erupted it was perceived as a galvanizing moment for the postrevolutionary government as well as for Iranian society. The Jewish leadership instantaneously showed solidarity and called for the Jewish youths to join the army and support the war effort. This was another manifestation of strong national identity, which does not conflict with religious affiliations.

The subject that remained most problematic for Jews was the association with Zionism in the broader Iranian consciousness. Although alternative interpretations for Zionism, as a concept, were put forth by Iranian Jews, it was still a shadow hanging over their loyalty to Iran and put it in question. Even in their hour of crisis, most of the Iranian Jews did not leave for Israel, and the overwhelming majority of those who left, decided on the United States rather than Israel. Another fact that is always worth considering is that even today, Iran still has the biggest Jewish community in the Middle East outside Israel.

Conclusion

IT IS RARE IN HISTORY that the interests of global superpowers, local political elites, and minority groups converge to serve all three communities equally. When one attempts to describe the moment of the Allied armies' invasion in August 1941, however, this convergence of interests is the explanation that fits best. The Allies needed to remove Reza Shah in order to confront whatever Nazi influence existed in Iran and to access transportation routes and much-needed oil between central Asia and the Persian Gulf freely. The then crown prince, Mohammad Reza Pahlavi, wanted to preserve the dynasty his father established and to resist public demands among the Iranian political elite to restore the Qajar monarchy or even to turn Iran into a republic. The minorities, although not fully aware of the possibilities of the hour, which would include unprecedented political and personal freedoms, happily overturned some of the policies instituted by Reza Shah, such as the Iranianization of the minorities' schools.

The Iran that the Allied armies left in 1945–1946 was utterly different from the one they had occupied only a few years earlier. By the mid-1940s Mohammad Reza Shah had already lifted many of the bans on political organizations and the freedom of press, and a massive urbanization process swept the country. This book has examined the social transformations Jewish individuals and institutions in Iran experienced during this period. The political and social changes influenced Jews just as they did their non-Jewish compatriots. They took advantage of the freedoms offered, but more than that, they took advantage of their improving legal status and the changes in the country's ethos that arose from Mohammad Reza Shah's nation building.

This new ethos detached religious and ethnic affiliations from the politics of national belonging and removed many of the official and social obstacles that had prevented Jews from fully integrating until that point. As Jews began their integration into the general society, they also started building new allegiances. Now they were not only connected vertically to the Shah and the government but also connected horizontally with their fellow Iranians.

Besides political activism and urbanization, the main vehicle for grander amendments was the educational system. Jewish schools provided first and foremost for Jewish communities, but by the 1960s Jews' educational and professional success encouraged non-Jews to take the same route and increasingly enroll in the Jewish schools. Once again, these developments opened up the Jewish institutions to broader collaborations and deepened the connection between Jewish and non-Jewish Iranians. As this connection progressed, religious affiliations weakened. The Shah disconnected Islam from the nation, forcing secularization and Westernization. He emphasized the pre-Islamic elements in Iranian culture and connections between the country and the West. Jews adapted this process to challenge the older (and more religious) guards of the Jewish establishment, and their communities began to politicize.

The radical politicization became evident as Jews participated in the activities of the oppositional student movements, the underground Tudeh organizations, and internal Jewish organizations, such as afterschool activities in a socialist-oriented camp and the Association of Jewish Iranian Intellectuals (AJII). AJII was instrumental in creating the hybrid identity that played out so clearly in the events leading to the revolution in 1979.

The Iranian Revolution of 1979 encompassed all strata of Iranian society, regardless of education, religion, vocation, or economic class, excluding only the political elite. The Jewish community was mostly divided in its support of the revolution. On the one hand, they possessed a great deal of freedom under Pahlavi. On the other hand, many of them participated in professional unions and truly sympathized with their fellow revolutionaries. The AJII led the way among Jewish revolutionary sympathizers. This revolution became a watershed moment in the Jewish history of Iran. For the first time, Jews acted in an organized way to support a national cause that exceeded the narrow goals of the community. Not all of those who aided the revolution did so on ideological grounds. Many accounts indicate that participants acted in the name of universal humanitarian values and personal relationships.

This episode in Iranian history suggests the unintended consequences of Mohammad Reza Pahlavi's nation-building project. This project aimed to create a unified nation that would make Iranian national identity stronger than any communal belonging, and indeed, as can be seen from much of the evidence, many of the participants did rank their Iranian identity and national identity higher than any other component of identity. When the time arrived, they prioritized standing shoulder to shoulder with their compatriots over advancing myopic community needs or goals. Jewish groups' contributions to the revolution remained somewhat obscured, however, partly because key Jewish leaders did not want to attract too much attention to the seemingly vulnerable community in Iran. Nevertheless, they played a part in the Islamic revolution and thus Iranian history.

In the postrevolutionary period Jews adjusted once again to a new nation-building project, this time better equipped with a higher social status that eased the effect of the new government's Islamicization policies. The same ideals and allegiances that led many Jews to participate in the revolution drove them to actively shape the new Iran after the 1979 revolution. Jews faced many challenges after the turmoil but held on to their achievements of the previous decades. The Jewish leadership felt a responsibility to support the new regime and to influence policy changes from within the government. The writing of the new constitution, and Jewish support of the Iran-Iraq War in the 1980s, highlighted the stakes of this responsibility.

Postscript
Toward a New Historiography

SPEND TEN MINUTES WITH AN IRANIAN Jew and he or she will not hesitate to tell you that Jewish existence in Iran goes back 2,700 years before the Islamic Republic appeared. Jews want to preserve this status in their homeland. "Jews here have great Iranian roots—they love Iran. Personally, I would stay in Iran no matter what. I speak in English, I pray in Hebrew, but my thinking is Persian," says Siamak Moreh-Sedeq, the Jewish deputy in the Majlis and a prominent leader of the roughly twenty-five thousand Jews still living in Iran.[1] This quote demonstrates the deeply rooted connection Iranian Jews feel to their country after a world war and expansive social developments, and nearly four decades after the revolution.

"The Iranian Jews are the most researched non-Muslim religious minorities in Iran," asserts Eliz Sanasarian.[2] While his claim may be empirically correct, this research finds that the majority of scholarship within this historical genre limits itself to a single metanarrative that describes the Jewish minority as an isolated community with very limited interactions. However, as this book proves, the studies of the Iranian community have not considered the Jews' environment and broader society or major social changes and trends that transformed the Jewish community and Iranian society as a whole. The historiographical solution is to conduct research that does not confine itself to isolated analysis of the Jewish community in Iran but rather explores the different groups that together compose Iranian society. This study, rather than examining only Jewish life and intercommunal interactions, provides a critical perspective on the general Iranian society. To carry out this kind of research, scholars must continue to locate new sources. The sources that reveal much of the social structure reside in the relief organizations' archives. The involvement of so many organizations in the reshaping of the society introduced many new forces from within the Jewish community and uncovered the ways Jewish institutions operated in collaboration with non-Jewish institutions.

How much attention has been given to Iranian Jewish identities in Iran and in the Iranian diaspora in Israel and the United States, for example? Not much, I would argue. Israel successfully assumed the role of (or rather the reputation for being) the protector of the Jews worldwide. With the descent of Iran and Israel into bitter rhetoric and a regional rivalry, the voices, identities, and culture of Iranian Jews lost their place, which is unfortunate because they could illuminate and enrich the conversations we have on a regular basis in Israel and the West regarding Iran. The ordinary layman in the United States or Israel (or Europe, for that matter) holds the notion that Iran is the enemy of the Jews, and not just Israel. Relatively few know that Iran is home to the second-largest Jewish population in the Middle East outside Israel. Very few know that Jews are relatively free to worship, celebrate their holidays, and even travel abroad (even to Israel). The conclusion we must draw is that the Iranian Jews did not just decide to stay in Iran in 1979 after the revolution; rather, they make this decision every day.

They decided to stay, but they knew and still know that they have to fight for their place, and occasionally they make progress; other times, setbacks prevail. In 1999 the Jewish community launched a new publication aimed at continuing the mission of *Tamuz* from the previous decade. Featured some of the same writers as *Tamuz*, the new publication, *Ofeq Bina*, gave publicity to the debates on Iranian Jewish identity, burning social issues, Iranian politics, and more.[3] We can see in *Ofeq Bina* once again the trajectory toward the increasing involvement of the Jews, which this book has highlighted frequently. Under the presidency of reformist Sayyid Mohammad Khatami, Jews experienced greater integration, after years of hardships for them and the country during the Iran-Iraq War and the death of Ruhullah Khomeini. President Khatami championed the policy of "discourse of civilizations" (*Goftigu-yi tamadun-ha*), and he implemented it on the domestic level, as he did on the international level. Two interesting events are worth mentioning in this context. First, on the Jewish holiday of Tu Bi'Shvat in 2004, President Khatami conducted an official visit to the Tehran synagogue of Yousef-Abad. This visit was perceived by the Iranian Jews as more than a showing of goodwill on behalf of the president.[4] For them it was a sign that they belong. The second event took place on April 8, 2005, during the funeral of Pope John Paul II. During the funeral the then president of Israel, Iranian-born Moshe Katsav, and President Khatami shook hands and briefly exchanged memories from their shared childhood in Yazd, Iran. The two leaders later promptly denied that any handshake took place, but world media captured that moment with the two in the same narrow frame.[5] It must also be mentioned that setbacks took place under Khatami's presidency as well. For example, the arrest of thirteen Jews from Shiraz on different counts of espionage for Israel hit Iran's Jewish population by surprise, and only after the last of them was released from prison did the cloud of this affair vanish from over their heads, as well as their future.[6]

Shortly afterward, Khatami ended his second term and, as sanctioned by the Iranian constitution, he could not run for a third consecutive term. In the 2005 elections the former mayor of Tehran, Mahmoud Ahmadinejad, defeated in a landslide the former president, Ayatollah Akbar Hashemi Rafsanjani. President Ahmadinejad cultivated his reputation as a populist in Iran and a Holocaust denier abroad. Under his presidency Iran took a different direction in its interactions with the West. Ahmadinejad insisted on expanding the Iranian nuclear program (despite arguing that the program is peaceful), which prompted international sanctions. He also convened a "scholarly" conference in Tehran to question the authenticity of the Holocaust and invited artists to participate in a Holocaust cartoon competition. It is this obsession with the Holocaust that has earned him his reputation as a Holocaust denier, and it has also fortified the arguments of critiques of Iran that Iran is essentially an unredeemable anti-Semitic country. Maurice Motamed, the Jewish deputy in the Majlis at the time, spoke in the parliament and slammed the president's Holocaust denial.[7] During Ahmadinejad's tenure as president, tensions between Israel and Iran ran high. His utterances regarding the Holocaust presented him not just as anti-Zionist—or anti-Israel, the official stance of the government since 1979—but also as anti-Semite. For Israel they unmasked Iran's anti-Semitic inclinations, therefore revealing Iran as an imminent danger for Israel, for Jews worldwide, and especially for Iranian Jews. This provided a fertile ground for conspiracies and rumors that attempted to portray the situation of the Jews in Iran as extremely fragile. On May 19, 2006, the

Canadian *National Post* published an article by Amir Taheri arguing that Jews would now be required to wear a yellow badge to identify them. The story was proved wrong pretty quickly; however, for those who were looking to attach blazing anti-Semitism to Iran, this story never died.[8]

Ahmadinejad famously quoted Ayatollah Khomeini saying that "this regime that is occupying Qods [Jerusalem] should disappear from the pages of history." In the press and public memory, the translation was "Israel should be wiped off the map"—a mistranslation that was disseminated partly by hype-seeking media and partly by Israel, which was very determined to sway the global public opinion in its favor. And, of course, the mistranslation perfectly fitted the image of Iran as an intolerant place for Jews. Although it looked like an armed conflict was inevitable, and the Israeli prime minister, Benjamin Netanyahu, did not make a secret of his wishes to see a coordinated attack on Iran, we saw something rather surprising.[9] In 2012, as Netanyahu made the case in the UN against Iran and tried to garner world support for an attack and sanctions on Iran, the Israeli public overwhelmingly opposed the attack. More interestingly, Iranian-born Israelis or Israelis of Iranian descent were more prone to oppose the attack in Iran and seek peaceful resolution. This goes against their groups' respective positions on national politics.[10]

In 2013 President Ahmadinejad finished his second term, and the moderate conservative (backed by the reformist movement) Hassan Rouhani was elected in a landslide, against the odds. Rouhani's campaign focused mainly on reconciliation with the West, and it proposed to do so by reaching a nuclear agreement that would remove sanctions and improve the economic situation in Iran. Shortly after being elected, Rouhani addressed the Jewish world in appeasing messages. On Rosh Ha-Shana in 2013 he tweeted a new-year blessing to the Jews worldwide and especially the Iranian Jews: "As the sun is about to set here in #Tehran I wish all Jews, especially Iranian Jews, a blessed Rosh Hashanah."[11] His foreign minister, Mohammad Javad Zarif, did the same, tweeting, "Happy Rosh Hashanah," and, following a response from Christine Pelosi, the daughter of the Democratic American lawmaker, regarding the Holocaust denial, he added that "Iran never denied it. The man who was perceived to be denying it is now gone."[12] For the UN General Assembly that year, President Rouhani took the Jewish deputy in the Majlis, Moreh-Sedeq, with him. Israel framed it as "smiles attack."[13] In a 2015 interview with NBC, Zarif responded to Netanyahu's allegations about Iran's anti-Semitism:

It is unfortunate that Mr. Netanyahu now totally distorts realities of today. . . . He even distorts his own scripture. If you read the book of Esther, you will see that it was the Iranian king who saved the Jews. . . . It is truly, truly regrettable that bigotry gets to the point of making allegations against an entire nation which has saved Jews three times in its history: once during that time of a prime minister who was trying to kill the Jews, and the king saved the Jews; again during the time of Cyrus the Great, where he saved the Jews from Babylon, and during the Second World War, where Iran saved the Jews.[14]

Following the relative opening of Iran after the nuclear agreement was reached, several American news outlets, such as NPR and the Jewish *Forward*, sent reporters to Iran to talk with the Iranian Jews; there, they found a safe and proud Jewish community and discovered that in some ways the Jews of Iran feel safer than their coreligionists in Europe:

Saturday is a workday in Iran's capital, and women in chadors and men in business suits hurried by us without so much as a glance. Moreover, the night before, when several hundred worshippers gathered for Friday night services at the Yousef Abad Synagogue in North Tehran, I noticed, too, that the sanctuary's large entrance remained open to the street as people spilled out for breaks to shmooze in crowds on the sidewalk outside. No security of any kind was in sight. "Compared to Europe," boasted Dr. Siamak Moreh Sedgh, the Jewish community's elected representative in Iran's parliament, "synagogues here are one of the safest places."[15]

Rouhani's government gave Iranian Jews a prominent place in the national conversation, yet again reassuring them of their belonging in the Iranian nation, under his administration perhaps more than those of other presidents. His cabinet passed a law accommodating the Sabbath as a holy day for Jewish students, excusing them from attending school on that day.[16] And perhaps the greatest gesture made by the Iranian government to show that the Jews are part and parcel of the Iranian national story became evident in December 2014, when the government unveiled a memorial for the Jewish martyrs of the Iran-Iraq War. With many prominent politicians and clergy in attendance, the Jewish community as a whole was finally recognized as being part of the postrevolutionary Iranian society—every part of it.[17]

In June 2014 the Israeli Knesset made the Day to Mark the Departure and Expulsion of Jews from the Arab Countries and Iran into a law.[18] Every year on November 30 (a day after the UN General Assembly's approval of the partition plan), Israelis will commemorate the destruction and expulsion of the Jewish communities in the Arab world and Iran. During the Knesset session, one of this bill's sponsors, Member of Knesset Nissim Ze'ev (Shas; Orthodox-Sephardi) said, "This law commemorates the exodus and the expulsion from the Arab countries and Iran, cherishes the history of those Jews, and the suffering our forefathers and their forefathers endured when they left the Arab countries until they came into Eretz Yisrael."[19] Indeed, many communities were forced out of their homelands following 1948 under various circumstances; other communities left en masse for other reasons. Many of them immigrated to Israel, others to Europe and the Americas. But the Jewish communities of Iran at no point were subject to expulsion. This attempt to lump together all those histories aims to erase the differences between the communities and to blur the simple fact that many Jews of certain communities chose to remain in their homeland, despite its being Muslim, and even an enemy at times. Iranian Jews who left Iran, whether to the United States, Europe, or Israel, overwhelmingly modified their Iranian identity but maintained it as their principal one. And so, since the mid-twentieth century, the Iranian Jewish diaspora has formed communities in Los Angeles, New York, London, Tel Aviv, and other major cities. And still, as mentioned, the largest Jewish community in the Middle East outside Israel is in Iran. They choose to be there, and they choose to stay there, because Iran is their Homeland and Zion is their direction of prayers.

Notes

Preface

1. Amnon Netzer added that compared to Jews from other Middle Eastern countries, Iranian Jews were significantly less literate and poorly trained. Amnon Netzer, "Ha'aretz ve'yehudiy'ha," in *Iran*, ed. Haim Saadoun (Jerusalem: Yad Ben-Zvi, 2005), 9–26.

Introduction

1. Today, the estimated number of Jews in Iran greatly fluctuates. The numbers are between ten thousand and thirty-five thousand, although most sources agree on twenty-five thousand, based on membership in synagogues and clubs. Charles London, *Far from Zion: In Search of a Global Jewish Community* (New York: William Morrow, 2009), 192–226; Scott Peterson, "In Ahmadinejad's Iran, Jews Still Find a Space," *Christian Science Monitor*, April 27, 2007, http://www.csmonitor.com/2007/0427/p01s03-wome.html.

2. For example, see the following discussions on the Azeris, Kurds, Zoroastrians, Armenians, Assyrians, and more: Adam H. Becker, *Revival and Awakening: American Evangelical Missionaries in Iran and the Origins of Assyrian Nationalism* (Chicago: University of Chicago Press, 2015); Rasmus Christian Elling, *Minorities in Iran: Nationalism and Ethnicity After Khomeini* (New York: Palgrave Macmillan, 2013); Denise Natali, *The Kurds and the State: Evolving National Identity in Iraq, Turkey, and Iran*, Modern Intellectual and Political History of the Middle East (Syracuse, NY: Syracuse University Press, 2005); Monica Ringer, *Pious Citizens: Reforming Zoroastrianism in India and Iran* (Syracuse, NY: Syracuse University Press, 2014); and Eliz Sanasarian, *Religious Minorities in Iran* (Cambridge: Cambridge University Press, 2000).

3. These two books show the dominant trends in writing national history in Iran in the formative years: Farzin Vejdani, *Making History in Iran: Education, Nationalism, and Print Culture* (Stanford, CA: Stanford University Press, 2015); Reza Zia-Ebrahimi, *The Emergence of Iranian Nationalism: Race and the Politics of Dislocation* (New York: Columbia University Press, 2016).

4. For more on the settlement of Jews in Iran in the late antiquity, see Parvaneh Pour-shriati, "New Vistas on the History of Iranian Jewry in Late Antiquity, Part I: Patterns of Jewish Settlement in Iran," in *The Jews of Iran: The History, Religion, and Culture of a Community in the Islamic World*, ed. Houman M. Sarshar (London: I. B. Tauris, 2014), 1–32.

5. Amnon Netzer, "Ha-Kehila Ha-Yehudit Be-Iran," in *Yehudei Iran: Avaram, Morash-tam ve-Zikatam Le-Eretz Ha-Kodesh*, ed. Amnon Netzer (Jerusalem: Beit Koresh, 1988), 3–4.

6. During the Mongol Ilkhanid period (1258–1335), in which Iran suffered devastating destruction, unparalleled in that time, that is identified by historians as the greatest disaster Iran had encountered, Jews and Christians had a mixed experience. Before they had converted to Islam, the Mongols practiced a more tolerant policy and did not charge minorities the Jezyeh tax. We have less information on the second part of the Mongol rule in Iran, but it is reasonable to believe that following the ascendance of Abu Sa'id, the approach to minorities changed as well. Homa Katouzian, *The Persians: Ancient, Medieval and Modern Iran* (New Haven, CT: Yale University Press, 2010), 100–104. Netzer adds that although Jews suffered, just like other non-Jewish Iranians, from the horrors of the Mongol occupation, and many of them died, in parts of the Mongol period Jews enjoyed an economic and cultural blossoming, as well as relative religious tolerance. Netzer, "Ha-Kehila Ha-Yehudit Be-Iran," 6.

7. Vera B. Moreen, "The Safavid Era," in *Esther's Children: A Portrait of Iranian Jews*, ed. Houman Sarshar (Beverly Hills, CA: Center for Iranian Jewish Oral History; Philadelphia: Jewish Publication Society, 2002), 63.

8. Habib Levy, *Comprehensive History of the Jews of Iran: The Outset of the Diaspora* (Costa Mesa, CA: Mazda Publishers in association with the Cultural Foundation of Habib Levy, 1999), 260.

9. Moreen, "Safavid Era," 64.

10. Moreen, 73.

11. There is an abundance of scholarship on the story of the crypto-Jews of Mashhad. The forced conversions had shaped the community for over a century, and in many ways they still serve as an identifier for the Mashhadi community in Israel and the United States. For example, see Hilda Nissimi, "Memory, Community, and the Mashhadi Jews During the Underground Period," *Jewish Social Studies* 9, no. 3 (2003): 76–106; Hilda Nissimi, "Individual Redemption and Family Commitment: The Influence of Mass Immigration to Israel on the Crypto-Jewish Women of Mashhad," *Nashim: A Journal of Jewish Women's Studies & Gender Issues*, no. 18 (2009): 39; and Haideh Sahim, "Two War, Two Cities, Two Religions: The Jews of Mashhad and the Herat Wars," in *The Jews of Iran: The History, Religion, and Culture of a Community in the Islamic World*, ed. Houman M. Sarshar (London: I. B. Tauris, 2014), 75–108.

12. See the following sources for more about the professional and social opportunities introduced by the missionaries: Michael P. Zirinsky, "Imperial Power and Dictatorship: Britain and the Rise of Reza Shah, 1921–1926," *International Journal of Middle East Studies* 24, no. 4 (November 1992): 639–63; Michael P. Zirinsky, "Harbingers of Change: Presbyterian Women in Iran, 1883–1949," *American Presbyterians* 70, no. 3 (1992): 173–86;

Michael P. Zirinsky, "A Panacea for the Ills of the Country: American Presbyterian Education in Inter-war Iran," *Iranian Studies* 26, no. 1/2 (1993): 119–37; Michael P. Zirinsky, "Inculcate Tehran: Opening a Dialogue of Civilizations in the Shadow of God and the Alborz," *Iranian Studies* 44, no. 5 (September 2011): 657–69; Thomas M. Ricks, "Alborz College of Tehran, Dr. Samuel Martin Jordan and the American Faculty: Twentieth-Century Presbyterian Mission Education and Modernism in Iran (Persia)," *Iranian Studies* 44, no. 5 (September 2011): 627–46; and Becker, *Revival and Awakening.*

13. Mehrdad Amanat explains the enchantment of Baha'ism as an opportunity to convert to a sort of indigenous religion without being labeled as a "new convert" (*jadid ul-Islam*), as well as an opportunity to preserve family history as part of the individual identity. Mehrdad Amanat, *Jewish Identities in Iran: Resistance and Conversion to Islam and the Baha'i Faith*, Library of Modern Religion 9 (London: I. B. Tauris, 2011), 3–6.

14. Janet Afary, "From Outcastes to Citizens: Jews in Qajar Iran," in Sarshar, *Esther's Children*, 154.

15. Rubin identifies epistemological differences between the Ottoman perceptions of the codification process and the mostly Western understanding of it. The gaps are applicable to some of the discussion on the Iranian movement. Avi Rubin, "Modernity as a Code: The Ottoman Empire and the Global Movement of Codification," *Journal of the Economic and Social History of the Orient* 59, no. 5 (November 7, 2016): 828–56; Avi Rubin, *Falling Stars: Ottoman Rule of Law and the Modern Political Trial* (Syracuse, NY: Syracuse University Press, 2018); See Fariba Zarinebaf's illuminating research on the influence of the Ottoman movement on the Iranian constitutional movement. Fariba Zarinebaf, "From Istanbul to Tabriz: Modernity and Constitutionalism in the Ottoman Empire and Iran," *Comparative Studies of South Asia, Africa and the Middle East* 28, no. 1 (July 5, 2008): 154–69.

16. The Zoroastrians were indeed represented by their own representative, whereas Jews and Armenians were asked to allow Sayyid 'Abdullah Bihbahani and Sayyid Muhammad Tabataba'i to represent them. In the second Majlis, all the recognized minority communities were allowed to send their own representatives. Janet Afary, *The Iranian Constitutional Revolution, 1906–1911: Grassroots Democracy, Social Democracy and the Origins of Feminism* (New York: Columbia University Press, 1996), 70; Afary, "From Outcastes to Citizens," 164–73.

17. For a fuller discussion of the connection between the Pahlavi nation-building project and religious reforms that gave room for religious minorities' integration, see Janet Afary, "Foundations for Religious Reform in the First Pahlavi Era," *Iran Nameh* 30, no. 3 (Fall 2015): 46–87.

18. Netzer, "Ha-Kehila Ha-Yehudit Be-Iran," 12.

19. Saba Soomekh, *From the Shahs to Los Angeles: Three Generations of Iranian Jewish Women Between Religion and Culture* (Albany: State University of New York Press, 2012), 42–43.

20. Salo Baron, "Ghetto and Emancipation: Shall We Revise the Traditional View?," *Menorah Journal* 14, no. 6 (1928): 515–26.

21. Baron, 524–25.

22. There is a continuous debate about this topic. Whereas Norman A. Stillman and Aron Rodrigue present the critical approach that finds a history of intolerance, to a certain degree, Mark R. Cohen compares social and religious influences on the emergence of the myth (of Jewish Islamic harmony) or the countermyth. Mark R. Cohen, "Islam and the Jews: Myth, Counter-myth, History," *Jerusalem Quarterly* 38 (1986): 125–37; Norman A. Stillman, *The Jews of Arab Lands in Modern Times* (Philadelphia: Jewish Publication Society, 2003); Aron Rodrigue, *Jews and Muslims: Images of Sephardi and Eastern Jewries in Modern Times* (Seattle: University of Washington Press, 2003); See also a roundtable discussion in the *International Journal of Middle East Studies* with relevant interventions: Orit Bashkin, "The Middle Eastern Shift and Provincializing Zionism," *International Journal of Middle East Studies* 46, no. 3 (August 2014): 577–80; Sarah Abrevaya Stein, "The Field of In Between," *International Journal of Middle East Studies* 46, no. 3 (August 2014): 581–84; Michelle U. Campos, "Between Others and Brothers," *International Journal of Middle East Studies* 46, no. 3 (August 2014): 585–88; Jonathan Marc Gribetz, "'To the Arab Hebrew': On Possibilities and Impossibilities," *International Journal of Middle East Studies* 46, no. 3 (August 2014): 589–92; Rami Ginat, "Jewish Identities in the Arab Middle East: The Case of Egypt in Retrospect," *International Journal of Middle East Studies* 46, no. 3 (August 2014): 593–96; Aomar Boum, "'The Virtual Genizah': Emerging North African Jewish and Muslim Identities Online," *International Journal of Middle East Studies* 46, no. 3 (August 2014): 597–601; and Lior Sternfeld, "Jewish-Iranian Identities in the Pahlavi Era," *International Journal of Middle East Studies* 46, no. 3 (August 2014): 602–5.

23. Baron, "Ghetto and Emancipation," 525.

24. Daniel Tsadik, *Between Foreigners and Shi'is: Nineteenth-Century Iran and its Jewish Minority* (Stanford, CA: Stanford University Press, 2007), 1.

25. This book was originally published in Persian as a three-volume comprehensive history of the Jews of Iran and was translated into English in 1999 in Los Angeles, where Levy lived until his passing. Levy, *Comprehensive History*; Habib Levy, *Tarikh-i Yahud-i Iran* (Tehran: Barukhim, 1956).

26. Nahid Pirnazar, "Habib Levy," in *Jewish Communities of Iran: Entries on Judeo-Persian Communities Published by the Encyclopedia Iranica*, ed. Houman Sarshar (New York: Encyclopedia Iranica Foundation, 2011), 412–14.

27. Habib Levy, *Khatirat-i Man* (Beverly Hills, CA: Habib Levy Cultural and Educational Foundation, 2002), 198.

28. See Levy's accounts of the following: "Flood of Anti-Semitism" (281), "Climax of Anti-Semitism" (288–97), "Intensification of Anti-Semitism During the Reign of Shah Abbas II" (318–19), and "The Loss of King's Dagger and the Riot Against Jews" (319–20), in Levy, *Comprehensive History*.

29. Haggai Ram, *Iranophobia: The Logic of an Israeli Obsession* (Stanford, CA: Stanford University Press, 2009); see esp. 96–119 for the most comprehensive critique of the Israeli academic and popular understanding of Iran.

30. Ram. 101.

31. Meir Ezri, *Mi Va-Khem Mi-Kol 'Amo* (Or Yehuda, Israel: Hed Arzi, Sifriyat Ma'ariv, 2001).

32. Haim Tsadok, *Yahadut Iran bi-tekufat ha-shoshelet ha-Pahlavit: Yehude Iran ve-Erets Yisrael (1935–1978)* (Tel Aviv: Meyatseg, 1991), 48–51; Ram, *Iranophobia*.

33. Tsadok, *Yahadut Iran bi-tekufat ha-shoshelet ha-Pahlavit*, 13. See also Tsadok, 13–22, 318–60, 521–24.

34. Levy explains that the MAPAI (Mifleget Po'ale Eretz Yisra'el [National Council of the Workers' Party of the Land of Israel]) socialist government and its policies prevented him from immigrating to Israel, because the taxes levied on him would have proved too heavy a burden. Levi, *Khatirat-i Man*, 200.

35. Yosef Hayim Yerushalmi, *Zakhor: Jewish History and Jewish Memory*, Samuel and Althea Stroum Lectures in Jewish Studies (Seattle: University of Washington Press, 1996), 94.

36. Yerushalmi, 94.

37. The term *ghetto* appears in many documents in reference to Jewish neighborhoods in Iran, but it had never been used in writing by Iranian Jews themselves.

38. Notable in this category are these books that contextualize Jewish local histories with modern Middle Eastern history: Orit Bashkin, *New Babylonians: A History of Jews in Modern Iraq* (Stanford, CA: Stanford University Press, 2012); Joel Beinin, *The Dispersion of Egyptian Jewry: Culture, Politics, and the Formation of a Modern Diaspora*, Contraversions 11 (Berkeley: University of California Press, 1998); Aomar Boum, *Memories of Absence: How Muslims Remember Jews in Morocco* (Stanford, CA: Stanford University Press, 2013); Michelle U. Campos, *Ottoman Brothers: Muslims, Christians, and Jews in Early Twentieth-Century Palestine* (Stanford, CA: Stanford University Press, 2011); Julia Phillips Cohen, *Becoming Ottomans: Sephardi Jews and Imperial Citizenship in the Modern Era* (Oxford: Oxford University Press, 2014); Rami Ginat, *A History of Egyptian Communism: Jews and Their Compatriots in Quest of Revolution* (Boulder, CO: Lynne Rienner, 2011); Abigail Jacobson and Moshe Naor, *Oriental Neighbors: Middle Eastern Jews and Arabs in Mandatory Palestine* (Waltham, MA: Brandeis University Press, 2016); Joshua Schreier, *Arabs of the Jewish Faith: The Civilizing Mission in Colonial Algeria*, Jewish Cultures of the World (New Brunswick, NJ: Rutgers University Press, 2010); Joshua Schreier, *The Merchants of Oran: A Jewish Port at the Dawn of Empire*, Stanford Studies in Jewish History and Culture (Stanford, CA: Stanford University Press, 2017); and Sarah Abrevaya Stein, *Saharan Jews and the Fate of French Algeria* (Chicago: University of Chicago Press, 2014).

39. David Yeroushalmi, *The Jews of Iran in the Nineteenth Century Aspects of History, Community, and Culture* (Leiden: Brill, 2009); Mehrdad Amanat, *Jewish Identities in Iran*.

40. Tsadik, *Between Foreigners and Shi'is*, 3.

41. Avraham Cohen makes this intervention regarding educational institutions. He points out that the basic form of Jewish religious schooling was "maktab khanah" or "khanah-i mullah," thus borrowing from the Iranian Muslim vernacular. The teacher in these institutions was interchangeably "mullah," "khalifah," or "hakham." Even though Cohen used these terms to vividly demonstrate the level of Iranian Jews' acculturation, he drew profoundly different conclusions from those shared by revisionist historians regarding assimilation and sociocultural integration. I want to thank Haggai Ram for directing me to this telling example, and I am also grateful to Avraham Cohen for

providing his publications to use for this research. Cohen, "'Maktab,'" "Iranian Jewry," and "Substantive Changes in Jewish Education in Persia," in *The Jews of Iran: Their Past, Legacy and Connection to the Land of Israel* (in Hebrew), edited by Amnon Netzer (Tel Aviv: Beit Koresh, 1988); Ram, *Iranophobia*, 119nn36–37.

42. The Tudeh Party is the Iranian Communist Party that was established in the wake of the Allied Armies' occupation in 1941. The two most important works on the Tudeh Party are perhaps Ervand Abrahamian's *Iran Between Two Revolutions* and Maziar Behrooz's *Rebels with a Cause: The Failure of the Left in Iran*. Both books are extremely important and illuminating but, again, leave much of the discussion on the ethnic and religious elements of the party out of the conversation. Ervand Abrahamian, *Iran Between Two Revolutions* (Princeton, NJ: Princeton University Press, 1982); Maziar Behrooz, *Rebels with a Cause: The Failure of the Left in Iran* (London: I. B. Tauris, 1999).

Chapter 1

1. See two important works on Iranian nationalism: Afshin Marashi, *Nationalizing Iran: Culture, Power, and the State, 1870–1940* (Seattle: University of Washington Press, 2008); and Zia-Ebrahimi, *Emergence of Iranian Nationalism.*

2. For example, see the following on the formation of German and American colonies, the creation of Western spaces in Tehran, and more: Jennifer Jenkins, "Hjalmar Schacht, Reza Shah, and Germany's Presence in Iran," *Iran Nameh* 30, no. 1 (Spring 2015): 20–46; Jennifer Jenkins, "Experts, Migrants, Refugees: Making the German Colony in Iran, 1900–1934," in *German Colonialism in a Global Age*, ed. Bradley Naranch and Goeff Eley (Durham, NC: Duke University Press, 2014), 147–69; Nile Green, "Fordist Connections: The Automotive Integration of the United States and Iran," *Comparative Studies in Society and History* 58, no. 2 (April 2016): 290–321, https://doi.org/10.1017/S0010417516000086; and Mikiya Koyagi, "The Vernacular Journey: Railway Travelers in Early Pahlavi Iran, 1925–50," *International Journal of Middle East Studies* 47, no. 4 (November 2015): 745–63, https://doi.org/10.1017/S0020743815000963.

3. Dr. Curt Eric Neumann, the founder of Iran's biggest pharmaceutical companies, as well as Reza Shah's personal physician, was a German Jew. Fariborz Mokhtari, *In the Lion's Shadow: The Iranian Schindler and His Homeland in the Second World War* (Stroud, UK: History Press, 2011), 69n220; Ahmad Mahrad, "Sarnivisht-i Iraniyan-i Yahudi Tay-Yi Jang-i Jahani-Yi Duvvum Dar Urupa," in *Yahudiyan-i Irani Dar Tarikh-i Mu'asir*, ed. Homa Sarshar (Beverly Hills, CA: Center for Iranian Jewish Oral History; Philadelphia: Jewish Publication Society, 1999), 3:59–108. Atina Grossmann mentions the many German Jews who had arrived in Iran during the 1930s and worked as engineers, architects, construction managers, teachers, legal advisers, secretaries, and physicians. Many of them came to Iran and lived there as "Europeans, oddly privileged, adventurers, in exotic colonial or semi-colonial non-Western societies." Atina Grossmann, "Remapping Survival: Jewish Refugees and Lost Memories of Displacement, Trauma, and Rescue in Soviet Central Asia, Iran, and India," *Simon Dubnow Institute Yearbook* 15 (2016): 84–87.

4. See the fascinating story of Herzfeld and his relations with Germany and Iran: Jennifer Jenkins, "Excavating Zarathustra: Ernst Herzfeld's Archaeological History of Iran,"

Iranian Studies 45, no. 1 (January 2012): 1–27. Also see the telling family history of Grossmann: Atina Grossmann, "Versions of Home: German Jewish Refugee Papers out of the Closet and into the Archives," *New German Critique* 90 (Autumn 2003): 95–122; Atina Grossmann, "Remapping Relief and Rescue: Flight, Displacement, and International Aid for Jewish Refugees During World War II," *New German Critique* 117, vol. 39, no. 3 (Fall 2012): 61–79.

5. Jennifer Jenkins, "Iran in the Nazi New Order, 1933–1941," *Iranian Studies* 49, no. 5 (September 2, 2016): 727–51.

6. Germany used its vast influence in Iran to lay foundations for military and intelligence operations. See Adrian O'Sullivan, *Nazi Secret Warfare in Occupied Persia (Iran): The Failure of the German Intelligence Services, 1939–45* (New York: Palgrave Macmillan, 2014); and Adrian O'Sullivan, *Espionage and Counterintelligence in Occupied Persia (Iran): The Success of the Allied Secret Services, 1941–45* (New York: Palgrave Macmillan, 2015).

7. In Reza Azari Shahrizayi's collection of Iranian archival documents, one finds correspondence between Iranian diplomats in Europe and Turkey that discusses the issue of allowing Jewish professionals to immigrate to Iran. The list included Jewish university professors in all academic fields, including art, biology, engineering, archeology, philology, medicine, and mathematics. These individuals had been removed from their positions after the Nazis usurped power. Reza Azari Shahrizayi, *Dawlat-i Iran va Mutikhassisan-i Muhajir-i Almani (1310–1319) [1931–1940]* (Tehran: Intisharat-i Sazman-i Asnad-i Milli-i Iran, 1374 [1996]), 35–47. Turkey instituted a similar program to place German Jewish and non-Jewish scientists in Turkish universities. Several hundred of them (with their families) immigrated to Turkey. Corry Guttstadt also mentions that pro-Nazi academics were awarded positions in Turkish universities, suggesting that the program supported, at least in part, a utilitarian rather than humanitarian agenda. Corry Guttstadt, *Turkey, the Jews, and the Holocaust*, first English-language ed. (Cambridge: Cambridge University Press, 2013), 84–89.

8. See two articles by Shaul Bakhash about the events leading to the occupation and the different calculations the British and Soviets had to make: Shaul Bakhash, "Britain and the Abdication of Reza Shah," *Middle Eastern Studies* 52, no. 2 (March 3, 2016): 318–34; and Shaul Bakhash, "'Dear Anthony,' 'Dear Leo': Britain's Quixotic Flirtation with Dynastic Change in Iran During World War II," *Iran Nameh* 30, no. 4 (2016): 24–37.

9. For more on the fascinating relationship between German Jews living in Iran and the Nazi diplomatic mission in the capital, see Grossmann, "Remapping Survival," 87–88.

10. In 1941, following Reza Shah's abdication, the political sphere opened up and witnessed mass and wide participation of every group of Iranian society, from the far right to the radical left. Such an opening merits the title "Liberal Age" not because it necessarily allowed the espousal of liberal values but because it allowed the political game to take place. See Homa Katouzian, *Iranian History and Politics* (New York: Routledge, 2002); Nikki Keddie, *Modern Iran: Roots and Results of Revolution* (New Haven, CT: Yale University Press, 2003); and Fakhreddin Azimi, *Iran: The Crisis of Democracy: From the Exile of Reza Shah to the Fall of Musaddiq* (London: I. B. Tauris, 2009).

11. Accurate numbers are extremely difficult to obtain. Every state or organization involved in the treatment of refugees reported different numbers. It varies from 115,000 at

the low end, reported by the Soviet authorities (who had every incentive to minimize how many people they deported and imprisoned), to 400,000, reported by the Iranian Foreign Ministry (which arguably had a vested interest in inflating numbers). Aid organizations such as the International Red Cross and the JDC suggest total numbers fluctuating from 150,000 to 300,000 across the war years. The number of troops has been estimated to be 500,000 by the Soviet, American, and British armies.

12. Julian Bharier, "A Note on the Population of Iran, 1900–1966," *Population Studies* 22, no. 2 (July 1, 1968): 273–79, https://doi.org/10.2307/2173024.

13. I am using the term *cosmopolitan* with the same caution and awareness prompted by Will Hanley. In this chapter and later I refer to the Iranian cosmopolitanism not as a top-down project but rather as something that emerged from below, graced the many over the few, and created a juncture of interests between the Pahlavi vision and the social-political-cultural reality. Will Hanley, "Grieving Cosmopolitanism in Middle East Studies," *History Compass* 6, no. 5 (September 2008): 1346–67, https://doi.org/10.1111/j.1478-0542.2008.00545.x.

14. The situation was not always as rosy as one might assume. Tensions existed between Poles and Iranians, between ethnic Poles and Ukrainians, and between Jews and non-Jews. While hinted at in this chapter, the substance and details of these hostilities go far beyond the scope of this research. For more information, see David Engel, *Facing a Holocaust: The Polish Government-in-Exile and the Jews, 1943–1945* (Chapel Hill: University of North Carolina Press, 1993), 50–55; and Keith Sword, *Deportation and Exile: Poles in the Soviet Union, 1939–48*, Studies in Russia and East Europe (New York: St. Martin's in association with School of Slavonic and East European Studies, University of London, 1994), 60–88. Other conflicts among refugees were registered in accounts of the Red Cross and JDC.

15. Mokhtari, *In the Lion's Shadow*.

16. For prime examples of research on Fascism and reactions to Nazism, see Israel Gershoni and James Jankowski, *Confronting Fascism in Egypt: Dictatorship Versus Democracy in the 1930s* (Stanford, CA: Stanford University Press, 2010); Israel Gershoni, ed., *Arab Responses to Fascism and Nazism: Attraction and Repulsion* (Austin: University of Texas Press, 2014); and Jeffrey Herf, *Nazi Propaganda for the Arab World* (New Haven, CT: Yale University Press, 2010).

17. Guttstadt, *Turkey*.

18. "NKVD Instructions on 'Anti-Soviet Elements,'" in *The Polish Deportees of World War II: Recollections of Removal to the Soviet Union and Dispersal Throughout the World*, ed. Tadeusz Piotrowski (Jefferson, NC: McFarland, 2004), 203.

19. The number of Polish citizens (prisoners and deportees) that the Soviet authorities sent to Gulags in Siberia, jails, camps in the Soviet Union, forced labor in mines, and other forms of resettlement fluctuate and are greatly contested. The official Soviet number is less than 390,000. However, this number is by all counts deceptive and much deflated. More reliable sources suggest numbers between 1.25 million and 1.7 million. Jan Tomasz Gross, *Revolution from Abroad: The Soviet Conquest of Poland's Western Ukraine and Western Belorussia*, expanded ed. (Princeton, NJ: Princeton University Press, 2002), 187–96.

20. The Soviet authorities confiscated vast tracts of private property, even from people who were not necessarily affluent. Jan Tomasz Gross reveals that apartments in occupied cities were confiscated in order to house Soviet officers and bureaucrats. Gross, 189–90.

21. Most of the deportees were ethnic Poles; however, Ukrainians, Belorussians, Lithuanians, and other Polish groups were also included. Among them were some eighty thousand Jews from the Soviet territories of Poland and Ukraine. Of these, 20 percent were Jews who had fled the Nazi-occupied zone. In the entire Soviet zone, there were almost two million Jews, many of whom had initially supported the Soviet occupation (for obvious reasons) and, therefore, were less likely to be deported. Piotrowski, *Polish Deportees of World War II*, 3–5; Gross, *Revolution from Abroad*, 28–35.

22. "Soviet-Polish Agreement: Partition Treaty with Germany Denounced," *Times* (London), July 31, 1941.

23. Civilians were transferred to many other locations as well. Lebanon, India, territories in Africa, New Zealand, and Mexico were especially welcoming to Polish refugees. Piotrowski, *Polish Deportees of World War II*.

24. Large numbers of refugees ended up in India. Admittedly, their impact was less significant than that of the Polish refugees in Iran. However, they did establish a few Polish institutions, including a Polish hospital that treated large numbers of wartime refugees. "Current Topics: Fire Compensation Poles' Own Hospital," *Times of India*, June 3, 1944.

25. Britain first contemplated changing dynasties in Iran and restoring the Qajar dynasty, or abolishing the monarchy altogether. Eventually it was decided that Mohammad Reza Pahlavi would inherit his father's crown. Reza Shah abdicated following the Anglo-Soviet invasion, and Mohammad Reza became the new Shah. Leo Amery to Anthony Eden, May 16, 1941, E/2283, National Archives, Kew, England (hereafter TNA).

26. 'Ali-Reza Karimi and Sayyid-'Ali Karimi provide an account of the crisis of famine and inflation in Iran as the Polish refugees were entering the country. 'Ali-Reza Karimi and Sayyid-'Ali Karimi, "Lehastani'ha-yi Muhajer Dar Iran," *Tarikh Mu'asir Iran* 3, no. 9 (1379 [1999–2000]): 16–22.

27. Iranian Legation, London, to Ministry of Foreign Affairs, Tehran, April 3, 1942, TNA HW 12/275/103011 (regarding Iranian protest at the arrival of the Poles); Associated Press, "British Carrying Food for the People of Iran," *New York Times*, August 26, 1941, also mentioned in Karimi and Karimi, "Lehastani'ha-yi Muhajer Dar Iran," 22.

28. Contrary to the Allies' assurances, famine spread during the war years in Iran, along with other economic crises. Abbas Amanat, *Iran: A Modern History* (New Haven, CT: Yale University Press, 2017), 503–8.

29. Henrietta K. Buchman to Mr. Pearlstein, March 8, 1943, 1933/44/712. There is also documentation of JDC involvement in the Lend-Lease Act of 1941, as a circular transaction containing information regarding refugees. For example, see Charles Passman to George T. Washington Esq., June 25, 1944, JDCA 1933/44/712.

30. Overseas News Agency, "More Poles Reach Iran," *New York Times*, November 5, 1942.

31. John N. Greely, "Iran in Wartime: Through Fabulous Persia, Hub of the Middle East, Americans, Britons, and Iranians Keep Sinews of War Moving to the Embattled

Soviet Union," *National Geographic Magazine*, August 1943, 152, http://tinyurl.galegroup .com/tinyurl/6NwYC4.

32. Irena Beaupré-Stankiewicz, Danuta Waszczuk-Kamieniecka, and Jadwiga Lewicka-Howells, eds., *Isfahan—City of Polish Children* (Sussex: Association of Former Pupils of Polish Schools, Isfahan and Lebanon, 1989), 63.

33. To protect the identities of interviewees and for methodological reasons, I have used pseudonyms exclusively throughout the discussions of my research. Roman, therefore, is not his real name.

34. Interview with Roman, July 15, 2013.

35. As mentioned earlier, the Anders Army relied on Polish refugees to whom Stalin granted amnesty in 1941. General Anders led troops under the command of the British Army. The Anders Army was meant to fight on the new fronts in the Middle East and North Africa. Interview with Roman.

36. "Niku Karan Israil Ra Bishnasid," *'Alim-i Yahud*, June 3, 1945.

37. Much has been written about Yaldei Tehran, so this part of the story may be somewhat familiar to the general reader. It could be speculated that this story is known because of the role it plays in the greater Zionist narrative. Most of the orphans were received by Jewish and Zionist organizations, and the overwhelming majority of them were transferred to Palestine/Israel shortly after their arrival in Tehran. For more information, see Devorah 'Omer, *The Teheran Operation: The Rescue of Jewish Children from the Nazis: Based on the Biographical Sketches of David and Rachel Laor* (Washington, DC: B'nai B'rith Books, 1991).

38. Many refugee testimonials reflect appreciation for Iranian hospitality. Although tensions existed between the different groups of refugees (ethnic tensions, anti-Semitic events, etc.), the Iranian people were overwhelmingly acknowledged for their genuine support. 'Omer, 165–68.

39. Piotrowski, *Polish Deportees of World War II*, 115.

40. "Makatib-i Safir-i Inglis dar Tihran, Vizaratkhanah-i Umur-i Kharijah, Ustandar-i Khurasan va Nukhust Vazir dar Khusus-i Vurud-i Muhajirin-i Lahistani az Shuravi bih Iran," in *Asnadi Az Ishghal-i Iran Dar Jang-i Jahani-i Duvvum, Jald-i Svvum*, ed. Moham-mad Hosein Salehi Maram (Tehran, Iran: Markaz-i Pazhuhish va Asnad-i Riyasat-i Jum-huri, 2011), 3:301.

41. "Report on Visit to Bagdad and Teheran," November 2–9, 1942, JDCA 1933/44/712. This report mentions the involvement of wealthy and generous Iraqi Jews; the Ashkenazi background of Mr. and Mrs. Hirsch Sand is assumed because of their name.

42. Karimi and Karimi, "Lehastani'ha-yi Muhajer Dar Iran," 39.

43. See especially Shaul Sehayik, *Parashah 'Alumah: Korot Mifgasham Shel Alfei Hay-alim Yehudim Polanim 'Im Yehudim Be-Iraq Uve-Iran Bashanim 1942–1943* (Tel Aviv: self published, 2003), 50–58.

44. This number only includes children under the age of fourteen and those who were not attending boarding or military school.

45. Beaupré-Stankiewicz, Waszczuk-Kamieniecka, and Lewicka-Howells, *Isfahan*, 122–42.

46. Beaupré-Stankiewicz, Waszczuk-Kamieniecka, and Lewicka-Howells, 307.

47. While many of the publications about Poland and Polish deportees discuss (even briefly) the Iranian episode, books on the Middle East during that period tend to focus on fascist inclinations, or the greater war schemes, and rarely mention these stories. See, for example, Halik Kochanski, *The Eagle Unbowed: Poland and the Poles in the Second World War* (Cambridge, MA: Harvard University Press, 2012); Beaupré-Stankiewicz, Waszczuk-Kamieniecka, and Lewicka-Howells, *Isfahan*; Piotrowski, *Polish Deportees of World War II*; and Kenneth K. Koskodan, *No Greater Ally: The Untold Story of Poland's Forces in World War II* (Oxford: Osprey, 2009).

48. Piotrowski, *Polish Deportees of World War II*, 105.

49. "Sanad-i shumarah 25/2," in Maram, *Asnadi Az Ishghal-i Iran Dar Jang-i Jahani-i Duvvum*, 303.

50. Piotrowski, *Polish Deportees of World War II*, 106.

51. "Report on Visit to Bagdad and Teheran," November 2–9, 1942.

52. The hardships of the exile are described in detail in Beaupré-Stankiewicz, Waszczuk-Kamieniecka, and Lewicka-Howells, *Isfahan*.

53. Greely, "Iran in Wartime," 133.

54. Greely, 139–40.

55. Greely, 140.

56. *Ittila'at*, 10 Ordibehesht 1321 [April 30, 1942], cited in Karimi and Karimi, "Lehastani'ha-yi Muhajer Dar Iran," 37.

57. *Ittila'at*, 12 Khordad 1321 [June 2, 1942], cited in Karimi and Karimi, 37.

58. 'Abd al-Rahim Ja'fari, *Dar Justuju-yi Subh: Khatirat-i 'Abd al-Rahim Ja'fari, Bunyanguzar-i Mu'assisah-i Intisharat-i Amir Kabir* (Tehran: Ruzbihan, 2004), 1:228.

59. *Ittila'at*, 26 Mordad 1321 [August 22, 1942], cited in Karimi and Karimi, "Lehastani'ha-yi Muhajer Dar Iran," 34.

60. Although most Polish refugees hailed from the middle and upper socioeconomic classes, some were indeed poor and, especially after their arrival in Tehran, engaged in prostitution. From other accounts I gather that many of the European prostitutes were Russian rather than Polish. Anwar Faruqi, "Forgotten Polish Exodus to Persia," *Washington Post*, November 23, 2000, https://www.washingtonpost.com/archive/politics/2000/11/23/forgotten-polish-exodus-to-persia/2b106c08-e61c-4c36-8102-fb2e114c9bff/.

61. Greely, "Iran in Wartime," 140.

62. Ida Meftahi, "Body National in Motion: The Biopolitics of Dance in the Twentieth-Century Iran" (PhD diss., University of Toronto, 2013), 12.

63. Greely, "Iran in Wartime," 152.

64. Reuters, "Polish Troops in Iraq and Iran," *New York Times*, November 7, 1942.

65. "Report on Visit to Bagdad and Teheran," November 2–9, 1942. Greely also mentions that many Polish women became waitresses and barmaids. Greely, "Iran in Wartime," 152.

66. Sayre also was a reporter at large for the *New Yorker* during World War II, and some of his wartime reports were published in the magazine. Joel Sayre, *I Served in the Persian Gulf Command* (Isfahan, 1945), 22.

67. Sayre, 22–23. Greely also reported about this story. Greely, "Iran in Wartime," 152.

68. Sinai quoted in Faruqi, "Forgotten Polish Exodus to Persia."

69. Karimi and Karimi, "Lehastani'ha-yi Muhajer Dar Iran," 37.

70. As both Iranian and JDC documents demonstrate, the Polish representative in Russia and the Russian forces administering this operation on the Russian side had no clear idea of how many refugees and Polish military personnel were still to cross the border to Iran. In some instances the crews on the Iranian side had to deal with the sudden arrival of thousands of refugees a day when they had expected none. Karimi and Karimi, "Lahistaniha-yi muhajir dar iran," 12–13.

71. Henrietta K. Buchman to Mr. Pearlstein, March 8, 1943.

72. Memorandum, February 11, 1943, JDCA 1933/44/712.

73. "Report on Visit to Bagdad and Teheran," November 2–9, 1942.

74. "Pole Urges Moscow to Release 800,000: Stanczyk Waives Land Dispute—Roosevelt Extols Courage," *New York Times*, May 4, 1943.

75. Henriette K. Buchman to Isaac B. Seligson, April 2, 1943, JDCA 1933/44/712.

76. Harry Viteles to American Joint Distribution Committee, March 29, 1943, JDCA 1933/44/712.

77. "Delegation du CICR en Iran au Comite International de la Croix-Rouge," August 19, 1944, BG 017/07-114, International Red Cross Archives (hereafter CICR), Geneva, Switzerland.

78. "Delegation du CICR en Iran au Comite International de la Croix-Rouge," August 25, 1944, CICR BG 017/07-114.

79. Beaupré-Stankiewicz, Waszczuk-Kamieniecka, and Lewicka-Howells, *Isfahan*, 362.

80. Karimi and Karimi, "Lehastani'ha-yi Muhajer Dar Iran," 34.

81. Petersen's mother arrived in Tehran in 1942 through Bandar-i Pahlavi and joined the Anders Army. This film beautifully depicts the story of the Polish refugees—from the horrors of Siberia to the grueling journey to Iran, and all the tragedies that befell them before they eventually settled in Iran. Annette Mary Olsen and Katia Forbert Petersen, dirs., *My Iranian Paradise*, Denmark: Sfinx Film/TV, 2008.

82. Faruqi, "Forgotten Polish Exodus to Persia."

83. Parisa Damandan, *Portrait Photographs from Isfahan: Faces in Transition, 1920–1950* (London: Saqi; The Hague: Prince Claus Fund Library, 2004).

84. In a letter to the British ambassador, Polish refugees in Isfahan wrote that "this territory is not secure for us." The letter refers to British plans for evacuation from Iran, based on the Allied commitment to Iran from 1941 to 1942 that supported refugee resettlement in the first place. It is possible that a sense of impermanence among refugees promoted fear and instability; political unrest was fairly widespread in Iran at this time. [Polish refugees in Iran] to Sir Reader Bullard, August 30, 1945, TNA FO 799/25.

85. [Polish refugees in Iran] to Sir Reader Bullard, August 30, 1945.

86. For example, see postwar agreements between Britain and the United States regarding the resettlement of refugees. These agreements were intended to create conditions in postwar Poland favorable to the establishment of democracy so that Polish refugees would return home in greater numbers. Telegram, June 22, 1945, TNA FO 799/25.

87. Hamid Naficy, *A Social History of Iranian Cinema* (Durham, NC: Duke University Press, 2011), 4:34.

88. Nir Shohet, *Sipurah Shel Golah: Perakim Be-Toldot Yahadut Bavel Le-Doroteha* (Jerusalem: ha-Agudah le-kidum ha-Mehker veha-Yetsirah, 1981), 121.

89. For more about the cultural ties between Iran and Iraq, with emphasis on minority communities, see Houchang E. Chehabi, "Iran and Iraq: Intersocietal Linkages and Secular Nationalisms," in *Iran Facing Others: Identity Boundaries in a Historical Perspective*, edited by Abbas Amanat and Farzin Vejdani (New York: Palgrave Macmillan, 2012), 191–216. For more on the Iraqi Jewish community in Iran, see Arlene Dallalfar, "Iraqi Jews in Iran," in *Esther's Children: A Portrait of Iranian Jews*, ed. Houman Sarshar (Beverly Hills, CA: The Center for Iranian Jewish Oral History, 2002), 277–81.

90. See especially Abbas Shiblak, *Iraqi Jews: A History of the Mass Exodus* (London: Saqi, 2005), 33–54, table 2, p. 39, table 5, p.49.

91. The accounts of the Farhud show the horrors the Iraqi Jews experienced in those two days, and the way it forever changed their relationship with their country. Bashkin, *New Babylonians*, 112–40; Dallalfar, "Iraqi Jews in Iran"; David Sitton, *Sephardi Communities Today* (Jerusalem: Council of Sephardi and Oriental Communities, 1985), 42–45; Shohet, *Sipurah Shel Golah*, 163–78; Esther Meir-Glitzenstein, *Zionism in an Arab Country: Jews in Iraq in the 1940s* (London: Routledge, 2014), 13–39.

92. For more about the relations of the Iraqi Jewish community with the Zionist movement, see Meir-Glitzenstein, *Zionism in an Arab Country*, 134–58, 256–57.

93. Interview with Hayyim, June 25, 2013. Hayyim is in his seventies today and lives in North America.

94. "Report on Iran and Suggestions for the Year 1951," JDCA 45/54-506, September 1950

95. Shohet, *Sipurah Shel Golah*, 141.

96. Shohet, 91.

97. Interview with Hayyim, June 25, 2013. For more information regarding negotiations and plans to resettle Iraqi Jews in Israel, see Bashkin, *New Babylonians*, 185–202.

98. Interview with Hayyim, June 25, 2013.

99. Interview with Daud, June 25, 2013.

100. Interview with Hayyim, June 25, 2013.

101. This view was at the center of an ideological struggle within the Zionist movement in Iran and opened the door to interpreting Zionism in different ways. For a more in-depth discussion, see Chapters 2 and 4.

102. Dallalfar, "Iraqi Jews in Iran," 277.

103. Dallalfar, 277.

104. For more on cultural aspects of the usage of "Arabs" and "'Ajams," see Chehabi, "Iran and Iraq"; Jalal Al-e Ahmad, *The Israeli Republic*, trans. Samuel Thrope (New York: Restless Books, 2013).

105. Interview with Daud, June 25, 2013.

106. In fact, Basson first arrived in Iran in the 1930s to work as a contractor. However, Tehran did not become his permanent residence until the 1940s.

107. Opening an event hall as part of the school's complex generated revenues that helped the school access cutting-edge technology and retain independence from community budgets.

108. Dallalfar, "Iraqi Jews in Iran," 281.

109. To the best of my knowledge, Berukhim was the first non-Iraqi to occupy this position. "Interview with Barukh Berukhim," September 25, 1998, Center for Iranian Jewish Oral History (hereafter CIJOH), Los Angeles, CA.

110. The JDC report from 1967 suggests that Ettefaq enjoyed financial stability. This stability resulted in part from the support of wealthy Iraqis and in part from tuition fees. The report clearly indicates that Ettefaq had been opened to non-Iraqi Jewish students (in fact, over half the students were Iranian youths). However, the report also predicts an increased future enrollment of Iraqi Jewish students, given the community's fear of Iraqi students assimilating in "American sponsored schools." "Annual Report 1967," JDCA AR 65/74-0111, December 1967.

111. "Re: Situation of Iraqis in Iran," JDCA 65/74-0111, May 28, 1965.

112. Guttstadt, *Turkey*.

Chapter 2

1. For references on Jews' support of Communist parties in the Middle East, see Bashkin, *New Babylonians*; Sami Michael, *Gevulot Ha-Ruah: Sihot 'im Rubik Rozental, Kav Adom* (Tel Aviv: ha-Kibuts ha-me'uhad, 2000); and Ginat, *History of Egyptian Communism*. Regarding the general tendency of minorities to support leftist political organizations, see Tony Judt and Timothy Snyder, *Thinking the Twentieth Century* (New York: Penguin, 2012); and Zygmunt Bauman, *Modernity and the Holocaust* (Ithaca, NY: Cornell University Press, 1989).

2. The Zoroastrians had better leverage vis-à-vis the constitutional committees and were eventually permitted to have their own elected representative become part of the first Majlis. All three communities were allowed to be fully represented by their own elected officials starting with the second Majlis. Afary, *Iranian Constitutional Revolution*, 69–71, 262–63.

3. In 1920 the Communist Party of Iran/Persia was established and had connections with the Comintern congress. The end of this party and several other Communist endeavors came when Stalin and the Soviet Union opted to support Reza Shah, turning against the party's leadership. Several incidents, including the trial of the fifty-three prisoners, and anti-Communist legislation sealed the first chapter of Iranian Communism, though it inevitably became part of the early history of the Tudeh Party, as demonstrated here. Cosroe Chaquèri, *The Soviet Socialist Republic of Iran, 1920–1921: Birth of the Trauma*, Pitt Series in Russian and East European Studies 21 (Pittsburgh: University of Pittsburgh Press, 1995). Also see especially Sepehr Zabih, *The Left in Contemporary Iran: Ideology, Organisation, and the Soviet Connection* (London: Croom Helm; Stanford, CA: Hoover Institution Press, 1986), 1–68.

4. David N. Yaghoubian, *Ethnicity, Identity, and the Development of Nationalism in Iran* (Syracuse, NY: Syracuse University Press, 2014), 137.

5. For a detailed account of the appearance of the Tudeh in the context of the war, see Sepehr Zabih, *The Communist Movement in Iran* (Berkeley: University of California Press, 1966), 71–122.

6. Abrahamian mentions this reputation because the party's opponents cited it to discredit the organization. Abrahamian, *Iran Between Two Revolutions*, 452.

7. Beinin, *Dispersion of Egyptian Jewry*; Ginat, *History of Egyptian Communism*; Bashkin, *New Babylonians*; Judt and Snyder, *Thinking the Twentieth Century*; Bauman, *Modernity and the Holocaust*; Renée Poznanski, *Jews in France During World War II*, Tauber Institute for the Study of European Jewry (Waltham, MA: Brandeis University Press in association with the United States Holocaust Memorial Museum; Hanover, NH: University Press of New England, 2001); Alma R. Heckman, "Radical Nationalists: Moroccan Jewish Communists 1925–1975" (PhD diss., University of California, Los Angeles, 2015); Alma Heckman, "Multivariable Casablanca: Vichy Law, Jewish Diversity, and the Moroccan Communist Party," in "Jews of Morocco and the Maghreb: History and Historiography," special issue, *Hespéris-Tamuda* 51, no. 3 (2016): 13–34.

8. Ministry of Fuel and Power, "Anglo-Iranian Oil Company: Malingering Employees and Labour Disputes," 1944, TNA FO 371/40158; Ervand Abrahamian, *The Coup: 1953, the CIA, and the Roots of Modern U.S.-Iranian Relations* (New York: New Press, 2013), 22–23.

9. Faryar Nikbakht, "Yahudiyan Dar Nihzatha va Ahzab-i Siyasi," in *Terua*, ed. Homa Sarshar (Beverly Hills, CA: Center for Iranian Jewish Oral History; Philadelphia: Jewish Publication Society, 1996), 79–81.

10. Nikbakht, 81.

11. Abrahamian also mentions border proximity as a factor in Soviet influence. The Soviets enthusiastically supported groups rebelling against Iran's central government. Abrahamian, *Iran Between Two Revolutions*, 386.

12. Iraj Farhoumand, "Iraniyan-i Yahudi va Hizb-i Tudah-i Iran," in *Yahudiyan-i Irani Dar Tarikh-i Mu'asir*, ed. Homa Sarshar (Beverly Hills, CA: Center for Iranian Jewish Oral History; Philadelphia: Jewish Publication Society, 2000), 119–24.

13. Judt and Snyder, *Thinking the Twentieth Century*, 98. Bauman made a similar point on the Communist appeal to Jews. See Bauman, *Modernity and the Holocaust*.

14. Michael, *Gevulot Ha-Ruah*, 50–121.

15. Interview with Pinhas, May 15, 2014.

16. Farhoumand, "Iraniyan-i Yahudi va Hizb-i Tudah-i Iran," 111.

17. Zabih, *The Left in Contemporary Iran*, 3.

18. Crucial disagreements split the Tudeh Party on several occasions. There were instances when a leadership vacuum opened the way to incompetence in the local Iranian political sphere. At times, Soviet interests seemed to be prioritized over Iranian interests. However, as both Zabih and Maziar Behrooz demonstrate, prioritization of Soviet interests was the exception and not the rule. Maziar Behrooz, *Rebels with a Cause: The Failure of the Left in Iran* (London: I. B. Tauris, 2000); Sepehr Zabih, *The Communist Movement in Iran* (Berkeley: University of California, 1966). Cosroe Chaquèri, on the other hand, suggests much greater involvement of the Soviets in the creation and control of the Tudeh

Party. Chaquèri backed his research with convincing evidence found in the Comintern archives; however, as previously mentioned, the party underwent several splits over the question of foreign involvement. Cosroe Chaquèri, "Did the Soviets Play a Role in Founding the Tudeh Party in Iran?," *Cahiers du Monde Russe* 40, no. 3 (July 1, 1999): 497–528, https://doi.org/10.2307/20171142.

19. Interview with Habib, June 24, 2013.

20. On the pretext of standardizing school curricula and creating a unified system, Reza Shah issued a decree that shut down community and religious schools in 1938.

21. Yaghoubian, *Ethnicity*, 140–43.

22. The Soviets actively supported and funded candidates elected to the Majlis, and intervened in elections of the Armenian representative as well. See Yaghoubian, *Ethnicity*, 138–39; and Abrahamian, *Iran Between Two Revolutions*, 186.

23. Abrahamian, *Iran Between Two Revolutions*, 201–2; Jaleh Pirnazar, "Yahudiyan-i Iran, Huvviyyat-i Milli va Ruznamahnigari," in Sarshar, *Yahudiyan-i Irani Dar Tarikh-i Mu'asir*, 25.

24. *Nissan* was not officially connected to the Tudeh Party. Its status as a semiofficial newspaper stemmed from Anvar's proximity to the party's leadership and his ability to communicate their messages efficiently when *Mardum*, *Rahbar*, or *Razm* was censored.

25. Pirnazar, "Yahudiyan-i Iran, Huvviyyat-i Milli va Ruznamahnigari," 25–26.

26. "Tashkilat-i Sayunist Alatidast-i Imperialism Amrika," *Nissan*, 17 Ordibehesht 1332 [May 7, 1953], 1, 4.

27. At one point in the article, the author refers to MAPAM as the "right-wing" party. This is certainly a mistake, as MAPAM not only was known as a socialist party in the Israeli political spectrum but was also solidly committed to Stalin. "Tiror Afkar va Taftish 'Aqayid bi-Vasilah Dulat Amrikayii Benguriun dar Isra'il Idamah Darad," *Nissan*, 17 Ordibehesht 1332 [May 7, 1953], 1, 3.

28. Arnold Krammer, *The Forgotten Friendship: Israel and the Soviet Bloc, 1947–53* (Urbana: University of Illinois Press, 1974), 134. Judd Teller reports that the Soviet security forces murdered 433 Jewish artists and intellectuals after 1948. See Judd L. Teller, *The Kremlin, the Jews, and the Middle East* (New York: T. Yoseloff, 1957); and Jacob Ari Labendz, "Renegotiating Czechoslovakia: The State and the Jews in Communist Central Europe: The Czech Lands, 1945–1990" (PhD diss., Washington University, Saint Louis, 2014), 51–52, 65. The assault on Soviet Jewish artists began even before the events of fall 1948. In January of that year, Soviet security forces in Belarus murdered Solomon Mikhoels, who led both the Moscow State Jewish Theater and the Jewish Anti-Fascist Committee. The Soviet anti-Zionist campaign culminated in 1952 with the trial and execution of fifteen functionaries of the latter organization, along with ten others. See Joshua Rubenstein, Vladimir Pavlovich Naumov, and Ester Wolfson, eds., *Stalin's Secret Pogrom: The Postwar Inquisition of the Jewish Anti-Fascist Committee*, abridged ed., Annals of Communism (New Haven, CT: Yale University Press, 2001). The Doctors' Plot was a series of government attacks on a group of Moscow doctors and officials, predominantly Jewish, between 1952 and 1953. These individuals were accused of plotting to assassinate Stalin and other senior officials between 1948 and 1953. Stalin's death in 1953 put an end to this persecution and

the case was dropped. The Prague trials concerned the 1952 Slánský affair that took place in Czechoslovakia. Like the Doctors' Plot, this was yet another "show trial" of fourteen Communist officials, eleven of them Jews. These individuals were accused of having Trotskyite leanings, supporting Yugoslavia's Josip Broz Tito, and engaging in Zionist conspiracy. The majority of the defendants were hanged in Prague, but three received life imprisonment. I want to thank Jacob Ari Labendz for assistance with this information.

29. "Matbu'at va Mardum Isra'il Tahrikat Zid-i Shuru-yi Bingurin Ra Mahkum Mikunand," *Nissan*, 17 Ordibehesht 1332 [May 7, 1953], 1.

30. "Guftigu Ba Khvanandigan," *Nissan*, 17 Ordibehesht 1332 [May 7, 1953], 3.

31. "Sukhani Chand Darbarih-yi Mas'alih-i Yahud," *Nissan*, 22 Murdad 1332 [August 13, 1953], 1, 4.

32. "Khulasih Nizr Hizb-i Susyalist Chip-i Israiil Darbarah-yi 'Musailah Yahud,'" *Nissan*, 22 Murdad 1332 [August 13, 1953], 1, 3.

33. See "Zadigi Yahudiyan Rumani Dar Guzashteh va Hal," *Nissan*, 22 Murdad 1332 [August 13, 1953], 1–2; and "Man Az Israiil Baz Migardam," *Nissan*, 22 Murdad 1332 [August 13, 1953], 1, 3.

34. "Khulasih Nizr Hizb-i Susyalist Chip-i Israiil," *Nissan*, 22 Murdad 1332 [August 13, 1953], 1, 3.

35. "Halivud Digar Jai Hunarmandan Nist," *Nissan*, 17 Ordibehesht 1332 [May 7, 1953], 1, 3.

36. "Majlis Yadibud," *Nissan*, 22 Murdad 1332 [August 13, 1953], 1, 4.

37. "Istiqbal Bi-nazir Yahudiyan Abadan Az Ruznamih Nissan," *Nissan*, 17 Ordibehesht 1332 [May 7, 1953], 1, 3.

38. Pirnazar, "Yahudiyan-i Iran, Huvviyyat-i Milli va Ruznamahnigari."

39. In an article on Jewish publications of this era, Amnon Netzer categorized some of the newspapers discussed in this chapter. Netzer asserts that *Nissan*, edited by Anvar, was directly connected to the Tudeh, whereas he describes *Bani-Adam* as merely "leftist; pro-Tudeh." Interestingly, newspapers like *Israiil* and *'Alim-i Yahud* are categorized as "general" (*'Alim-i Yahud*) and "social-Zionist" (*Israiil*). However, Netzer added that Jewish Tudeh sympathizers wrote for both newspapers and that they even formed the majority of *Israiil's* editorial board. This contribution by Netzer demonstrates, perhaps better than other statistics, the degree to which Jews embraced leftist political ideologies at the time. Amnon Netzer, "Ha-'Itonut Ha-Yehudit," in *Iran*, ed. Haim Saadoun (Jerusalem: Yad Ben-Zvi, 2005), 141–54.

40. "Jashn Aghaz Chiharmin Sal-i Istiqlal: Israil Ra Bimilat-i Israil Tabrik Miguyim," *Bani-Adam*, 14 Ordibehesht 1331 [May 4, 1952], 1, 3. Interestingly, this issue also included excerpts from the Israeli Declaration of Independence.

41. For another perspective on the relationship between Zionism and anticolonialism, and its subsequent influence on the founding fathers of Pakistan, see Faisal Devji, *Muslim Zion: Pakistan as a Political Idea* (Cambridge, MA: Harvard University Press, 2013).

42. The second part of the article is confusing chronologically. There are a few references to 1949 as the year of Israel's establishment as a state, instead of 1948. "Jashn Aghaz Chiharmin Sal-i Istiqlal," *Bani-Adam*, 14 Ordibehesht 1331 [May 4, 1952], 1, 3.

43. *Ha'Olam Ha'Zeh* was an Israeli weekly news magazine published between 1937 and 1993. Some still consider it to have been the proving ground of investigative journalism for generations of Israeli journalists. In 1950 Uri Avnery and Shalom Cohen purchased *Ha'Olam Ha'Zeh*. Under Avnery's leadership, the magazine developed a markedly antiestablishment, and often sensationalist, tone. Avnery and Cohen both entered politics, served in the Knesset (Avnery served twice, in 1965 and in 1969), and founded a new party, Ha'Olam Ha'Zeh, named after the magazine.

44. "Israiil va Jonbash'ha-i Azadi Talibanih Khavar Miyanih va Shumal Afriqa," *Bani-Adam*, 14 Ordibehesht 1331 [May 4, 1952], 1, 3.

45. Before 1948 Sneh was a member of the Jewish Agency and several Zionist organizations. In 1948 he joined MAPAM, where he rose to a leadership role, and he joined the Israeli Communist Party in 1954.

46. "Israiil va Jonbash'ha-i Azadi Talibanih Khavar Miyanih," *Bani-Adam*, 14 Ordibehesht 1331 [May 4, 1952], 1, 3.

47. "Intizarat Jami'ah Yahud Iran Az Majlis Hafdhum," *Bani-Adam*, 21 Ordibehesht 1331 [May 11, 1952], 1–2.

48. "Israiil va Jonbash'ha-i Azadi Talibanih Khavar Miyanih," *Bani-Adam*, 14 Ordibehesht 1331 [May 4, 1952], 3.

49. Eskandari mentions that in the conference of 1331 (1952), "the question of fighting against Fascism was especially important. A few people opposed it, but the vast majority voted for it and that is how we decided to start an anti-Fascist newspaper, and this led to Soviet intervention in our work." There is good reason to believe that the date of the conference, because of the content Eskandari mentions, actually took place ten years earlier, in 1321 (1942). Iraj Eskandari, Babak Amir Khusravi, and Faridun Azamur, *Khatirat-i Siyasi* (France, 1336 [1957]), 28.

50. The Hebra was the umbrella organization for Iran's Jewish community. Its leadership tended to be more conservative and Zionist.

51. The JDC was perceived by radical leftist organizations to be an American imperialist agent, by virtue of its representing American Jewish interests in the region. This view must be situated in the Cold War context, as this was a time when groups that, overall, lent support to the Soviet Union could not condone American activities or American organizations in their backyard.

52. Pirnazar, "Yahudiyan-i Iran, Huvviyyat-i Milli va Ruznamahnigari," 26–27.

53. "Divan Dadgastri Binalmilili Lahih Har Tasmimi Itikhad Konid Dar Rah Vurush Millat Iran Kuchaktarin Bin Tasiri Nakhvuhad Dhasht," *Bani-Adam*, 4 Khordad 1331 [May 25, 1952], 1, 3.

54. "Namunih-i Az Vaz'i Zandigi Yahudiyan Abadan," *Bani-Adam*, 11 Khordad 1331 [June 1, 1952], 1, 4.

55. In mid-1952 *Bani-Adam* sought to provide a forum for these forgotten voices by publicizing an appeal on behalf of Abadani Jews, an appeal written by fourteen members of Iran's Jewish community leadership. This letter, sent to the governor of Abadan, asked for the creation of election booths so that Abadan's four thousand Jews could participate in the general elections, thus insisting on their right to elect their (one) representative.

A copy of the letter was also sent to Prime Minister Mosaddeq, the governor of Tehran, the Tehran Jewish Society, *Etela'at*, and *'Alim-i Yahud*, and it was reprinted in *Bani-Adam*. "Faraman-dati Mukhtarim Abadan," *Bani-Adam*, 4 Khordad 1331 [May 25, 1952], 3.

56. "Barrasi Birnamih Intikhabati Aqayi Anvar," *Bani-Adam*, 11 Khordad 1331 [June 1, 1952], 1, 3.

57. "Shabu'ot, 'Id Tajlil Adalat va Azadi," *Bani-Adam*, 11 Khordad 1331 [June 1, 1952], 1, 3.

58. "Arzash-i Zan Dar Ijtima'," *Bani-Adam*, 9 Aban 1330 [November 1, 1951], 1, 3.

59. "Intikhabat," *Bani-Adam*. 9 Aban 1330 [1 November 1951]. Pp. 1–2.

60. Rahim Namvar, *Yadnameh Shahidan*.

61. I am grateful to Ervand Abrahamian for bringing this issue, and Namvar's publication, to my attention.

62. Mushfiq Hamadani, *Khatirat-i Nim-i Qarn-i Ruznamahnigari*, n.d., 276.

63. Orly R. Rahimian, "Irgun Ha-Kehila," in Saadoun, *Iran*, 153–54.

64. Goel Cohen, ed., *Bar Bal-i Khirad: Jami'ah-i Yahudiyan-i Iran va Haftad Sal Rahbari-Yi Mazhabi, Gam Bah Gam Ba Hakham Yedidiya Shofet Dar Kashan, Tehran, va Los Angeles* (Los Angeles: Educational Foundation of Hacham Yedidia Shofet, 2010), 372–73.

65. Cohen, 373.

66. Interview with Ardeshir, November 17, 2013.

67. Interview with Ardeshir.

68. See more on Kashani's political history in Abbas Milani, *Eminent Persians: The Men and Women Who Made Modern Iran, 1941–1979*, 2 vols. (Syracuse, NY: Syracuse University Press; New York: Persian World, 2008), 1:343–49; and Jacob Abadi, *Israel's Quest for Recognition and Acceptance in Asia: Garrison State Diplomacy*, Israeli History, Politics, and Society 34 (London: Frank Cass, 2004), 39.

Chapter 3

1. The Balfour Declaration was a letter delivered by Lord Balfour on behalf of the British government to the Zionist movement on November 2, 1917. The letter expressed British support for the establishment of a Jewish homeland in Palestine. While the intention and meaning of this declaration continue to be debated, it is considered to be the most significant diplomatic achievement of the Zionist movement.

2. Levy, *Comprehensive History of the Jews*, 510.

3. Levy, 508–9.

4. It would appear that affiliation with a broader coalition such as that of the Zionists, a sense of empowerment inherent in education, and the ability to organize and exercise their civil rights had already created new options for Jews. These changing circumstances emboldened Jews to negotiate a place in Iranian society. Incidents of anti-Semitic harassment, which in the past had been accommodated in order to avoid conflict, were now taken to the police and authorities. Alignment with the Zionist movement clearly resulted in increased political and social agency for Iranian Jews. Levy, 516–18.

5. Ezri, *Mi Va-Khem Mi-Kol 'Amo*, 17–51.

6. Tsadok, *Yahadut Iran bi-tekufat ha-shoshelet ha-Pahlavit*, 30–41.

7. Amnon Netzer, *Yehude Iran Be-Yamenu* (Jerusalem: Hebrew University of Jerusalem Press, 1981), 10.

8. For more on Loqman Nahurai, see Rahimian, "Irgun Ha-Kehila," 86–87. For Levy's account on the rift between Nahurai and Hayyim, see Levy, *Comprehensive History of the Jews*, 523–39. Also see Jaleh Pirnazar, "Yahudiyan-i Iran, Huvviyyat-i Milli va Ruznamahn-igari"; and Sanasarian, *Religious Minorities in Iran*, 180.

9. Meir Sasson, "Ha-Tziyonut ve-Ha-'aliya," in *Iran*, ed. Haim Saadoun (Jerusalem: Yad Ben-Zvi, 2005), 160–61.

10. Amnon Netzer, "Shemuel Haim," in Sarshar, *Jewish Communities of Iran*, 406–7.

11. Thirty thousand Iranian Jews left for Israel during those years, and an additional seventeen thousand Iraqi Jews passed through Iran en route to the same destination. Ezri, *Mi Va-Khem Mi-Kol 'Amo*, 51.

12. Interview with Pinhas, May 15, 2014.

13. The governing body of the Jewish community in Mandatory Palestine was the Jewish Agency. At the helm of the Jewish Agency was David Ben-Gurion, leader of the first incarnation of the current Israeli Labor Party (originally referred to as MAPAI). Solel Boneh became an essential part of the Israeli project of state building after 1948 and continued working in Iran and elsewhere through 1979. Yehouda Shenhav, "The Phenomenology of Colonialism and the Politics of 'Difference': European Zionist Emissaries and Arab-Jews in Colonial Abadan," *Social Identities* 8, no. 4 (December 2002): 521–44.

14. *Yishuv* (Hebrew: settlement) refers to the community of Jewish residents in Mandatory Palestine under the leadership of the Jewish Agency. The term, introduced in the 1880s, denotes those Jews living in the land of Israel before 1948.

15. A wide swath of literature exists on the origins of the Zionist movement in the context of European modernism and colonialism and in regard to Mizrahi Jews (Jews of the Middle East and North Africa). For example, Theodor Herzl, founding father of Zionism, alludes to the model, utopian society as essentially European (including spoken language, education, and culture). For more, see Theodor Herzl, *The Jewish State* (New York: Dover, 1988); Theodor Herzl, *Altneuland: The Old-New-Land* (Charleston, SC: WLC, 2009); Aziza Khazzoom, *Shifting Ethnic Boundaries and Inequality in Israel: or, How the Polish Peddler Became a German Intellectual*, Studies in Social Inequality (Stanford, CA: Stanford University Press, 2008); and Haggai Ram, "Between Homeland and Exile: Iranian Jewry in Zionist/Israeli Political Thought," *British Journal of Middle Eastern Studies* 35, no. 1 (April 2008): 1–20.

16. Ram, "Between Homeland and Exile." Orit Bashkin discusses the circumstances under which the Iraqi Jews were welcomed in Israel. Large parts of this discussion remain relevant in the case of the Iranian Jews. Orit Bashkin, *Impossible Exodus: Iraqi Jews in Israel* (Stanford, CA: Stanford University Press, 2017), 3–20; Shenhav, "Phenomenology of Colonialism"; Yehouda Shenhav, *The Arab Jews: A Postcolonial Reading of Nationalism, Religion, and Ethnicity* (Stanford, CA: Stanford University Press, 2006); Ella Shohat, "The Invention of the Mizrahim," *Journal of Palestine Studies* 29, no. 1 (1999): 5–20.

17. Sasson, "Ha-Tziyonut ve-Ha-'aliya," 163.

18. "Iran-Propaganda," KKL5/17801/276-5, Central Zionist Archives (hereafter CZA), Jerusalem, Israel. *n.d.*

19. Sasson, "Ha-Tziyonut ve-Ha-ʿaliya," 166–68.

20. "Declaration of Establishment of State of Israel," *Official Gazette*, no. 1, May 14, 1948, available at Israel Ministry of Foreign Affairs, http://www.mfa.gov.il/mfa/foreign policy/peace/guide/pages/declaration%20of%20establishment%20of%20state%20of%20 israel.aspx.

21. In his monumental work on the 1948 Arab-Israeli War, Benny Morris makes a compelling case that November 30, 1947, is the actual date that war commenced, the day after the UN passed the partition plan resolution. Morris describes the period between November 1947 and May 1948 as a civil war. Benny Morris, *Righteous Victims: A History of the Zionist-Arab Conflict, 1881–2001* (New York: Vintage Books, 2001).

22. Notably, Ayatollah Abolqasim Kashani was one of the prominent politicians who tried to organize Iranian military and paramilitary assistance for Palestine. Ultimately, not even one Iranian soldier joined the belligerent parties.

23. Stanley Abramovitch, "Report on Iran and Suggestions for the Year 1953," August 1952, JDCA AR 45/54-505.

24. In 1947 Iran's Jewish population numbered one hundred thousand. Most sources suggest that between 1948 and 1951, one-third of these individuals left for Israel, whereas the aforementioned numbers actually demonstrate that only one-fifth of Iran's Jews immigrated in those years. See the annotated table in Sasson, "Ha-Tziyonut ve-Ha-ʿaliya," 169. Also see the JDC report "12,000 Iraqi Jews Passed Through Tehran," September 1950, JDCA AR 45/54-506. The JDC report suggests that between May 1948 and June 1951 only 17,919 Iranian Jews immigrated to Israel. See June 1952, JDCA AR 45/54-505.

25. *Aliyah* refers to the return of the Jewish people in diaspora to Israel. The word *Aliyah* derives from the verb meaning "to ascend" (in a spiritual sense). By immigrating to the Holy Land, one ascends in holiness; therefore, the act of "making Aliyah" is one of Zionism's basic tenets.

26. Stanley Abramovitch, JDC Tehran, to JDC Paris, November 8, 1951, JDCA 45/54-505.

27. One who makes Aliyah is referred to as *Oleh* (masc.) or *Olah* (fem.). The plural forms are *Olim* (masc.) and *Olot* (fem.).

28. In 1952 there were 4,236 Olim, and in 1953 the number declined to 1,114. From 1953 onward the numbers waned to only a few hundred every year. Sasson, "Ha-Tziyonut ve-Ha-ʿaliya," 169.

29. There are indications that political parties like the Pan-Iranist Party, along with Muslim clerics inspired by Kashani, incited violence against Jews, especially in the provinces. "Executive Committee Meeting," November 30, 1949, JDCA AR 45/54-506.

30. On migration to Tehran from the villages, see "Report on a Visit to Iran—November 8th–30th, 1948," November 29, 1948, JDCA AR 45/54-506. On anti-Jewish actions, see "Memorandum," November 30, 1949, JDCA AR 45/54-506.

31. Report, September 1950, JDCA AR 45/54-506.

32. W. G. Dildine, "Persian Moslems Join Jews as Refugees to Palestine," *Washington Post*, August 1950.

33. For a credible introduction to the Ma'abarot issue, see Bryan K. Roby, *The Mizrahi Era of Rebellion: Israel's Forgotten Civil Rights Struggle, 1948–1966* (Syracuse, NY: Syracuse University Press, 2015), 86–109.

34. Stanley Abramovitch, JDC Tehran, to JDC Paris, November 8, 1951, JDCA AR 45/54-505.

35. Stanley Abramovitch, JDC Tehran, to JDC Paris, December 9, 1951, JDCA AR 45/54-505.

36. Stanley Abramovitch, JDC Tehran, to JDC Paris, December 9, 1951, JDCA AR 45/54-505.

37. "Report on Visit to Kashan, Isfahan, Shiraz, Rafsanjan, and Yazd: December 10–December 21, 1952," JDCA AR 45/54-505. One will note that letters containing these same sentiments were sent by recent emigrants from Morocco and Iraq.

38. Stanley Abramovitch, JDC Tehran, to JDC Paris, November 8, 1951, JDCA AR 45/54-505.

39. Stanley Abramovitch, JDC Tehran, to JDC Paris, January 16, 1952, JDCA AR 45/54-505. The stream of return migration from Israel to Iran continued through the 1960s. In August 1960, about eighty families demonstrated outside the Jewish Agency's offices in Tel Aviv, demanding assistance to return to "their homeland." Protesters complained that they had been discriminated against in both housing and labor placement. Moreover, they resented the fact that while the majority of the residents of their Ma'abara from other countries had already been provided permanent housing, Persians were still living in Amishav (the name of the Ma'abara near Petah-Tikva) and had been there for over ten years. In the demonstration they held signs such as the following: "Protest against lawlessness in Israel—Long live Persia!" See Yesha'ayahu Avi'am, "80 Mishpahot mi- 'olei paras dorshot lahahziran la-moledet,'" *Ma'ariv*, August 7, 1960.

40. "Report on Visit to Kashan, Isfahan, Shiraz, Rafsanjan, and Yazd: December 10–December 21, 1952," JDCA AR 45/54-505.

41. Stanley Abramovitch, JDC Tehran, to JDC Paris, December 26, 1951, JDCA AR 45/54-505.

42. "The Persian Consulate General in Jerusalem," July 17, 1951, 345/17, Israel State Archives (hereafter ISA), Jerusalem, Israel. According to correspondence from this time, the Iranian consul notified the Israeli Ministry of Foreign Affairs that, as of July 7, 1951, the Iranian embassy in Amman would be responsible for Iranian interests in Israel and Palestine. The Iranian government also refused to pay rent for use of the consulate building, as this property had belonged to a Palestinian before 1948. Iran's position was one of protest. The Iranian consul argued that Israel owned the property illegally, having "confiscated" it from its rightful Palestinian owner.

43. The AIU was a Jewish French worldwide educational network with schools throughout the Orient, from Morocco to Iran to the Ottoman Empire (and later Turkey). The mission of this organization was to "civilize" Jews of the Orient and, through proper education, bring them culturally closer to France and Western Europe. For more about the

AIU, see Rodrigue, *Jews and Muslims*; and Aron Rodrigue, *French Jews, Turkish Jews: The Alliance Israélite Universelle and the Politics of Jewish Schooling in Turkey, 1860–1925*, Modern Jewish Experience (Bloomington: Indiana University Press, 1990). For more on the AIU specifically within the Iranian context, see Avraham Cohen, "Tmurot Mahutiyot Ba'hinikh Ha'yehudi Be'paras," in *Yehudei Iran: Avaram, Morashtam ve-Zikatam Le-Eretz Ha-Kodesh*, ed. Amnon Netzer (Holon, Israel: Beit Koresh, 1988), 68–76.

44. Habib Levy, "Report on Zionism in Iran, by Doctor Habib Levy: The Situation of the Jews in Diaspora," December 20, 1953, ISA S41/449/2.

45. "Report on Iran and Suggestions for the Year 1953: Tehran, August 1952," August 1952, JDCA AR 45/54-505 (4704).

46. Levy, "Report on Zionism in Iran."

47. Interestingly, the inclination of Jewish youths to support Tudeh and other communist or socialist organizations remained of considerable concern until 1962 (and admittedly later). Yeshayahu Haran, who worked with the Jewish Agency and World Zionist Organization as early as 1949, wrote in a 1962 letter that the "overwhelming majority of [Iranian] Jewish youth is under influence of leftist organizations, but knows nothing about ongoing [events] in Israel." Yeshayahu Haran to Mr. A. Efrat, September 26, 1962, CZA S/64/194.

48. Levy, "Report on Zionism in Iran."

49. Ezri, *Mi Va-Khem Mi-Kol 'Amo*, 60.

50. For further information regarding Mosaddeq's influence on political and social developments outside Iran, see Lior Sternfeld, "Iran Days in Egypt: Mosaddeq's Visit to Cairo in 1951," *British Journal of Middle Eastern Studies* 43, no. 1 (January 2, 2016): 1–20, https://doi.org/10.1080/13530194.2015.1060151.

51. Arab politicians pressured Mosaddeq and like-minded political colleagues, such as Ayatollah Kashani, to reverse Iranian recognition of Israel and cut all diplomatic and economic ties. For example, see Albion Ross, "Move Behind Withdrawal of Recognition of Israel: Consolidation of Arab Views on Isolationism," *Times of India*, July 6, 1951, 5.

52. While Mosaddeq took a more pragmatic approach to Israel, a number of senior members in his National Front Party opposed Israel on ideological grounds. For example, one of Mosaddeq's foreign ministers and a secular politician, Fatemi, vehemently opposed any relations between Iran and Israel. So, of course, did Kashani, who connected popular politics with religious appeal and whose powerful position as a "nationalist" cleric in many ways foreshadowed the emergence of Ruhullah Khomeini. Mosaddeq's own party, the National Front, championed a policy of national economy, asserting that the natural resources of Iran should serve Iran and not Britain or any other nation.

53. For a broader study on the Periphery Doctrine, see Yossi Alpher, *Periphery: Israel's Search for Middle East Allies* (Lanham, MD: Rowman and Littlefield, 2015).

54. Yosef Nedava, "Mosaddeq Be-doro Ke-Ahashverosh Be-doro," *Ha-Boker*, October 12, 1951.

55. Nedava, "Mosaddeq Be-doro Ke-Ahashverosh Be-doro."

56. See Joel Beinin's book for an excellent discussion on MAPAM. One can hardly overemphasize the central role this party played in the formative years of the State of

Israel. Joel Beinin, *Was the Red Flag Flying There? Marxist Politics and the Arab-Israeli Conflict in Egypt and Israel, 1948–1965* (Berkeley: University of California Press, 1990); Eli Tzur, "Mapam and the European and Oriental Immigrations," in *Israel: The First Decade of Independence*, ed. S. Ilan Troen and Noah Lucas, SUNY Series in Israeli Studies (Albany: State University of New York Press, 1995), 543–56.

57. Cable from N. Raanan and B. Qadem Sion to Executive of the Zionist Organization in Jerusalem, April 9, 1951, CZA S41/449/2.

58. "MAPAM Pe'ila . . . Gam Be-Paras," *Yedioth Ahronoth*, October 10, 1951.

59. "Israel- Iran Relations," ISA 2410/11; "Iran General," ISA 2565/24; Uri Bialer, *Oil and the Arab-Israeli Conflict, 1948–63*, St. Antony's Series (New York: St. Martin's Press in association with St. Anthony's College, Oxford, 1999), 171–93.

60. For more about the extensive military and strategic geopolitical relationship, see Trita Parsi, *Treacherous Alliance: The Secret Dealings of Israel, Iran, and the United States* (New Haven, CT: Yale University Press, 2008); and Alpher, *Periphery*; more can be found in Ezri, *Mi Va-Khem Mi-Kol 'Amo*; and Tsadok, *Yahadut Iran bi-tekufat ha-shoshelet ha-Pahlavit*.

61. Read more on Jewish education in Iran in this period in Lior Sternfeld, "Reclaiming Their Past: Writing Jewish History in Iran During the Mohammad Reza Pahlavi and Early Revolutionary Periods (1941–1989)" (PhD diss., University of Texas at Austin, 2014); Rodrigue, *French Jews, Turkish Jews*; and Avraham Cohen, "Tmurot Mahutiyot Ba'hinikh Ha'yehudi Be'paras."

62. The schools of the AIU, ORT, and Otzar Ha-Torah, as well as smaller schools, had exchanged courses and classes among the institutions. For example, AIU faculty offered language classes at ORT, Otzar Ha-Torah teachers taught language and religion classes at ORT, and the AIU received vocational training from ORT instructors. Files on ORT and the AIU can be found in JDCA AR 45/54-505.

63. It should be noted that in the late 1940s the Jewish Agency accused the JDC of anti-Zionist activity because the agency invested too much time and excessive resources in supporting Jewish life in Iran—instead of convincing Iranian Jews to relocate to Israel. Merrill A. Rosenberg, "Relations Between JDC & JA in Iran," October 16, 1974, JDCA AR 65/74-0107.

64. Avraham Cohen, "Tmurot Mahutiyot Ba'hinukh Ha'yehudi Be'paras," 75.

65. "Visit to Iran," n.d., JDCA AR 65/74-0110; "Annual Report 1969," n.d., JDCA AR 65/74-0110.

66. Ilyas Ishhaqyan, *Hamrah Ba Farhang: Gushah'i Az Tarikh-i Mu'assasah-i Alyans Dar Iran/Khatirat-i Ilyas Ish aqyan* (Los Angeles, CA: Sina, 2008), 441.

67. This was before Israel's involvement in training and collaborating with the SAVAK [*Sazman-i Ettela'at va Amniyat-i Keshvar*, Organization of National Intelligence and Security] (Iran's secret police) became public knowledge. See Ram, *Iranophobia*, 57–60; and Ezri, *Mi Va-Khem Mi-Kol 'Amo*, 61–65.

68. For example, see the following on Israel's projects in sub-Saharan Africa: Haim Yacobi, *Israel and Africa: A Genealogy of Moral Geography*, Routledge Studies in Middle Eastern Geography 1 (Abingdon, UK: Routledge, 2016).

69. For excellent analysis of Israel's projects in Qazvin, see Neta Feniger and Rachel Kallus, "Expertise in the Name of Diplomacy: The Israeli Plan for Rebuilding the Qazvin Region, Iran," *International Journal of Islamic Architecture* 5, no. 1 (March 1, 2016): 103–34, https://doi.org/10.1386/ijia.5.1.103_1. For other Israeli projects in Iran, of different nature, see Neta Feniger and Rachel Kallus, "Israeli Planning in the Shah's Iran: A Forgotten Episode," *Planning Perspectives* 30, no. 2 (April 3, 2015): 231–51, https://doi.org/10.1080/02665433.2014.933677.

70. For example, on competitions in basketball, volleyball, and table tennis between Tehran University and the Hebrew University of Jerusalem (first round in Tehran and second in Jerusalem), see Menahem Sadinsky, "Ha-universita huzmena le-hitmoded 'im michlelet Tehran," *Ma'ariv*, November 5, 1961, 15. Also see the following item on a boxing match between Tel Aviv and Tehran: "Mit'agrefei Tehran ve-Tel-Aviv itmodedu hayom be-Be'er Sheva," *Ma'ariv*, June 29, 1960, 10. The match was conducted in Beersheba.

71. Ezri, *Mi Va-Khem Mi-Kol 'Amo*, 326.

72. Michael Zand, "Ha-Dimuy Shel Ha-Yehudi Be-'eynei Ha-Iranim Le'ahar Milhemet Ha-Olam Ha-Sheniya (1945–1979)," *Pe'amim* 29 (1986): 119–26; Eldad Pardo, "Iran Ve-Yisrael: Yisrael Kemofet Be-'einei Ha-Smol Ha-Irani Be-Shnot Ha-Shishim," *'Iyunim Bitkumat Yisrael*, no. 22 (2004): 337–65.

73. Interview with Daryoush Ashouri, July 29, 2016.

74. The Kayhan Institute is a think tank and research institute affiliated with the *Kayhan International* newspaper.

75. Interview with Abolhassan Bani-Sadr, Paris, July 28, 2016.

76. Jalal Al-e Ahmad, *Occidentosis: A Plague from the West*, trans. Hamid Algar (Berkeley: Mizan, 1984).

77. Jalal Al-e Ahmad, *Safar bih vilayet-i 'Izrail* (Tehran: Intisharat-i Ravaq, 1363 [1984]), 58; my translation. See also the English translation, Jalal Al-e Ahmad, *The Israeli Republic: Jalal Al-e Ahmad, Islam, and the Jewish State*, trans. Samuel Thrope (Brooklyn, NY: Restless Books, 2017), iBook ed., 66.

78. Al-e Ahmad, *Safar bih vilayet-i 'Izrail*, 59; my translation.

79. Entry in the kibbutz guest book, 1963, p. 112, Kibbutz Ayelet Ha'Shahar Archive.

80. A vibrant discussion continues among scholars regarding whether Al-e Ahmad actually wrote the last chapter. Some argue that his brother wrote it following Al-e Ahmad's death. See the most recent translation and introduction by the translator, Samuel Thrope: Al-e Ahmad, *Israeli Republic*. Also see my detailed review of this translation: Lior Sternfeld, "The Israeli Republic, by Jalal Al-e Ahmad (2014)," Not Even Past, March 5, 2014, https://notevenpast.org/the-israeli-republic-by-jalal-al-e-ahmad-2014/.

81. Houchang E. Chehabi, "The Politics of Football in Iran," *Soccer & Society* 7, no. 2–3 (April 2006): 233–61; Houchang E. Chehabi, "Jews and Sport in Modern Iran," in *Yahudiyan-i Irani Dar Tarikh-i Mo'aser*, ed. Homa Sarshar and Houman Sarshar (Beverly Hills, CA: Center for Iranian Jewish Oral History, 2001), 4:3–24.

82. For more on this controversy, see Chehabi, "Politics of Football in Iran."

83. Secret report from Ambassador Meir Ezri to Foreign Ministry, May 28, 1968, ISA H/442/8.

84. For more about Iranian intellectuals and Zionism, see Lior Sternfeld, "Pahlavi Iran and Zionism: An Intellectual Elite's Short-Lived Love Affair with the State of Israel," Ajam Media Collective, March 7, 2013, http://ajammc.com/2013/03/07/pahlavi-iran-and-zionism -an-intellectual-elites-short-lived-love-affair-with-israel/.

85. See the documentary by director Dan Shadur in which a former security officer at the Israeli embassy recounts the screening of Israeli movies on the embassy's walls and large crowds assembling to watch. Dan Shadur, dir., *Before the Revolution: The Untold Story of the Israeli Paradise in Iran* (Tel Aviv: Heymann Brothers Films, 2013). Also see Lior Sternfeld, "'In This Room There Is No Islam': The Shah's 'Special Relationship' with Iran's Israeli Community," *+972 Magazine* (blog), June 8, 2013, http://972mag.com/in-this-room -there-is-no-islam-the-shahs-special-relationship-with-irans-israeli-community/73273/.

86. Advertisement in the author's possession.

87. Porat also performed at the Shah's palace at Prince Reza Pahlavi's birthday party. Another Israeli singer whose international career began in Tehran was Mike Brandt. Interview with Tova Porat, Israel, June 29, 2016. I thank Mrs. Porat for granting an interview and for providing this information.

88. *Halachic*: related to the Halacha, or Jewish religious laws.

89. Delegation in Tehran, ISA A/375/12/8.

90. Delegation in Tehran, ISA A/375/12/128.

91. Delegation in Tehran, ISA A/375/12/42.

92. Yossef Ness, director of the Aliyah Department in Tehran, to Tzvi Luria, chair of the Organization Department, Jewish Agency, July 30, 1961, CZA S/64/194/1106.

93. Tsadok, *Yahadut Iran bi-tekufat ha-shoshelet ha-Pahlavit*, 310–12.

94. See the letter written by Yeshayahu Haran regarding the situation of Jewish establishments in Iran: "[Zionist activists in Tehran] wrote personally to the prime minister through the Israeli embassy and asked his personal intervention. . . . It is necessary to send a [Jewish Agency] department representative; however, he must not be the member of any leftist party." Yeshayahu Haran to Mr. A. Efrat, September 26, 1962, CZA S/64/194.

95. "Minutes from Board Meeting on Haran's Visit to Iran," October 13, 1961, CZA S/64/194/A35.

96. Amir Taheri, "Iran's Minorities: The Jews," *Kayhan International*, February 8, 1969. See also embassy in Tehran to Foreign Office, February 10, 1969, ISA H/442/8/227.

Chapter 4

This chapter is partly based on these articles: Lior Sternfeld, "The Revolution's Forgotten Sons and Daughters: The Jewish Community in Tehran during the 1979 Revolution," *Iranian Studies* 47, no. 6 (November 2, 2014): 857–69, https://doi.org/10.1080/00210862.2014 .948744; and Lior Sternfeld, "Yahudiyan Faramush Shodeh-Ye Enqelab Iran," *Iran Nameh* 28, no. 4 (Winter 2013): 16–22.

1. On January 19, 2017, the Plasco Building collapsed in a tragic fire. "Tehran Fire: 20 Dead in Plasco Building Collapse," Al Jazeera, January 19, 2017, http://www.aljazeera.com /news/2017/01/tehran-fire-170119082905960.html.

2. Back in the day, before the revolution, the hospital was known as Kanun-i Kheir Khva, Kurush-i Kabir, or the Jewish Charity Hospital. It was established by Doctor Ruhollah Sapir and was named after him following the revolution, as relayed in this chapter.

3. As seen in previous chapters, Jewish Iranian historiography usually deem the Pahlavi era as a golden age, mostly because of the irrefutable progress Jews made during the reign of Mohammad Reza. This view has been reinforced by many leaders of the community, such as Kohan, who was the Jewish representative in the Majlis (1975–1979). See Yousef Kohan, *Yousef Kohan: Guzarish va Khaṭirat-i Faʿaliyatʿha-yi Siyasi va Ijtimaʿi* (Los Angeles: International Printing, 1993), 303.

4. Sanasarian, *Religious Minorities in Iran*.

5. David Menashri, "The Pahlavi Monarchy and the Islamic Revolution," in *Esther's Children: A Portrait of Iranian Jews*, ed. Houman Sarshar (Beverly Hills, CA: Center for Iranian Jewish Oral History; Philadelphia: Jewish Publication Society, 2002), 395.

6. Sitton, *Sephardi Communities Today*, 184.

7. Random anecdotal evidence appeared about Armenians protesters against the Shah's regime, but there is much yet to be studied about political communal organizations affiliated with religious minorities in this era.

8. Jeremi Suri, *Power and Protest: Global Revolution and the Rise of Detente* (Cambridge, MA: Harvard University Press, 2005), 2, 274n7.

9. Most prominent among them were Taqi Arani and Khalil Maliki, Afshin Matin-Asgari, *Iranian Student Opposition to the Shah* (Costa Mesa, CA: Mazda, 2002), 20–22.

10. Matin-Asgari, 27–28.

11. Matin-Asgari, 30.

12. Abbas Milani, *The Shah* (New York: Palgrave Macmillan, 2011), 287.

13. On the context of the global aspects of the Iranian Communist movement, see Eskandar Sadeghi-Boroujerdi, "The Origins of Communist Unity: Anti-colonialism and Revolution in Iran's Tri-continental Moment," *British Journal of Middle Eastern Studies*, August 2017, 1–27.

14. It was preceded by the formation of an inclusive governing elected body that represented the different factions. Matin-Asgari, *Iranian Student Opposition to the Shah*, 43–49.

15. Matin-Asgari, 86.

16. Interview with Mihrdad, January 22, 2013.

17. Interview with Mihrdad.

18. David Menashri, "The Jews in Iran: Between the Shah and Khomeini," in *Anti-Semitism in Times of Crisis*, ed. Sander Gilman (New York: New York University Press, 1991), 360.

19. Interview with Habib, June 24, 2013.

20. Kohan provides another account of the events, which is interesting in light of Kohan's own affiliation with the old guard and his political position:

By the spring of 1979, the legal term of the Jewish Association leadership was also coming to an end. The Jewish University Students Organizations, the youth and graduate societies had submitted a unified list of candidates among which were the names of only two members of the present Association. The rest of the Association members, those who were known as the

"National Fund Group" had produced their own list. After several meetings, seminars and other activities, finally the candidates of the former group won the majority, and the community was faced by a new Association. In the new Association, Engineer Aziz Daneshrad who had been a member of the Association in the past was elected as the Chairman. The reason for the defeat of the "National Fund Group" in a few words was that these gentlemen preferred connections over qualifications when recruiting their colleagues; instead of selecting experts and knowledgeable people they were after people who would obediently follow the head of the Fund. Also, by concentrating all the financial affairs and by controlling all the funds, they intended to ensure the obedience of all active organizations for themselves. The organizations on the other hand, and in particular the University Students and the youth, would not acquiesce anyway, and demanded that the National Fund disperse each organization's respective expenses without conditions, according to their bylaws, without interfering with the leadership and the activities of the organizations. For the extended quotations from this memoir I used translations by Faryar Nikbakht with Aziz Kohan's permission. Kohan, *Yousef Kohan*, 302.

21. Editorial, "Fa'aliyyat-i Sah Salah-i Jami'ah-i Rawshanfikran-i Kalimi-yi Iran," *Tamuz*, September 25, 1981.

22. I would like to thank Karmel Melamed for referring me to this interview and contributing his own knowledge to this research; Karmel Melamed, "Escape, Exile, Rebirth: Iranian Jewish Diaspora Alive and Well in Los Angeles," *Jewish Journal*, September 4, 2008, http://jewishjournal.com/news/los_angeles/community/65726/escape-exile-rebirth-iranian -jewish-diaspora-alive-and-well-in-los-angeles/.

23. Interview with Hushang, May 15, 2011.

24. In any case, a few months later, in the summer of 1978 they failed to be reelected. Netzer, *Yehude Iran Be-Yamenu*, 21.

25. Read more about Taliqani and his pivotal role in the revolution in: Hamid Dabashi, *Theology of Discontent* (New York: New York University Press, 1993), 216–72.

26. Netzer, *Yehude Iran Be-Yamenu*, 22; "Fa'aliyyat-i Sah Salah-i," 6.

27. Amnon Netzer, "Yehudei Iran, Yisrael, ve-Ha-Republiqah Ha-Islamit Shel Iran," *Gesher* 26 (Spring–Summer 1980): 48.

28. Netzer, 49.

29. "Ma Yahudiyan Mizrakhi Hastim va Fiqh Ghani Darim," Iranjewish.com, Summer 1388 [2009], http://www.iranjewish.com/Essay/Essay_36_mizrakhi.htm.

30. "Doktor Manuchehr Aliyasi," 7Dorim.com, accessed July 7, 2011, http://www .7dorim.com/tasavir/Namayandeh_Eliasi.asp.

31. Interview with Dr. Jalali, May 15, 2011.

32. Interview with Dr. Jalali. Kohan remembered the day very similarly. Given that Kohan was at odds with Jalali, I believe it validates the account. Kohan, *Yousef Kohan*, 312.

33. "I'zam-i Ekip-i Pizashki-yi Ayatollah Taliqani," *Kayhan International*, April 24, 1979.

34. Goel Cohen, *Az Kargaran Ta Kar-Afarini* (Geneva: Sina, 2011), 190–91.

35. Netzer, *Yehude Iran Be-Yamenu*, 22.

36. Interview with Hushang, May 15, 2011.

37. Interview with Hushang.

38. Interview with Mihrdad, January 22, 2013.

39. Goel Cohen, *Bar Bal-i Khirad*, 390.

40. Interview with Mihrdad, January 22, 2013.

41. Cohen, *Bar Bal-i Khirad*, 390.

42. Madrasah-i 'Alavi was a girls' school in Tehran. It was known to be an opposition-supporting institution. Upon his return from exile, Khomeini first resided there.

43. Interview with Habib, June 24, 2013.

44. Interview with Dr. Jalali, May 15, 2011.

45. M. Shehpar, "Bimaristan-i Sapir Dar Jarayan-i Inqilab," *Tamuz*, July 11, 1979, 1.

46. Shehpar, 4.

47. Shehpar, 4.

48. Netzer, *Yehude Iran Be-Yamenu*, 22.

49. "Nishani Az Vahdat-i Milli Dar Bimaristan-i Duktur Sapir," IranJewish.com, Esfand 1386 [February-March 2008], http://www.iranjewish.com/Essay/Essay_34_farsi _bimarestan_sepir.htm.

50. Kohan, *Yousef Kohan*, 310–11.

51. Shadur, *Before the Revolution*.

52. Interview with Mihrdad, January 22, 2013.

53. Golisurkhi was identified with some of the guerilla movements. His trial was televised and had a tremendous impact on the young revolutionaries. His iconic image became one of the symbols of the revolution. Read more about him in Behrooz, *Rebels with a Cause*, 69–70.

54. Interview with Dr. Jalali, May 15, 2011.

55. Interview with Simin, March 27, 2011.

56. I am thankful to Rabbi Dr. Oren Steinitz for his advice and clarification on this important issue.

57. "Mas'ulin-i Bimaristan-i Doktor Sapir dar jalasat-i haftagi-yi Jami'ah-yi Rawshan-fikran-yi Yahudi-yi Iran," *Tamuz*, January 28, 1982, 7.

58. The Mujahidin-i Khalq had gone through several organizational changes from its beginning to its modern-day (or even post-1977) structure. The movement was part of the Liberation Front of Iran, and its ideology and activity were inspired by numerous political movements that preceded its appearance. Bazargan and Taliqani were influenced by the National Front of Mosaddeq. For more on the ideology and genealogy of the movement, see Houchang E. Chehabi, *Iranian Politics and Religious Modernism: The Liberation Movement of Iran Under the Shah and Khomeini* (Ithaca, NY: Cornell University Press, 1990), 210–13.

59. Zabih, *The Left in Contemporary Iran*, 69–119.

60. As Mihrdad said in his interview, this generation sought to break the boundaries of the community, and many of them dated and got married to partners outside the community, mostly Muslims. Interview with Mihrdad, January 22, 2013.

61. "Ms. Edna Sabet—Iran Human Rights Memorial," Human Rights & Democracy for Iran, accessed November 13, 2013, http://www.iranrights.org/english/memorial-case —4056.php.

62. Email correspondence with Parvin, July 16, 2012.

63. See also Jaleh Pirnazar's thoughtful comments about Sabet and other marginalized Jewish political activists in Iranian (and Jewish) historiography: Jaleh Pirnazar, "Voices of Marginality: Diversity in Jewish Iranian Women's Memoirs and Beyond," in *The Jews of Iran: The History, Religion, and Culture of a Community in the Islamic World*, ed. Houman M. Sarshar, International Library of Iranian Studies 53 (London: Tauris, 2014), 201.

64. Theda Skocpol, *States and Social Revolutions: A Comparative Analysis of France, Russia, and China* (Cambridge: Cambridge University Press, 1979), 171.

65. Trita Parsi beautifully describes the gaps between the harsh rhetoric of the revolutionary government and its eventual deeds, both domestically and internationally. Although Iran was the most vocal supporter of the Palestinian cause, this rhetoric was seldom followed up by actions. Also, despite calling the US and Israel "Big Satan" and "Small Satan," respectively, Iran continued to deal with both when the regime considered it beneficial for its long-term policies. Moreover, Parsi shows that Israel and pro-Israel lobbyists in the US persistently pled policy makers to ignore the Iranian rhetoric and to evaluate only its actions. Trita Parsi, *Treacherous Alliance: The Secret Dealings of Israel, Iran, and the United States* (New Haven, CT: Yale University Press, 2008).

66. Menashri, "Pahlavi Monarchy," 396.

67. Netzer, *Yehude Iran Be-Yamenu*, 22.

68. Ovadia Yosef was born in Baghdad under the name Abdallah Yosef. After his tenure as Israel's chief Sephardi rabbi, he established and became the spiritual leader of the Shas Party, the main political organization of Sephardi religious Jews in Israel. As the spiritual leader of Shas, he issued a religious ruling in support of Prime Minister Yitzhak Rabin and his peace negotiations with the Palestinians. He passed away in Jerusalem in 2013.

69. Netzer, *Yehude Iran Be-Yamenu*, 24.

70. Israel is the only the place that we can speak of as demonstrating a systematic overlapping of Judaism and Zionism.

71. It should be noted that Elqaniyan was arrested for the first time in 1975, well before the revolution. Back then he was arrested, as part of the Shah's antiprofiting campaign, for currency manipulation and overcharging for goods. Abrahamian, *Iran Between Two Revolutions*, 497–98.

72. Editorial, "Imam: Hisab-i jami'ah-i yahud ghayr az jami'ah-i sahyunist ast," *Ittila'at*, May 14, 1979, 5.

73. Editorial, "Sahyunism barayi yahudiyan-i irani ashk-i timsah mirizad," *Ittila'at*, May 14, 1979, 3.

74. Netzer, *Yehude Iran Be-Yamenu*, 26.

75. Interview with Mihrdad, January 22, 2013.

76. "Darbarih-yi Mizgard Tilivizyuni," *Tamuz*, July 4, 1979.

77. "Darbarih-yi Mizgard Tilivizyuni."

78. Interview with Ishaq, October 3, 2012.

79. "Darbarih-yi Mizgard Tilivizyuni."

80. Later, Daneshrad explained the connections between Zionism and world imperialism: "The truth is that Zionism is part of the system of world imperialism that works to

secure global capitalism through the means of Zionist capitalists. As a result Zionism today is both colonialist and servant of the American imperialism." "Darbarih-Yi Mizgard Tilivizyuni."

81. "Dabirkhanih-i Majlis-i Khibrigan-i Rahbari: Khibrigan-i Tadvin-i Qanun-i Assasi," Majleskhobaregan.ir, accessed June 15, 2014, http://www.majleskhobregan.ir/fa/tadvinGhanon.html.

82. Afary, *Iranian Constitutional Revolution*.

83. 'Aziz Daneshrad, "Nazariyat-i Jami'iah Rawshanfikran Yahudi Iran Dar Barayi Qanun-i Asasi," *Tamuz*, July 4, 1979.

84. Daneshrad, "Nazariyat-i Jami'iah Rawshanfikran Yahudi Iran Dar Barayi Qanun-i Asasi." It became Article 64 of the constitution in its final form. That article reads,

> There are to be two hundred seventy members of the Islamic Consultative Assembly which, keeping in view the human, political, geographic and other similar factors, may increase by not more than twenty for each ten-year period from the date of the national referendum of the year 1368 [1989] of the solar Islamic calendar. The Zoroastrians and Jews will each elect one representative; Assyrian and Chaldean Christians will jointly elect one representative; and Armenian Christians in the north and those in the south of the country will each elect one representative. The limits of the election constituencies and the number of representatives will be determined by the law. (*Constitution of the Islamic Republic of Iran* [Tehran: Islamic Consultative Assembly, 1980]).

Daneshrad refers in his article in *Tamuz* to that constitutional article. See also the protocols of the constitutional assembly regarding this article: Sayyid Javvad Vari'i, *Mabani va Mustanidat Qanun-i Asasi Bih Rivayat Qanunguzar* (Qum, Iran: Intisharat-i Dabirkhanah-i Majlis-i Khibrigan-i Rahbari, 1385 [2006]), 389–93.

85. Interview with Mihrdad, January 22, 2013.

86. See, for example, the discussion of the debates over Article 43 in the section "Economy and Financial Affairs," in Vari'i, *Mabani va Mustanidat Qanun-i Asasi Bih Rivayat Qanunguzar*, 311–24.

87. Sanasarian also shows that during the period of the constitutional assembly, both Ayatollah Hossein Ali Muntaziri and Ayatollah Taliqani made clear in their Friday sermons that Jews are an integral part of Iranian society and that any criticism should be directed at Israel and Zionism and not Iranian Jews. Sanasarian, *Religious Minorities in Iran*, 63–64; Vari'i, *Mabani va Mustanidat Qanun-i Asasi Bih Rivayat Qanunguzar*, 232–35.

88. "Muhajirat Ma'akus Az Israil: Sahyunist'ha Dar bayn-i Bast-i Kamil," *Tamuz*, November 19, 1981.

89. "Bimunasibat-i Ruz-i Quds: I'ilmiya Jami'ah-yi Rawshanfikran-i Yahudi Iran," *Tamuz*, July 29, 1981.

90. "Nasl-i javan-i kalimi-yi Iran bidar shudah ast," *Tamuz*, May 6, 1982, 3.

91. Approximately fifteen Jews were killed in the war with Iraq. Maryam Sinaiee, "Iran's Jews Feel Very Much at Home," *The National*, October 7, 2008, http://www.thenational.ae/news/world/middle-east/irans-jews-feel-very-much-at-home.

92. Vizarat-i farhang va irshad islami- Dabirkhaneh-yi shura-yi hamahangi va nizarat bar amr tarvij farhang isar va shahadat, *Yadnameh-Yi Hamvatanaan-i Bargozide-Yi*

Isaargar-i Masihi, Zartushti va Kalimi (Tehran: Vizarat-i farhang va irshad islami, 1390 [2011]), 47–54.

93. The construction of the complex began in 1972 and ended in 1979, just after the revolution. Feniger and Kallus, "Israeli Planning."

94. See Parsi's excellent account of this period: Parsi, *Treacherous Alliance*, 91–126.

95. The story with some of the ethnic minorities was different. Many of the members of the postrevolutionary clerical elite were Azeris, a group that flourished in the new society. Among them one can find the current supreme leader, Sayyid 'Ali Khamenei, and the prime minister during the war with Iraq, Mir Husayn Musavi.

Postscript

1. Peterson, "In Ahmadinejad's Iran, Jews Still Find a Space."

2. Sanasarian, *Religious Minorities in Iran*, 44.

3. This is not the only Jewish publication in postrevolutionary Iran. Still today, the Jewish Students' Association of Iran publishes *Parvaz*, which deals with a wide range of topics that Jewish Iranian students can relate to, providing coverage of community events, political debates, and women's rights in Judaism and even publishing critiques of books, movies, and music.

4. See reports on this visit and excerpts of the speeches by the Jewish dignitaries and President Khatami: "Arash Abaie—Visit to the Tehran Synagogue," *Nahum Goldmann Fellowship Alumni Magazine*, accessed February 19, 2017, http://members.ngfp.org/Month /Month_Item.2004-03-26.0421.

5. Yoav Stern, "Katsav Greets Assad, Iran's Khatami During Pope's Funeral," *Haaretz*, April 8, 2005, http://www.haaretz.com/news/katsav-greets-assad-iran-s-khatami-during -pope-s-funeral-1.155501; Associated Press, "Iranian President Denies Israeli Handshake," NBC News, April 9, 2005, http://www.nbcnews.com/id/7443548/ns/world_news/t/iranian -president-denies-israeli-handshake/.

6. John F. Burns, "Arrests Shake Ancient Roots of Iran's Jews," *New York Times*, October 17, 1999, http://www.nytimes.com/1999/10/17/world/arrests-shake-ancient-roots-of -iran-s-jews.html.

7. Ewen MacAskill, Simon Tisdall, and Robert Tait, "Lone Jewish MP Confronts Ahmadinejad on Holocaust but Stresses Loyalty to Iran," *Guardian*, June 27, 2006, https:// www.theguardian.com/world/2006/jun/28/iran.israel.

8. In a number of televised interviews (the first cited here was with Piers Morgan), Ahmadinejad reiterated that his position is against Israel and not against Jews. He said that he would not have issues with his children marrying Jews. *Piers Morgan Tonight*, "Interview with Iranian President Mahmoud Ahmadinejad," RealClearPolitics, September 24, 2012, http://www.realclearpolitics.com/articles/2012/09/24/interview_with _iranian_president_mahmoud_ahmadinejad_115574.html ; Mark Hughes, "Mahmoud Ahmadinejad: 'I Would Have No Problem with Children Marrying a Jew,'" *Telegraph*, September 24, 2012, http://www.telegraph.co.uk/news/worldnews/middleeast/iran /9563627/Mahmoud-Ahmadinejad-I-would-have-no-problem-with-children-marrying-a -Jew.html.

9. Charly Wegman, "Peres Says Attack on Iran 'More and More Likely,'" Mail & Guardian, November 6, 2011, http://mg.co.za/article/2011-11-06-peres-says-attack-on-iran -more-and-likely/.

10. Tara Mahtafar, "Q&A | Meir Javedanfar: How Israelis (Including Iranian Israelis) Read Iran," Frontline—Tehran Bureau, May 23, 2012, http://www.pbs.org/wgbh/pages /frontline/tehranbureau/2012/05/qa-meir-javedanfar-how-israelis-including-iranian -israelis-read-iran.html; Jasmin Ramsey, "Poll: More Israelis Oppose Military Attack on Iran, View Obama Favorably," LobeLog, November 30, 2012, http://lobelog.com/poll -more-israelis-oppose-military-attack-on-iran-view-obama-favorably/ ; Michael Car- michael, "Poll: Majority of Jewish Israelis Oppose Attack on Iran," Global Research, August 16, 2012, http://www.globalresearch.ca/poll-majority-of-jewish-israelis-oppose -attack-on-iran/32378; Shibley Telhami, "Israeli Public Opinion After the November 2012 Gaza War," Brookings (blog), November 30, 2001, https://www.brookings.edu/on-the -record/israeli-public-opinion-after-the-november-2012-gaza-war/. Also see this story and video of Iranian Israelis in Little Tehran in Tel Aviv and their perspective on the relations between Israel and Iran: Fionnuala Sweeney, "Iranian Jews in Israel Wary, Hoping for the Best," CNN, March 5, 2012, http://www.cnn.com/2012/03/05/world/meast/iranian -jews-israel/.

11. Hassan Rouhani (@HassanRouhani), "As the sun is about to set here in #Tehran I wish all Jews, especially Iranian Jews, a blessed Rosh Hashanah," Twitter, September 4, 2013, https://twitter.com/hassanrouhani/status/375278962718412800?lang=en; Hassan Rouhani (@HassanRouhani), "May our shared Abrahamic roots deepen respect & bring peace & mutual understanding. L'Shanah Tovah. #RoshHashanah," Twitter, Septem- ber 13, 2015, https://twitter.com/hassanrouhani/status/643067027389837312?lang=en.

12. Javad Zarif (@JZarif), "Happy Rosh Hashanah," Twitter, September 4, 2013, https://twitter.com/jzarif/status/375617854214660097?lang=en ; Javad Zarif (@JZarif), "@sfpelosi Iran never denied it. The man who was perceived to be denying it is now gone. Happy New Year," Twitter, September 5, 2013, https://twitter.com/jzarif/status /375617854214660097?lang=en.

13. Reuters, "Benjamin Netanyahu to Warn Barack Obama Not to Trust Iran 'Smiles,'" Telegraph, September 30, 2013, http://www.telegraph.co.uk/news/worldnews/middleeast /iran/10343904/Benjamin-Netanyahu-to-warn-Barack-Obama-not-to-trust-Iran-smiles .html.

14. Barak Ravid, "Iran: We Saved the Jews Three Times; Netanyahu Should Learn His- tory," Haaretz, March 5, 2015, http://www.haaretz.com/israel-news/1.645497.

15. Larry Cohler-Esses, "How Iran's Jews Survive in Mullahs' World," Forward, Au- gust 18, 2015, http://forward.com/news/319269/irans-jews-win-secure-place-in-mullahs -world-with-strings-attached/. See also Steve Inskeep, "Iran's Jews: It's Our Home and We Plan to Stay," NPR, February 19, 2015, http://www.npr.org/sections/parallels/2015/02/19 /387265766/irans-jews-its-our-home-and-we-plan-to-stay.

16. "Rouhani Accommodates Iran's Jewish Students," Al-Monitor, February 17, 2015, http://www.al-monitor.com/pulse/originals/2015/02/iran-hassan-rouhani-iranian-jews .html.

17. "Runmai-Yi Az Bina-Yi Yadbud Shohada-Yi Kalimi Dar Bihishtiyeh-i Tihran (ISNA; Iranian Students News Agency)," text, ایسنا, December 15, 2014, http://www.isna .ir/photo/93092414438/رونمایی-از-بنای-یادبود-شهدای-کلیمی-در-بهشتیه-تهران.

18. The Knesset Website provides the official text of the law as appears now in the Israeli law book, "Day to Mark the Departure and Expulsion of Jews from the Arab Countries and Iran," http://fs.knesset.gov.il//19/law/19_lsr_303812.pdf.

19. See http://www.regthink.org/articles/שכתוב-ההסטוריה-של-יהודי-איראן; http://main .knesset.gov.il/Activity/plenum/Pages/SessionItem.aspx?itemID=2014402; http://www .knesset.gov.il/laws/data/law/2457/2457_2.pdf.

Bibliography

Archives

American Jewish Joint Distribution Committee Archives (JDCA), New York, NY
Center for Iranian Jewish Oral History (CIJOH), Los Angeles, CA
Central Zionist Archives (CZA), Jerusalem, Israel
International Red Cross Archives (CICR), Geneva, Switzerland
Israel State Archives (ISA), Jerusalem, Israel
Majlis Library (Kitabkhanih-yi Majlis), Tehran, Iran
National Archives, College Park, MD
National Archives (TNA), Kew, England
Presbyterian Historical Society, Philadelphia, PA

Periodicals and Newspapers

Persian

'Alim-i Yahud (Tehran)
Andishah va-Hunar (Tehran)
Bani-Adam (Tehran)
Daniyal (Tehran)
Gozaresh (Tehran)
Ittila'at (Tehran)
Ittila'at Haftegi (Tehran)
Kaviyan (Tehran)
Kayhan (Tehran)
Nissan (Tehran)
Parvaz (Tehran)
Tamuz (Tehran)
Ofeq Bina (Tehran)

Hebrew
Davar (Tel Aviv)
Ha'aretz (Tel Aviv)
Ha-Boker (Tel Aviv)
Yedioth Ahronoth (Tel Aviv)

English
Forward (New York)
Jerusalem Post (Jerusalem)
Kayhan International (Tehran)
London Times (London)
National Geographic (Washington, DC)
New York Times (New York)
Telegraph (London)
Times of India (Mumbai)
Times of Israel (Jerusalem)
Washington Post (Washington, DC)

Secondary Sources

Abadi, Jacob. *Israel's Quest for Recognition and Acceptance in Asia: Garrison State Diplomacy*. Israeli History, Politics, and Society 34. London: Frank Cass, 2004.

Abrahamian, Ervand. *The Coup: 1953, the CIA, and the Roots of Modern U.S.-Iranian Relations*. New York: New Press, 2013.

———. *Iran Between Two Revolutions*. Princeton, NJ: Princeton University Press, 1982.

Afary, Janet. "Foundations for Religious Reform in the First Pahlavi Era." *Iran Nameh* 30, no. 3 (Fall 2015): 46–87.

———. "From Outcastes to Citizens: Jews in Qajar Iran." In *Esther's Children: A Portrait of Iranian Jews*, edited by Houman Sarshar, 137–74. Beverly Hills, CA: Center for Iranian Jewish Oral History; Philadelphia: Jewish Publication Society, 2002.

———. *The Iranian Constitutional Revolution, 1906–1911: Grassroots Democracy, Social Democracy and the Origins of Feminism*. New York: Columbia University Press, 1996.

Al-e Ahmad, Jalal. *The Israeli Republic*. Translated by Samuel Thrope. New York: Restless Books, 2013.

———. *Occidentosis: A Plague from the West*. Translated by Hamid Algar. Berkeley: Mizan, 1984.

———. *Safar bih vilayet-i 'Izrail*. Tehran: Intisharat-i Ravaq, 1363 [1984].

'Alim-i Yahud. "Niku Karan Israil Ra Bishnasid." June 3, 1945.

Alpher, Yossi. *Periphery: Israel's Search for Middle East Allies*. Lanham, MD: Rowman and Littlefield, 2015.

Amanat, Abbas. *Iran: A Modern History*. New Haven, CT: Yale University Press, 2017.

Amanat, Mehrdad. *Jewish Identities in Iran: Resistance and Conversion to Islam and the Baha'i Faith*. Library of Modern Religion 9. London: I. B. Tauris, 2011.

Associated Press. "Iranian President Denies Israeli Handshake." NBC News, April 9, 2005. http://www.nbcnews.com/id/7443548/ns/world_news/t/iranian-president-denies -israeli-handshake/.

Azimi, Fakhreddin. *Iran: The Crisis of Democracy: From the Exile of Reza Shah to the Fall of Musaddiq*. London: I. B. Tauris, 2009.

Bakhash, Shaul. "Britain and the Abdication of Reza Shah." *Middle Eastern Studies* 52, no. 2 (March 3, 2016): 318–34.

———. "'Dear Anthony,' 'Dear Leo': Britain's Quixotic Flirtation with Dynastic Change in Iran During World War II." *Iran Nameh* 30, no. 4 (2016): 24–37.

Baron, Salo. "Ghetto and Emancipation: Shall We Revise the Traditional View?" *Menorah Journal* 14, no. 6 (1928): 515–26.

Bashkin, Orit. *Impossible Exodus: Iraqi Jews in Israel*. Stanford, CA: Stanford University Press, 2017.

———. "The Middle Eastern Shift and Provincializing Zionism." *International Journal of Middle East Studies* 46, no. 3 (August 2014): 577–80.

———. *New Babylonians: A History of Jews in Modern Iraq*. Stanford, CA: Stanford University Press, 2012.

Bauman, Zygmunt. *Modernity and the Holocaust*. Ithaca, NY: Cornell University Press, 1989.

Beaupré-Stankiewicz, Irena, Danuta Waszczuk-Kamieniecka, and Jadwiga Lewicka-Howells, eds. *Isfahan—City of Polish Children*. Sussex: Association of Former Pupils of Polish Schools, Isfahan and Lebanon, 1989.

Becker, Adam H. *Revival and Awakening: American Evangelical Missionaries in Iran and the Origins of Assyrian Nationalism*. Chicago: University of Chicago Press, 2015.

Behrooz, Maziar. *Rebels with a Cause: The Failure of the Left in Iran*. London: I. B. Tauris, 1999.

Beinin, Joel. *The Dispersion of Egyptian Jewry: Culture, Politics, and the Formation of a Modern Diaspora*. Contraversions 11. Berkeley: University of California Press, 1998.

———. *Was the Red Flag Flying There? Marxist Politics and the Arab-Israeli Conflict in Egypt and Israel, 1948–1965*. Berkeley: University of California Press, 1990.

Bharier, Julian. "A Note on the Population of Iran, 1900–1966." *Population Studies* 22, no. 2 (July 1, 1968): 273–79. https://doi.org/10.2307/2173024.

Bialer, Uri. *Oil and the Arab-Israeli Conflict, 1948–63*. St. Antony's Series. New York: St. Martin's Press in association with St. Anthony's College, Oxford, 1999.

Boum, Aomar. *Memories of Absence: How Muslims Remember Jews in Morocco*. Stanford, CA: Stanford University Press, 2013.

———. "'The Virtual Genizah': Emerging North African Jewish and Muslim Identities Online." *International Journal of Middle East Studies* 46, no. 3 (August 2014): 597–601.

Burns, John F. "Arrests Shake Ancient Roots of Iran's Jews." *New York Times*, October 17, 1999. http://www.nytimes.com/1999/10/17/world/arrests-shake-ancient-roots-of-iran-s -jews.html.

Campos, Michelle U. "Between Others and Brothers." *International Journal of Middle East Studies* 46, no. 3 (August 2014): 585–88.

————. *Ottoman Brothers: Muslims, Christians, and Jews in Early Twentieth-Century Palestine*. Stanford, CA: Stanford University Press, 2011.

Carmichael, Michael. "Poll: Majority of Jewish Israelis Oppose Attack on Iran." *Global Research*, August 16, 2012. http://www.globalresearch.ca/poll-majority-of-jewish-israelis-oppose-attack-on-iran/32378.

Chaquèri, Cosroe. "Did the Soviets Play a Role in Founding the Tudeh Party in Iran?" *Cahiers du Monde Russe* 40, no. 3 (July 1, 1999): 497–528. https://doi.org/10.2307/20171142.

————. *The Soviet Socialist Republic of Iran, 1920–1921: Birth of the Trauma*. Pitt Series in Russian and East European Studies 21. Pittsburgh: University of Pittsburgh Press, 1995.

Chehabi, Houchang E. "Iran and Iraq: Intersocietal Linkages and Secular Nationalisms." In *Iran Facing Others: Identity Boundaries in a Historical Perspective*, edited by Abbas Amanat and Farzin Vejdani, 193–220. New York: Palgrave Macmillan, 2012.

————. *Iranian Politics and Religious Modernism: The Liberation Movement of Iran Under the Shah and Khomeini*. Ithaca, NY: Cornell University Press, 1990.

————. "Jews and Sport in Modern Iran." In *Yahudiyan-i Irani Dar Tarikh-i Mu'asir*, edited by Homa Sarshar and Houman Sarshar, 4:3–24. Beverly Hills, CA: Center for Iranian Jewish Oral History; Philadelphia: Jewish Publication Society, 2001.

————. "The Politics of Football in Iran." *Soccer & Society* 7, no. 2–3 (April 2006): 233–61.

Cohen, Avraham. "Iranian Jewry and the Educational Enterprise of Alliance Israélite Universelle" (in Hebrew). *Pe'amim* 22 (1985): 93–125.

————. "'Maktab': The Jewish 'Heder' in Persia" (in Hebrew). *Pe'amim* 14 (1982): 57–76.

————. "Tmurot Mahutiyot Ba'hinikh Ha'yehudi Be'paras." In *Yehudei Iran: Avaram, Morashtam ve-Zikatam Le-Eretz Ha-Kodesh*, edited by Amnon Netzer, 68–76. Holon, Israel: Beit Koresh, 1988.

Cohen, Goel. *Az Kargaran Ta Kar Afarini*. Geneva: Sina, 2011.

————, ed. *Bar Bal-i Khirad: Jami'ah-i Yahudiyan-i Iran va Haftad Sal Rahbari-Yi Mazhabi, Gam Bah Gam Ba Hakham Yedidiya Shofet Dar Kashan, Tehran, va Los Angeles*. Los Angeles: Educational Foundation of Hacham Yedidia Shofet, 2010.

Cohen, Julia Phillips. *Becoming Ottomans: Sephardi Jews and Imperial Citizenship in the Modern Era*. Oxford: Oxford University Press, 2014.

Cohen, Mark R. "Islam and the Jews: Myth, Counter-myth, History." *Jerusalem Quarterly* 38 (1986): 125–37.

Cohler-Esses, Larry. "How Iran's Jews Survive in Mullahs' World." *Forward*, August 18, 2015. http://forward.com/news/319269/irans-jews-win-secure-place-in-mullahs-world-with-strings-attached/.

Constitution of the Islamic Republic of Iran. Tehran: Islamic Consultative Assembly, 1980.

Dabashi, Hamid. *Theology of Discontent*. New York: New York University Press, 1993.

"Dabirkhanih Majlis Khabargan Rahbari: Khabragan-i Tadvin Qanun-i Assasi." Majleskhobaregan.ir, Accessed June 15, 2014. http://www.majleskhobregan.ir/fa/tadvin Ghanon.html.

Dallalfar, Arlene. "Iraqi Jews in Iran." In *Esther's Children: A Portrait of Iranian Jews*, edited by Houman Sarshar, 277–81. Beverly Hills, CA: Center for Iranian Jewish Oral History; Philadelphia: Jewish Publication Society, 2002.

Damandan, Parisa. *Portrait Photographs from Isfahan: Faces in Transition, 1920–1950*. London: Saqi; The Hague: Prince Claus Fund Library, 2004.

Daneshrad, Aziz. "Nazariyat-i Jami'iah Rawshanfikran Yahudi Iran Dar Barayi Qanun-i Asasi." *Tamuz*, July 4, 1979.

Devji, Faisal. *Muslim Zion: Pakistan as a Political Idea*. Cambridge, MA: Harvard University Press, 2013.

"Doktor Manuchehr Aliyasi." 7Dorim.com, Accessed July 7, 2011. http://www.7dorim.com/tasavir/Namayandeh_Eliasi.asp.

Elling, Rasmus Christian. *Minorities in Iran: Nationalism and Ethnicity After Khomeini*. New York: Palgrave Macmillan, 2013.

Engel, David. *Facing a Holocaust: The Polish Government-in-Exile and the Jews, 1943–1945*. Chapel Hill: University of North Carolina Press, 1993.

Eshaqian, Elias. *Hamrah Ba Farhang: Gushah'i Az Tarikh-i Mu'assasah-i Alyans Dar Iran/ Khatirat-i Ilyas Ishaqyan*. Los Angeles: Sina, 2008.

Eskandari, Iraj, Babak Amir Khusravi, and Faridun Azamur. *Khatirat-i Siyasi*. France, 1336 [1957].

Ezri, Meir. *Mi Va-Khem Mi-Kol 'Amo*. Or Yehuda, Israel: Hed Arzi, Sifriyat Ma'ariv, 2001.

Farhoumand, Iraj. "Iraniyan-i Yahudi va Hizb-i Tudah-i Iran." In *Yahudiyan-i Irani Dar Tarikh-i Mu'asir*, edited by Homa Sarshar, 107–34. Beverly Hills, CA: Center for Iranian Jewish Oral History; Philadelphia: Jewish Publication Society, 2000.

Faruqi, Anwar. "Forgotten Polish Exodus to Persia." *Washington Post*, November 23, 2000. https://www.washingtonpost.com/archive/politics/2000/11/23/forgotten-polish-exodus-to-persia/2b106c08-e61c-4c36-8102-fb2e114c9bff/.

Feniger, Neta, and Rachel Kallus. "Expertise in the Name of Diplomacy: The Israeli Plan for Rebuilding the Qazvin Region, Iran." *International Journal of Islamic Architecture* 5, no. 1 (March 1, 2016): 103–34. https://doi.org/10.1386/ijia.5.1.103_1.

———. "Israeli Planning in the Shah's Iran: A Forgotten Episode." *Planning Perspectives* 30, no. 2 (April 3, 2015): 231–51. https://doi.org/10.1080/02665433.2014.933677.

Gershoni, Israel, ed. *Arab Responses to Fascism and Nazism: Attraction and Repulsion*. Austin: University of Texas Press, 2014.

Gershoni, Israel, and James Jankowski. *Confronting Fascism in Egypt: Dictatorship Versus Democracy in the 1930s*. Stanford, CA: Stanford University Press, 2010.

Ginat, Rami. *A History of Egyptian Communism: Jews and Their Compatriots in Quest of Revolution*. Boulder, CO: Lynne Rienner, 2011.

———. "Jewish Identities in the Arab Middle East: The Case of Egypt in Retrospect." *International Journal of Middle East Studies* 46, no. 3 (August 2014): 593–96.

Greely, John N. "Iran in Wartime: Through Fabulous Persia, Hub of the Middle East, Americans, Britons, and Iranians Keep Sinews of War Moving to the Embattled Soviet Union." *National Geographic Magazine*, August 1943. http://tinyurl.galegroup.com/tinyurl/6NwYC4.

Green, Nile. "Fordist Connections: The Automotive Integration of the United States and Iran." *Comparative Studies in Society and History* 58, no. 2 (April 2016): 290–321. https://doi.org/10.1017/S0010417516000086.

Gribetz, Jonathan Marc. "'To the Arab Hebrew': On Possibilities and Impossibilities." *International Journal of Middle East Studies* 46, no. 3 (August 2014): 589–92.

Gross, Jan Tomasz. *Revolution from Abroad: The Soviet Conquest of Poland's Western Ukraine and Western Belorussia.* Expanded ed. Princeton, NJ: Princeton University Press, 2002.

Grossmann, Atina. "Remapping Relief and Rescue: Flight, Displacement, and International Aid for Jewish Refugees During World War II." *New German Critique* 117, vol. 39, no. 3 (Fall 2012): 61–79.

———. "Remapping Survival: Jewish Refugees and Lost Memories of Displacement, Trauma, and Rescue in Soviet Central Asia, Iran, and India." *Simon Dubnow Institute Yearbook* 15 (2016): 71–100.

———. "Versions of Home: German Jewish Refugee Papers out of the Closet and into the Archives." *New German Critique* 90 (Autumn 2003): 95–122.

Guttstadt, Corry. *Turkey, the Jews, and the Holocaust.* First English-language ed. Cambridge: Cambridge University Press, 2013.

Hamadani, Mushfiq. *Khatirat-i Nim-i Qarn-i Ruznamahnigari.* n.p., 1370 [1991].

Hanley, Will. "Grieving Cosmopolitanism in Middle East Studies." *History Compass* 6, no. 5 (September 2008): 1346–67. https://doi.org/10.1111/j.1478-0542.2008.00545.x.

Herf, Jeffrey. *Nazi Propaganda for the Arab World.* New Haven, CT: Yale University Press, 2010.

Herzl, Theodor. *Altneuland: The Old-New-Land.* Charleston, SC: WLC, 2009.

———. *The Jewish State.* New York: Dover, 1988.

Hughes, Mark. "Mahmoud Ahmadinejad: 'I Would Have No Problem with Children Marrying a Jew.'" *Telegraph*, September 24, 2012. http://www.telegraph.co.uk/news/worldnews/middleeast/iran/9563627/Mahmoud-Ahmadinejad-I-would-have-no-problem-with-children-marrying-a-Jew.html.

Inskeep, Steve. "Iran's Jews: It's Our Home and We Plan to Stay." NPR, February 19, 2015. http://www.npr.org/sections/parallels/2015/02/19/387265766/irans-jews-its-our-home-and-we-plan-to-stay.

Ittila'at. "Imam: Hisab-i Jami'ah-i Yahud Ghayr Az Jami'ah-i Sahyunist Ast." Editorial, May 14, 1979.

———. "Sahyunism Barayi Yahudiyan-i Irani Ashk-i Timsah Mirizad." Editorial, May 14, 1979.

Jacobson, Abigail, and Moshe Naor. *Oriental Neighbors: Middle Eastern Jews and Arabs in Mandatory Palestine.* Waltham, MA: Brandeis University Press, 2016.

Ja'fari, 'Abd al-Rahim. *Dar Justuju-yi Subh: Khatirat-i 'Abd al-Rahim Ja'fari, Bunyangu-zar-i Mu'assisah-i Intisharat-i Amir Kabir.* Tehran: Ruzbihan, 2004.

Jenkins, Jennifer. "Excavating Zarathustra: Ernst Herzfeld's Archaeological History of Iran." *Iranian Studies* 45, no. 1 (January 2012): 1–27.

———. "Experts, Migrants, Refugees: Making the German Colony in Iran, 1900–1934." In *German Colonialism in a Global Age*, edited by Bradley Naranch and Goeff Eley, 147–69. Durham, NC: Duke University Press, 2014.

———. "Hjalmar Schacht, Reza Shah, and Germany's Presence in Iran." *Iran Nameh* 30, no. 1 (Spring 2015): 20–46.

————. "Iran in the Nazi New Order, 1933–1941." *Iranian Studies* 49, no. 5 (September 2, 2016): 727–51.

Judt, Tony, and Timothy Snyder. *Thinking the Twentieth Century*. New York: Penguin, 2012.

Karimi, 'Ali-Reza, and Sayyid-'Ali Karimi. "Lehastani'ha-yi Muhajer Dar Iran." *Tarikh Mu'asir Iran* 3, no. 9 (1379 [1999–2000]): 7–40.

Katouzian, Homa. *Iranian History and Politics*. New York: Routledge, 2002.

————. *The Persians: Ancient, Medieval and Modern Iran*. New Haven, CT: Yale University Press, 2010.

Keddie, Nikki. *Modern Iran: Roots and Results of Revolution*. New Haven, CT: Yale University Press, 2003.

Keyhan. "E'ezam-i Akip Pezashki Ayatollah Taleqni." April 24, 1979.

Khazzoom, Aziza. *Shifting Ethnic Boundaries and Inequality in Israel: or, How the Polish Peddler Became a German Intellectual*. Studies in Social Inequality. Stanford, CA: Stanford University Press, 2008.

Kochanski, Halik. *The Eagle Unbowed: Poland and the Poles in the Second World War*. Cambridge, MA: Harvard University Press, 2012.

Kohan, Yousef. *Yousef Kohan: Guzarish va Khatirat-i Fa'aliyat'ha-Yi Siyasi va Ijtima'i*. Los Angeles: International Printing, 1993.

Koskodan, Kenneth K. *No Greater Ally: The Untold Story of Poland's Forces in World War II*. Oxford: Osprey, 2009.

Koyagi, Mikiya. "The Vernacular Journey: Railway Travelers in Early Pahlavi Iran, 1925–50." *International Journal of Middle East Studies* 47, no. 4 (November 2015): 745–63. https://doi.org/10.1017/S0020743815000963.

Krammer, Arnold. *The Forgotten Friendship: Israel and the Soviet Bloc, 1947–53*. Urbana: University of Illinois Press, 1974.

Levy, Habib. *Comprehensive History of the Jews of Iran: The Outset of the Diaspora*. Costa Mesa, CA: Mazda Publishers in association with the Cultural Foundation of Habib Levy, 1999.

————. *Khatirat-i Man*. Beverly Hills, CA: Habib Levy Cultural and Educational Foundation, 2002.

MacAskill, Ewen, Simon Tisdall, and Robert Tait. "Lone Jewish MP Confronts Ahmadinejad on Holocaust but Stresses Loyalty to Iran." *Guardian*, June 27, 2006. https://www.theguardian.com/world/2006/jun/28/iran.israel.

Mahrad, Ahmad. "Sarnivisht-i Iraniyan-i Yahudi Tay-Yi Jang-i Jahani-Yi Duvvum Dar Urupa." In *Yahudiyan-i Irani Dar Tarikh-i Mu'asir*, edited by Homa Sarshar, 3:59–108. Beverly Hills, CA: Center for Iranian Jewish Oral History; Philadelphia: Jewish Publication Society, 1999.

Mahtafar, Tara. "Q&A | Meir Javedanfar: How Israelis (Including Iranian Israelis) Read Iran." Frontline—Tehran Bureau, May 23, 2012. http://www.pbs.org/wgbh/pages/frontline/tehranbureau/2012/05/qa-meir-javedanfar-how-israelis-including-iranian-israelis-read-iran.html.

"Makatib-i Safir-i Inglis dar Tihran, Vizaratkhanah-i Umur-i Kharijah, Ustandar-i Khurasan va Nukhust Vazir dar Khusus-i Vurud-i Muhajirin-i Lahistani az Shuravi bih Iran." In *Asnadi Az Ishghal-i Iran Dar Jang-i Jahani-i Duvvum, Jald-i Svvum*, vol. 3, edited by Mohammad Hosein Salehi Maram, 301–302. Tehran, Iran: Markaz-i Pazhuhish va Asnad-i Riyasat-i Jumhuri, 2011.

Marashi, Afshin. *Nationalizing Iran: Culture, Power, and the State, 1870–1940*. Seattle: University of Washington Press, 2008.

Matin-Asgari, Afshin. *Iranian Student Opposition to the Shah*. Costa Mesa, CA: Mazda, 2002.

"Ma Yahudiyan Mizrakhi Hastim va Fiqh Ghani Darim." Iranjewish.com, Summer 1388 [2009], 2011. http://www.iranjewish.com/Essay/Essay_36_mizrakhi.htm.

Meftahi, Ida. "Body National in Motion: The Biopolitics of Dance in the Twentieth-Century Iran." PhD diss., University of Toronto, 2013.

Meir-Glitzenstein, Esther. *Zionism in an Arab Country: Jews in Iraq in the 1940s*. London: Routledge, 2014.

Melamed, Karmel. "Escape, Exile, Rebirth: Iranian Jewish Diaspora Alive and Well in Los Angeles." Jewish Journal, September 4, 2008, http://jewishjournal.com/news/los _angeles/community/65726/escape-exile-rebirth-iranian-jewish-diaspora-alive-and -well-in-los-angeles/.

Menashri, David. "The Jews in Iran: Between the Shah and Khomeini." In *Anti-Semitism in Times of Crisis*, edited by Sander Gilman. New York: New York University Press, 1991.

———. "The Pahlavi Monarchy and the Islamic Revolution." In *Esther's Children: A Portrait of Iranian Jews*, edited by Houman Sarshar, 379–402. Beverly Hills, CA: Center for Iranian Jewish Oral History; Philadelphia: Jewish Publication Society, 2002.

Michael, Sami. *Gevulot Ha-Ruah: Sihot 'im Rubik Rozental*. Kav Adom. Tel Aviv: ha-Kibuts ha-me'uhad, 2000.

Milani, Abbas. *Eminent Persians: The Men and Women Who Made Modern Iran, 1941–1979*. 2 vols. Syracuse, NY: Syracuse University Press; New York: Persian World, 2008.

———. *The Shah*. New York: Palgrave Macmillan, 2011.

Mokhtari, Fariborz. *In the Lion's Shadow: The Iranian Schindler and His Homeland in the Second World War*. Stroud, UK: History Press, 2011.

Moreen, Vera B. "The Safavid Era." In *Esther's Children: A Portrait of Iranian Jews*, edited by Houman Sarshar, 61–74. Beverly Hills, CA: Center for Iranian Jewish Oral History; Philadelphia: Jewish Publication Society, 2002.

Morris, Benny. *Righteous Victims: A History of the Zionist-Arab Conflict, 1881–2001*. New York: Vintage Books, 2001.

"Ms. Edna Sabet—Iran Human Rights Memorial." Human Rights & Democracy for Iran, accessed November 13, 2013. http://www.iranrights.org/english/memorial-case —4056.php.

Naficy, Hamid. *A Social History of Iranian Cinema*. Vol. 4. Durham, NC: Duke University Press, 2011.

Namvar, Rahim. *Yadnameh Shahidan*. n.p.: Intisharat-i hizb-i tudeh iran, 1964.

Natali, Denise. *The Kurds and the State: Evolving National Identity in Iraq, Turkey, and Iran*. Modern Intellectual and Political History of the Middle East. Syracuse, NY: Syracuse University Press, 2005.

Netzer, Amnon. "Ha'aretz Ve'yehudiy'ha." In *Iran*, edited by Haim Saadoun, 9–26. Jerusalem: Yad Ben-Zvi, 2005.

———. "Ha-Kehila Ha-Yehudit Be-Iran." In *Yehudei Iran: Avaram, Morashtam ve-Zikatam Le-Eretz Ha-Kodesh*, edited by Amnon Netzer, 3–20. Jerusalem: Beit Koresh, 1988.

———. *Yehude Iran Be-Yamenu*. Jerusalem: Hebrew University of Jerusalem Press, 1981.

———. "Yehudei Iran, Yisrael, ve-Ha-Republiqah Ha-Islamit Shel Iran." *Gesher* 26 (Spring–Summer 1980): 45–57.

New York Times. "Pole Urges Moscow to Release 800,000: Stanczyk Waives Land Dispute—Roosevelt Extols Courage." May 4, 1943.

Nikbakht, Faryar. "Yahudiyan Dar Nihzatha va Ahzab-i Siyasi." In *Terua*, edited by Homa Sarshar, 69–91. Beverly Hills, CA: Center for Iranian Jewish Oral History; Philadelphia: Jewish Publication Society, 1996.

"Nishani Az Vahdat-i Milli Dar Bimaristan-i Duktur Sapir." IranJewish.com, Esfand 1386 [February–March 2008]. http://www.iranjewish.com/Essay/Essay_34_farsi_bimarestan_sepir.htm.

Nissimi, Hilda. "Individual Redemption and Family Commitment: The Influence of Mass Immigration to Israel on the Crypto-Jewish Women of Mashhad." *Nashim: A Journal of Jewish Women's Studies & Gender Issues*, no. 18 (2009): 39.

———. "Memory, Community, and the Mashhadi Jews During the Underground Period." *Jewish Social Studies* 9, no. 3 (2003): 76–106.

'Omer, Devorah. *The Teheran Operation: The Rescue of Jewish Children from the Nazis: Based on the Biographical Sketches of David and Rachel Laor*. Washington, DC: B'nai B'rith Books, 1991.

O'Sullivan, Adrian. *Espionage and Counterintelligence in Occupied Persia (Iran): The Success of the Allied Secret Services, 1941–45*. New York: Palgrave Macmillan, 2015.

———. *Nazi Secret Warfare in Occupied Persia (Iran): The Failure of the German Intelligence Services, 1939–45*. New York: Palgrave Macmillan, 2014.

Overseas News Agency. "More Poles Reach Iran." *New York Times*, November 5, 1942.

Pardo, Eldad. "Iran Ve-Yisrael: Yisrael Kemofet Be-'einei Ha-Smol Ha-Irani Be-Shnot Ha-Shishim." *'Iyunim Bitkumat Yisrael*, no. 22 (2004): 337–65.

Parsi, Trita. *Treacherous Alliance: The Secret Dealings of Israel, Iran, and the United States*. New Haven, CT: Yale University Press, 2008.

Piers Morgan Tonight. "Interview with Iranian President Mahmoud Ahmadinejad." RealClearPolitics, September 24, 2012. http://www.realclearpolitics.com/articles/2012/09/24/interview_with_iranian_president_mahmoud_ahmadinejad_115574.html.

Piotrowski, Tadeusz, ed. *The Polish Deportees of World War II: Recollections of Removal to the Soviet Union and Dispersal Throughout the World*. Jefferson, NC: McFarland, 2004.

Pirnazar, Jaleh. "Voices of Marginality: Diversity in Jewish Iranian Women's Memoirs and Beyond." In *The Jews of Iran: The History, Religion, and Culture of a Community in the Islamic World*, edited by Houman M. Sarshar. International Library of Iranian Studies 53. London: Tauris, 2014.

———. "Yahudiyan-i Iran, Huvviyyat-i Milli va Ruznamahnigari." In *Yahudiyan-i Irani Dar Tarikh-i Mu'asir*, edited by Homa Sarshar, 13–46. Beverly Hills, CA: Center for Iranian Jewish Oral History; Philadelphia: Jewish Publication Society, 2000.

Pourshriati, Parvaneh. "New Vistas on the History of Iranian Jewry in Late Antiquity, Part I: Patterns of Jewish Settlement in Iran." In *The Jews of Iran: The History, Religion, and Culture of a Community in the Islamic World*, edited by Houman M. Sarshar, 1–32. London: I. B. Tauris, 2014.

Poznanski, Renée. *Jews in France During World War II*. Tauber Institute for the Study of European Jewry. Waltham, MA: Brandeis University Press in association with the United States Holocaust Memorial Museum; Hanover, NH: University Press of New England, 2001.

Rahimian, Orly R. "Irgun Ha-Kehila." In *Iran*, edited by Haim Saadoun, 77–96. Jerusalem: Yad Ben-Zvi, 2005.

Ram, Haggai. "Between Homeland and Exile: Iranian Jewry in Zionist/Israeli Political Thought." *British Journal of Middle Eastern Studies* 35, no. 1 (April 2008): 1–20.

———. *Iranophobia: The Logic of an Israeli Obsession*. Stanford, CA: Stanford University Press, 2009.

Ramsey, Jasmin. "Poll: More Israelis Oppose Military Attack on Iran, View Obama Favorably." LobeLog, November 30, 2012. http://lobelog.com/poll-more-israelis-oppose -military-attack-on-iran-view-obama-favorably/.

Ravid, Barak. "Iran: We Saved the Jews Three Times; Netanyahu Should Learn History." *Haaretz*, March 5, 2015. http://www.haaretz.com/israel-news/1.645497.

Reuters. "Benjamin Netanyahu to Warn Barack Obama Not to Trust Iran 'Smiles.'" *Telegraph*, September 30, 2013. http://www.telegraph.co.uk/news/worldnews/middleeast /iran/10343904/Benjamin-Netanyahu-to-warn-Barack-Obama-not-to-trust-Iran -smiles.html.

———. "Polish Troops in Iraq and Iran." *New York Times*, November 7, 1942.

Ricks, Thomas M. "Alborz College of Tehran, Dr. Samuel Martin Jordan and the American Faculty: Twentieth-Century Presbyterian Mission Education and Modernism in Iran (Persia)." *Iranian Studies* 44, no. 5 (September 2011): 627–46.

Ringer, Monica. *Pious Citizens: Reforming Zoroastrianism in India and Iran*. Syracuse, NY: Syracuse University Press, 2014.

Roby, Bryan K. *The Mizrahi Era of Rebellion: Israel's Forgotten Civil Rights Struggle, 1948–1966*. Syracuse, NY: Syracuse University Press, 2015.

Rodrigue, Aron. *French Jews, Turkish Jews: The Alliance Israélite Universelle and the Politics of Jewish Schooling in Turkey, 1860–1925*. Modern Jewish Experience. Bloomington: Indiana University Press, 1990.

———. *Jews and Muslims: Images of Sephardi and Eastern Jewries in Modern Times*. Seattle: University of Washington Press, 2003.

"Rouhani Accommodates Iran's Jewish Students." Al-Monitor, February 17, 2015. http:// www.al-monitor.com/pulse/originals/2015/02/iran-hassan-rouhani-iranian-jews.html.

Rubenstein, Joshua, Vladimir Pavlovich Naumov, and Ester Wolfson, eds. *Stalin's Secret Pogrom: The Postwar Inquisition of the Jewish Anti-Fascist Committee.* Abridged ed. Annals of Communism. New Haven, CT: Yale University Press, 2001.

Rubin, Avi. *Falling Stars: Ottoman Rule of Law and the Modern Political Trial.* Syracuse, NY: Syracuse University Press, 2018.

———. "Modernity as a Code: The Ottoman Empire and the Global Movement of Codification." *Journal of the Economic and Social History of the Orient* 59, no. 5 (November 7, 2016): 828–56.

"Runmai-Yi Az Bina-yi Yadbud Shohada-yi Kalimi Dar Bihishtiyeh-i Tihran (ISNA)." Text. ایسنا (ISNA), December 15, 2014. http://www.isna.ir/photo/93092414438 /در-بهشتیه-تهران-رونمایی-از-بنای-یادبود-شهدای-کلیمی-.

Sadeghi-Boroujerdi, Eskandar. "The Origins of Communist Unity: Anti-colonialism and Revolution in Iran's Tri-continental Moment." *British Journal of Middle Eastern Studies*, August 2017, 1–27.

Sahim, Haideh. "Two War, Two Cities, Two Religions: The Jews of Mashhad and the Herat Wars." In *The Jews of Iran: The History, Religion, and Culture of a Community in the Islamic World*, edited by Houman M. Sarshar, 75–108. London: I. B. Tauris, 2014.

Sanasarian, Eliz. *Religious Minorities in Iran.* Cambridge: Cambridge University Press, 2000.

Sarshar, Houman, ed. *Jewish Communities of Iran: Entries on Judeo-Persian Communities Published by the Encyclopedia Iranica.* New York: Encyclopedia Iranica Foundation, 2011.

Sasson, Meir. "Ha-Tziyonut ve-Ha-'aliya." In *Iran*, edited by Haim Saadoun, 157–72. Jerusalem: Yad Ben-Zvi, 2005.

Sayre, Joel. *I Served in the Persian Gulf Command.* Isfahan, 1945.

Schreier, Joshua. *Arabs of the Jewish Faith: The Civilizing Mission in Colonial Algeria.* Jewish Cultures of the World. New Brunswick, NJ: Rutgers University Press, 2010.

———. *The Merchants of Oran: A Jewish Port at the Dawn of Empire.* Stanford Studies in Jewish History and Culture. Stanford, CA: Stanford University Press, 2017.

Sehayik, Shaul. *Parashah 'Alumah: Korot Mifgasham Shel Alfei Hayalim Yehudim Polanim 'Im Yehudim Be-Iraq Uve-Iran Bashanim 1942–1943.* Tel Aviv: self-published, 2003.

Shahrizayi, Reza Azari. *Dawlat-i Iran va Mutikhassisan-i Muhajir-i Almani (1310–1319) [1931–1940].* Tehran: Intisharat-i Sazman-i Asnad-i Milli-i Iran, 1374 [1996].

Shehpar, M. "Bimaristan-i Sapir Dar Jarayan-i Inqelab." *Tamuz*, July 11, 1979.

Shenhav, Yehouda. *The Arab Jews: A Postcolonial Reading of Nationalism, Religion, and Ethnicity.* Stanford, CA: Stanford University Press, 2006.

———. "The Phenomenology of Colonialism and the Politics of 'Difference': European Zionist Emissaries and Arab-Jews in Colonial Abadan." *Social Identities* 8, no. 4 (December 2002): 521–44.

Shiblak, Abbas. *Iraqi Jews: A History of the Mass Exodus.* London: Saqi, 2005.

Shohat, Ella. "The Invention of the Mizrahim." *Journal of Palestine Studies* 29, no. 1 (1999): 5–20.

Shohet, Nir. *Sipurah Shel Golah: Perakim Be-Toldot Yahadut Bavel Le-Doroteha.* Jerusalem: ha-Agudah le-kidum ha-Mehker veha-Yetsirah, 1981.

Sinaiee, Maryam. "Iran's Jews Feel Very Much at Home." *The National*, October 7, 2008. http://www.thenational.ae/news/world/middle-east/irans-jews-feel-very-much-at -home.

Sitton, David. *Sephardi Communities Today*. Jerusalem: Council of Sephardi and Oriental Communities, 1985.

Skocpol, Theda. *States and Social Revolutions: A Comparative Analysis of France, Russia, and China*. Cambridge: Cambridge University Press, 1979.

Soomekh, Saba. *From the Shahs to Los Angeles: Three Generations of Iranian Jewish Women Between Religion and Culture*. Albany: State University of New York Press, 2012.

Stein, Sarah Abrevaya. "The Field of In Between." *International Journal of Middle East Studies* 46, no. 3 (August 2014): 581–84.

———. *Saharan Jews and the Fate of French Algeria*. Chicago: University of Chicago Press, 2014.

Stern, Yoav. "Katsav Greets Assad, Iran's Khatami During Pope's Funeral." *Haaretz*, April 8, 2005. http://www.haaretz.com/news/katsav-greets-assad-iran-s-khatami -during-pope-s-funeral-1.155501.

Sternfeld, Lior. "'In This Room There Is No Islam': The Shah's 'Special Relationship' with Iran's Israeli Community." *+972 Magazine* (blog), June 8, 2013. http://972mag.com/in -this-room-there-is-no-islam-the-shahs-special-relationship-with-irans-israeli -community/73273/.

———. "Iran Days in Egypt: Mosaddeq's Visit to Cairo in 1951." *British Journal of Middle Eastern Studies* 43, no. 1 (January 2, 2016): 1–20. https://doi.org/10.1080/13530194.2015 .1060151.

———. "The Israeli Republic, by Jalal Al-e Ahmad (2014)." Not Even Past, March 5, 2014. https://notevenpast.org/the-israeli-republic-by-jalal-al-e-ahmad-2014/.

———. "Jewish-Iranian Identities in the Pahlavi Era." *International Journal of Middle East Studies* 46, no. 3 (August 2014): 602–5.

———. "Pahlavi Iran and Zionism: An Intellectual Elite's Short-Lived Love Affair with the State of Israel." Ajam Media Collective, March 7, 2013. http://ajammc.com/2013/03 /07/pahlavi-iran-and-zionism-an-intellectual-elites-short-lived-love-affair-with-israel/.

———. "Reclaiming Their Past: Writing Jewish History in Iran During the Mohammad Reza Pahlavi and Early Revolutionary Periods (1941–1989)." PhD diss., University of Texas at Austin, 2014.

———. "The Revolution's Forgotten Sons and Daughters: The Jewish Community in Tehran During the 1979 Revolution." *Iranian Studies* 47, no. 6 (November 2, 2014): 857–69. https://doi.org/10.1080/00210862.2014.948744.

Stillman, Norman A. *The Jews of Arab Lands in Modern Times*. Philadelphia: Jewish Publication Society, 2003.

Suri, Jeremi. *Power and Protest: Global Revolution and the Rise of Detente*. Cambridge, MA: Harvard University Press, 2005.

Sweeney, Fionnuala. "Iranian Jews in Israel Wary, Hoping for the Best." CNN, March 5, 2012. http://www.cnn.com/2012/03/05/world/meast/iranian-jews-israel/.

Sword, Keith. *Deportation and Exile: Poles in the Soviet Union, 1939–48.* Studies in Russia and East Europe. New York: St. Martin's Press in association with School of Slavonic and East European Studies, University of London, 1994.

Tamuz. "Bimunasibat-i Ruz-i Quds: I'ilmiya Jamehe-Ye Ruwshanfikeran-i Yahudi Iran." July 29, 1981.

———. "Darbarih-Yi Mizgard Tilivizyuni." July 4, 1979.

———. "Fe'aliyat-i 3 Saleh-Ye Jame'eh-Ye Rushanfikran Kalimi-i Iran." Editorial, September 25, 1981.

———. "Mas'ulin-i Bimaristan-i Doktor Sapir Dar Jalasat-i Haftagi-yi Jami'ah-yi Rawshanfikran-yi Yahudi-yi Iran." January 28, 1982.

———. "Muhajirat Ma'akus Az Israil: Sahyunist'ha Dar Bayn-i Bast-I Kamil." November 19, 1981.

———. "Nasl-i Javan-i Kalimi-Yi Iran Bidar Shudah Ast." Editorial, May 6, 1982.

"Tehran Fire: 20 Dead in Plasco Building Collapse." Al Jazeera, January 19, 2017. http://www.aljazeera.com/news/2017/01/tehran-fire-170119082905960.html.

Telhami, Shibley. "Israeli Public Opinion After the November 2012 Gaza War." *Brookings* (blog), November 30, 2001. https://www.brookings.edu/on-the-record/israeli-public-opinion-after-the-november-2012-gaza-war/.

Teller, Judd L. *The Kremlin, the Jews, and the Middle East.* New York: T. Yoseloff, 1957.

The Times (London). "Soviet-Polish Agreement: Partition Treaty with Germany Denounced." July 31, 1941.

Times of India. "Current Topics: Fire Compensation Poles' Own Hospital." June 3, 1944.

Tsadik, Daniel. *Between Foreigners and Shi'is: Nineteenth-Century Iran and Its Jewish Minority.* Stanford, CA: Stanford University Press, 2007.

Tsadok, Haim. *Yahadut Iran bi-tekufat ha-shoshelet ha-Pahlavit: Yehude Iran ve-Erets Yisrael (1935–1978).* Tel Aviv: Meyatseg, 1991.

Tzur, Eli. "Mapam and the European and Oriental Immigrations." In *Israel: The First Decade of Independence*, edited by S. Ilan Troen and Noah Lucas, 543–56. SUNY Series in Israeli Studies. Albany: State University of New York Press, 1995.

Vari'i, Sayyid Javvad. *Mabani va Mustanidat Qanun-i Asasi Bih Rivayat Qanunguzar.* Qum, Iran: Intisharat-i Dabirkhanah-i Majlis-i Khibrigan-i Rahbari, 1385 [2006].

Vejdani, Farzin. *Making History in Iran: Education, Nationalism, and Print Culture.* Stanford, CA: Stanford University Press, 2015.

Vizarat-i farhang va irshad islami- Dabirkhaneh-yi shura-yi hamahangi va nizarat bar amr tarvij farhang isar va shahadat. *Yadnameh-Yi Hamvatanaan-i Bargozide-Yi Isaargar-i Masihi, Zartushti va Kalimi.* Tehran: Vizarat-i farhang va irshad islami, 1390 [2011].

Wegman, Charly. "Peres Says Attack on Iran 'More and More Likely.'" Mail & Guardian, November 6, 2011. http://mg.co.za/article/2011-11-06-peres-says-attack-on-iran-more-and-likely/.

Yacobi, Haim. *Israel and Africa: A Genealogy of Moral Geography.* Routledge Studies in Middle Eastern Geography 1. Abingdon, UK: Routledge, 2016.

Yaghoubian, David N. *Ethnicity, Identity, and the Development of Nationalism in Iran.* Syracuse, NY: Syracuse University Press, 2014.

Yerushalmi, Yosef Hayim. *Zakhor: Jewish History and Jewish Memory.* Samuel and Althea Stroum Lectures in Jewish Studies. Seattle: University of Washington Press, 1996.

Zabih, Sepehr. *The Communist Movement in Iran.* Berkeley: University of California Press, 1966.

———. *The Left in Contemporary Iran: Ideology, Organisation, and the Soviet Connection.* London: Croom Helm; Stanford, CA: Hoover Institution Press, 1986.

Zand, Michael. "Ha-Dimuy Shel Ha-Yehudi Be-'eynei Ha-Iranim Le'ahar Milhemet Ha-Olam Ha-Sheniya (1945–1979)." *Pe'amim* 29 (1986): 109–39.

Zarif, Javad (@JZarif). "@sfpelosi Iran never denied it. The man who was perceived to be denying it is now gone. Happy New Year." Twitter, September 5, 2013. https://twitter.com/jzarif/status/375617854214660097?lang=en.

Zarinebaf, Fariba. "From Istanbul to Tabriz: Modernity and Constitutionalism in the Ottoman Empire and Iran." *Comparative Studies of South Asia, Africa and the Middle East* 28, no. 1 (July 5, 2008): 154–69.

Zia-Ebrahimi, Reza. *The Emergence of Iranian Nationalism: Race and the Politics of Dislocation.* New York: Columbia University Press, 2016.

Zirinsky, Michael P. "Harbingers of Change: Presbyterian Women in Iran, 1883–1949." *American Presbyterians* 70, no. 3 (1992): 173–86.

———. "Imperial Power and Dictatorship: Britain and the Rise of Reza Shah, 1921–1926." *International Journal of Middle East Studies* 24, no. 4 (November 1992): 639–63.

———. "Inculcate Tehran: Opening a Dialogue of Civilizations in the Shadow of God and the Alborz." *Iranian Studies* 44, no. 5 (September 2011): 657–69.

———. "A Panacea for the Ills of the Country: American Presbyterian Education in Interwar Iran." *Iranian Studies* 26, no. 1/2 (1993): 119–37.

Filmography

Farhani, Ramin, dir. *The Jews of Iran.* Hilversum, Netherlands: NIK Media; Jerusalem: Ruth Diskin Films, 2005.

Itzhak, George, dir. *Reading Tehran in Tel Aviv.* New York, 2013.

Olsen, Annette Mary, and Katia Forbert Petersen, dirs. *My Iranian Paradise.* Denmark: Sfinx Film/TV, 2008.

Shadur, Dan, dir. *Before the Revolution: The Untold Story of the Israeli Paradise in Iran.* Tel Aviv: Heymann Brothers Films, 2013.

Sinai, Khosrow, dir. *The Lost Requiem.* Iran, 1983.

Index